Family Systems Theory Simplified

In this textbook for students and instructors of marriage and family therapy, Bethany C. Suppes offers a refreshed perspective of family systems therapy (FST), focusing on the importance of understanding its concepts and demonstrating how models of marriage and family therapy can appear practically in counseling.

In Part I, Suppes begins with a theoretical overview of FST, including the history of development, key theorists, and defining core concepts. In Part II, she focuses on application and explores nine key components of FST, identifying how various systemic therapy models apply these concepts. The book also covers the professional responsibilities of the systemic therapist and cultural considerations for those using the theory professionally.

Primarily written for those having their first exposure to the ideas of FST, it explains concepts in a language and structure that is more comprehensive and culturally aware than existing literature, aiming to improve the therapeutic process for both therapist and client.

Bethany C. Suppes is a marriage and family therapist and approved supervisor based in Spokane, Washington, USA. She has experience as a clinical director and assistant professor along with author and psychotherapist.

Family Systems Theory Simplified

Applying and Understanding Systemic Therapy Models

Bethany C. Suppes

NEW YORK AND LONDON

Cover image: © Getty Images

First published 2023
by Routledge
605 Third Avenue, New York, NY 10158

and by Routledge
4 Park Square, Milton Park, Abingdon, Oxon, OX14 4RN

Routledge is an imprint of the Taylor & Francis Group, an informa business

© 2023 Bethany C. Suppes

The right of Bethany C. Suppes to be identified as author of this work
has been asserted in accordance with sections 77 and 78 of the Copyright,
Designs and Patents Act 1988.

All rights reserved. No part of this book may be reprinted or reproduced or utilised
in any form or by any electronic, mechanical, or other means, now known or
hereafter invented, including photocopying and recording, or in any information
storage or retrieval system, without permission in writing from the publishers.

Trademark notice: Product or corporate names may be trademarks or registered trademarks,
and are used only for identification and explanation without intent to infringe.

Library of Congress Cataloging-in-Publication Data
A catalog record for this title has been requested

ISBN: 978-0-367-54206-1 (hbk)
ISBN: 978-0-367-54208-5 (pbk)
ISBN: 978-1-003-08819-6 (ebk)

DOI: 10.4324/9781003088196

Typeset in Galliard
by Newgen Publishing UK

Contents

Foreword	vii
Dedications and Acknowledgments	ix
Introduction	1

PART I
Theoretical Overview — 7

1	History of Family Systems Theory	9
2	Differentiating Therapeutic Theory and Clinical Modality	23
3	Roles and Responsibilities of the Therapist in Family Systems Theory	34

PART II
Theoretical Application — 49

4	FST Concept I: Wholeness	51
5	FST Concept II: You Cannot Not Communicate	68
6	FST Concept III: Context Is Key	90
7	FST Concept IV: Co-occurring Systems	114
8	FST Concept V: Boundaries	137
9	FST Concept VI: Circular Causality	162

vi *Contents*

PART III
Additional Considerations 183

10 Role of Individual Psychology in Family Systems Theory 185

11 Cultural Considerations of Family Systems Theory 198

Conclusion 216

References 218
Index 226

Foreword

Over the years, as a professor in several graduate counseling programs, I have come to recognize that there are two groups of students who seek the helping profession. There is one group of very bright students who delve into theory, research, and adore every second of their study. They ask important questions in class that almost outshine the other students, who sometimes frown at their knowledge, and feel intimidated by them. Those students often go on and do phenomenal research and prove that certain theories are worthy of future study. They often teach in graduate school after they graduate, expounding on theory and research. They enliven our field with statistics and results of what therapists do that work with families. Their work pushes us to understand the effectiveness of marriage and family therapy.

The other group also consists of bright students who are interested in *doing* marriage and family therapy and work very hard to learn the underpinnings of marriage and family therapy. They seek out textbooks that define each family therapy model, sometimes, skim the theory chapters, and hurry on to the interventions. They try to understand how each model works and come to class with important questions to ask, mostly to clarify what they have read. They want examples of cases because they learn better that way. In their eyes, most of what they read in their textbook is amazing. Yet, it is not always understandable. Their textbooks were probably written by a member of the first group I described.

This book, however, is for the second group. They are the ones who will go to work, day by day see families, push our field forward, and help humans interact so that their lives are meaningful, together.

Dr. Suppes was once a student in my graduate program. I often noticed that she walked the balance beam between both groups. I noticed early on that her writing was superb, along with her drive and passion for research. Her love of certain family therapy models meant that she was driven to understand how they worked and examine the outcomes. The joy of watching such a student made me excited. I told her often that her writing was amazing and she should write a book. Somehow, I knew that if more students could come to understand what Dr. Suppes understood through her efforts of learning the models and utilizing them with families, they too would share in Dr. Suppes' passion.

viii   *Foreword*

This book will finally provide the simplicity and clarification that students need to enter into the field of marriage and family therapy, with an understanding of systemic principles, key terms, theory about family, case studies, and explanations that make sense. Dr. Suppes has taken the sophisticated terminology and principles of marriage and family therapy, along with mentions of those early family therapists who transformed therapy, and provided the same information into an easy-to-read and casual manuscript that makes sense. Her descriptions are so clear and at times, fun, that one can almost feel that she is sitting next to the reader, like a friend talking about something fascinating to them.

When I interviewed Dr. Suppes for admission to our PhD program, I mentioned that my wish for her and all of our students was for them to make a contribution to the field. I am happy to write in this Foreword that Dr. Suppes has succeeded.

Linda Metcalf, PhD
Texas Wesleyan University
August, 2021

Dedications and Acknowledgments

This book would not have been possible without numerous indirect contributions and support from others. First, my parents and grandparents who showed me just how influential family can be. Your constant support and compassion helped me persevere through many challenges, including personal development, academic degrees, and now, this manuscript. Second, my loving partner who did not know this book (or a global pandemic) would be a significant character in the first few years of our relationship and persevered alongside me. Third, Dr. Linda Metcalf, who offered not only connection to publication opportunities but invaluable guidance on how to write a book people, hopefully, actually want to read. Fourth, Dr. Sara Blakeslee Salkil, who wrote on one of my tests in my master's program that she would not be surprised if I authored a theory text someday. To each of you, I offer my sincerest gratitude. Finally, my thanks to the many professors, peers, family, and friends who let me talk about this text repeatedly over its authorship. Please know I am constantly learning from you and hope you see flavors of your wisdom in this text as you offered it to me.

This book is dedicated to all those who helped my hope of publishing a book become a reality. I hope it is not the last.

Introduction

Two major factors contributed to the development of this book. First, I first entered academia from the faculty side, I was eager to teach the class introducing family systems theory. However, I quickly noticed from syllabi and my own experience that the textbook options were very…challenging. Of course, challenging is not bad. But these books were often dated, lacking in scope, and dare I say, white-washed. Several of my students were not reading the book because it was too complex, confusing, and to many of them, irrelevant. In typical new-professor fashion, I thought to myself, "I gotta find a way to reach them!"

So I set out to write a book about therapeutic models and how they use family systems theory practically. I wanted to create a book that both simplified the concepts – as the title implies – and demonstrates their usage in therapy. However, I quickly noticed a pattern. In my desire to bridge theory and reality, therapeutic modalities started to appear more and more connected, too. What one model described as well-differentiated, another called self-leadership, but they were essentially describing similar healthy personal identities. What one model called exceptions, another called sparkling moments, but both were describing an intervention focused on deviating focus from a problematic belief. Model after model, there were consistencies and themes. Through all the models, though, the concepts of family systems theory were there. They are a foundational understanding of how the world – and the people in the world – make sense.

The second major contributor to deciding to write this book was always my fascination with stories. I love stories. I love hearing the stories of my students and clients, telling me how they have grown and learned and how they can continue to grow and learn. They tell me about chapters in their lives that were difficult; sometimes they are still in that chapter. But I love to work with them from where they are, where they are still writing, still contributing to their future. Stories are how the world makes sense to me.

The first draft of this book was called "*A Therapist's Heroic Journey,*" in reference to the formulaic heroic journey of characters in fiction writing. Interestingly, the person who drew these parallels, Joseph Campbell, was influenced by Carl Jung's analytical psychology. The heroic journey includes four parts: The call to adventure, an initiation, a transformation or unification,

DOI: 10.4324/9781003088196-1

2 Introduction

and the heroic return. Within each of those steps, we see common occurrences – leaving the ordinary world, struggles to accept the call, connecting to a helper and/or mentor, undergoing great personal difficulty, eventually rising to that challenge, and eventually experiencing reward and atonement. This journey is a commonality across time, across cultures, and across audiences. While an author may add some flare or shift of expectation within these steps, they inevitably fall into place on this consistent timeline. In the same way, many therapeutic modalities may have various names and interventions, the goal seems to consistently be the same: To improve lives through the quality of meaningful relationships, and to help reach reward and atonement.

Therapeutic models demonstrate the variety of ways to explore a client's story. Models overlap because they utilize consistent core concepts, such as those of family systems theory. There are so many overlapping ideas in models because there are consistent truths in the therapeutic success and therapist worldviews. However, like new authors rewriting that same heroic journey in new and exciting tales of adventure, creative people keep finessing existing therapy models and making more! As a result, this book cannot possibly address all models. Instead, I selected ten systemic models that I know well. However, even in different models of therapy, we see core concepts that appear in all family systems therapies. We design these models because there is no perfect model that works for every client. The models can be just different enough to reach clients differently. In therapy models, there's no need to "reinvent the wheel." Instead, we seek new ways to reach underlying truths and use constructive language to convey that *change is possible, and they can make it happen.*

Over the course of this book, you will be exposed to several models of therapy that use family systems theory. As you read, I hope you consider each model and how well it matches your perception of the nature of humanity and potential for change. This qualifies as part of your *worldview.*

What Is Worldview?

Every person on the planet has a point of view. That point of view is the result of a lifetime of experience and unique balance of internal chemicals and brain processes. No two people, anywhere, ever, can have identical points of view. People can experience the same event and still have separate points of view. Siblings can grow up in the same house and remember it differently based on their individual experiences. A couple can have an argument and remember it differently based on their emotional response to the words that were exchanged. People can perceive professor competence differently based on past experiences and present expectations. These differences can also reflect a person's worldview.

As the morphemes of the phrase entails, a worldview is one's view of the world. It is a person's mindset of how the world works and how they feel about the world. A worldview is a life philosophy; it is how you view reality. This can include the presence (or absence) of hope, despair, indifference, faith, belief

Introduction 3

in human progress or global regression, or any number of other perspectives. I often use the metaphor of a filter. Your worldview filters your view of the world, making some ideas stand out or "stick" more than others. Have you heard the phrase, "seeing the world through rose-colored glasses"? This term meant that a person has a "rosy" worldview, one of hope and joy that does not focus on problems.

Even with intentionality, we cannot leave our worldview. It is a part of who we are. But we can account for how our frame of reference impacts us. As a therapist, we will inevitably have our own perspectives. The Freudian idea of the therapist being a blank slate is a human impossibility. We are people, too! We cannot ignore how our life has contributed to our identity, including our identity as a therapist. However, we can – and should – be intentionally aware of how our worldviews may influence our work as a therapist. Knowing our own limits, we can be intentional to make up the difference. Instead, it is my responsibility, as the therapist, to account for my worldview and create space to see from the client's worldview instead. After all, in the client's therapy, it is more important to focus on the client's worldview, not mine.

Introductory Vocabulary

Before we get into the concepts of family systems, I'd like to cover some vocabulary you will see throughout this book. These terms are common in marriage and family therapy practice, per the American Association of Marriage and Family Therapy (AAMFT). These terms will be used in the chapters to describe different family dynamics. I want to make sure you are familiar with them before we get further:

- *System:* A collection of interrelated units, often with relationship between them (Hall & Fagen, 1956). In the field of marriage and family therapy, that typically refers to families, but not always. In Chapter 1 when we talk about the history of the theory, you'll see that this broad language stems from its multidisciplinary application. In Chapter 7, you will see just how widely and precisely the term can be used.
- *Family-of-origin:* The family you come from. This can include a family you are born into and/or one into which you are adopted. Typically, this is tied to the family or families that raise you. It can also include people you have never met, like an absentee parent, strangers who birthed you then offered you up for adoption, and deceased family members. It can be complex as it also can include the people who also adopted or fostered you. Therefore, it is not just about blood relatives. However, that is the general source of one's identity. It is both nature and nurture, though I would argue the two are inseparable rather than dichotomous.
- Within families, we see two additional divisions across and through generations. *Vertical relationships* are those where the power is inequal between the two people in the relationship. This is typical between a parent and child, for example. Vertical relationships cross the generational

4   *Introduction*

gap. *Horizontal relationships*, as can likely be surmised, are relationships between people who are of an equal hierarchy. A typical family example could be a pair of siblings. These are most often seen in those of the same generation. These types of relationships are common and natural in systems.

- Depending on the presence of children in a family, families can fall into either adult- or child-centered patterns. An *adult-centered family* prioritizes the adults' needs and desires in the family system. This can include if the adults do not have children or if the children are grown and no longer depend on the adults in their life. Typically, when there are dependent children in the home, it will be a *child-centered family*. These families organize around the well-being and growth of the child(ren). Generally, this is not problematic. When the child's desires overtake or disable the adult's needs, it can bring an imbalance of boundaries, which will be covered in detail in Chapter 8.
- *Nuclear family:* The family one makes. This is often through romantic connection and/or childbearing. For children, family-of-origin and nuclear families are one and the same. When they are older and start developing independent relationships outside the family, particularly romantic relationships, they may form a new family. This does not replace the old one; it grows out of it. A nuclear family can also be the coming together of multiple families-of-origin to create a new family. This new family will have its own roles, rules, and rituals that will differ from each contributor's family-of-origin as they each decide how they want to imitate or avoid what they witnessed before.
- *Family roles:* Each member of a system, including a family, has a role to fill. These roles include identifying one's behavioral responsibilities to the system and division of power in the system. It determines a person's position of influence in the system, like a mother's influence over her children. The details of that influence depend on the situation, convenience, and one's obligations based on that role.
- *Family rules:* Regulation of behavioral expectations to keep the family stable and together. These rules can be overtly known or secretive and discreet. The rules can span generations, altering slightly perhaps. Rules can also be related to myths within the family, such as stories that make the family unique and family lessons to be learned. Rules are one way a family distinguishes itself from other systems and unite the family together. Rituals can do something similar.
- *Family rituals:* Activities the family system does together to further that bond and sense of togetherness. These rituals can occur at prominent events or regular small occurrences. Examples can include anything from regular family dinners to holiday traditions to sharing a moment of affection before going to work. These also are often passed down through generations as symbols of connection and family identity.

These terms will appear throughout the text, in all three parts of the book.

Overview of Content

Overall, this book is divided into three sections. The first is general information about family systems theory. This will include its history, the difference between theory and modality in systems-based therapeutic practices, and the role of the therapist in family systems therapy.

The second section is the description and application of the six core concepts: Wholeness, communication, context, co-occurring systems, boundaries, and circular causality. In each of these chapters, I will describe the concept in detail including how it applies to other family systems concepts. Next, I'll demonstrate how a few family therapy models use the concept both in its theory and therapeutic practice. After that, I will provide a case example, describing a client presenting to therapy. This will be followed by a description of how those models would approach that case, including specific interventions and example questions. Those example questions are not given in a particular order nor would they be asked sequentially. They reflect the different directions the therapist could take to address the clients' needs.

Please note that all the case examples are fictional and are not based on real people, scenarios, or client cases. That being said, they can demonstrate common dynamics that appear in therapy. The hope is that, while they are specific examples, you will be able to apply them and see how they apply to the different concepts introduced in this text. At the end of the chapter, I also include some reader reflection questions. These are meant to help you, my audience, connect to the material and consider on how the concepts of family systems theory relate to you and your life.

The third section of this book is brief but no less important. It focuses on how family systems theory perceives and treats individual mental health and the cultural considerations of each concept within family systems theory. It also acknowledges the cultural context of the theory's design and development. Originally this section was in Part I of the book, but a deepened familiarity with the concepts was deemed necessary to get the most out of it. So, it was added at the end. I hope that despite its brevity, you will give due consideration and emphasis to this portion of the book. Culture – including ethnicity, race, socioeconomic considerations, geographic location, and many others – is highly influential to family systems and impacts what families view as healthy or unhealthy attitudes and behaviors. I hope this section is enlightening and communicates the depth of consideration we must give this topic with our clients, too.

With this foundation of information, allow me to clarify one last thing. The purpose of this book is to help my audience, particularly therapists, understand and apply family systems theory. I hope to uncomplicate the concepts to the best of my ability. That being said, these concepts are difficult to spread out and look at one-by-one because they intersect so often.

Part I
Theoretical Overview

1 History of Family Systems Theory

Family systems theory began as the application of natural science concepts. It is general systems theory (GST) in social contexts; to use a term from the introduction, it is isomorphic. This includes philosophies of cybernetics, which is central to the theory. However, family systems theory uses concepts of social interaction theories, too. Among these philosophies, there are key researchers, particularly those who bridged GST to apply in families.

General Systems Theory

GST began as a mathematical construct, crafted in the context of World War II by Ludwig von Bertalanffy. GST contributed to wartime need of mathematical theories of predictability, where cybernetics originated. Though the theory gained popularity and clout in the 1940s, von Bertalanffy had been constructing the concepts since the 1920s. It gained traction in application to families in the 1950s and 1960s with continued research and overlap with social sciences.

The foundational belief of GST is that complex systems can demonstrate commonalities in organization and structure. The theory suggests that the relationships between elements contribute to their identity and development as much as the elements themselves. That is to say, we cannot fully understand something just by looking at its parts; we must also consider the relationship between the parts. Understanding these relationships will offer greater insight to the overall operation and capabilities of the parts. This idea can be found in technology, natural sciences, philosophy, and even people.

Let's give an example. A computer is made up of a body of hardware: A hard drive, motherboard, graphics card, central processing unit, and random access memory (RAM). Each part has a distinct role and capacity. However, those parts can only do so much independently. When brought together, they create a machine capable of developing and utilizing software. Software enables a computer to complete tasks. This can include systems software, like an operating system, or application software, such as games or specific tools such as Internet access or document-building programs. These tasks would not be possible without the hardware, and they work best when the hardware is functioning optimally (Cioffi-Revilla, 2017).

DOI: 10.4324/9781003088196-3

10 *Theoretical Overview*

Of course, this metaphor does not perfectly encapsulate the complexities of a family. We are people; we are more complex than computer equipment. But we can see the commonalities within the comparison. People offer so much independently (our "hardware"), but the relationships between us (the "software") bring out so much more than what is quantifiable. Other authors have offered other, more artistic metaphors: Music is more than a sequence of individual notes played by specific instruments; a picture is more than a collection of pixels or dabs of paint; beautiful works of literature are more than letters on a page.

More than a scientific theory, GST proposed a new way of thinking, of making sense of the world. It offered attention to the dynamic nature of relationships, particularly familial relationships (Whitchurch & Constantine, 1993). The tenants of family systems theory make sense because they are founded in GST concepts of interdependence, boundaries, hierarchies, and other topics this book will explore. Central to these concepts is that of cybernetics.

Cybernetics

Cybernetics came alongside GST during World War II, when studying communication was essential to understand manipulation of information to control behavior. Cybernetics and GST came together in concepts of feedback loops and homeostasis, which connect to how change happens in a system (Guttman, 1991). It also relates to systemic wholeness and interchangeability of the individual pieces within a system. In a family context, the pieces of the whole are members of a family.

Cybernetics' originator, Norbert Wiener, would provide the key attribute to family systems theory that other research lacked: Communication patterns that convey circular influence. According to Wiener, family members pass influence back and forth via feedback loops. These either encourage or discourage a particular behavior. Based on whether individual members of the family like or dislike a certain behavior, they respond in a way that encourages or discourages it. They either perpetuate or change patterns of behaviors, thoughts, and feelings in a relationship and in a family (Keeney, 1983). Cybernetics' concept of influence can present in two ways, depending on the perceived influence of those outside the system. These are called first- or second-order cybernetics.

First-Order Cybernetics

First-order cybernetics views the observer as an outsider of the system, not directly impacting the system. An observer could include many roles. They could be a passerby who does not interact with the system, such as someone that shares a bus route with you. It could be someone with whom the system briefly interacts, such as a waiter at a restaurant. It could also be a therapist with whom the family has regular contact. In these examples, the observer – the bus rider, waiter, or therapist – is an outsider. Per this perspective, the

History of Family Systems Theory 11

outsider does not influence the system directly, and the system does not influence the observer. From the outside, the viewer makes observations about the system that are objective and separate. However, this concept was considered not wholly realistic, so second-order cybernetics changed a few ideas.

Second-Order Cybernetics

Second-order cybernetics can be poetically summarized as the cybernetics of cybernetics. It recognizes, when observing a system, the observer both influences and is influenced by the system. The observer has personal perceptions that influence their observations. They will respond from this perception, not a purely objective stance. Similarly, the observed thing, such as a client in therapy, is influenced by both the presence of the observer and their potential input.

Here's a therapeutic example. A student client comes to therapy because they have been feeling very anxious. The therapist, or observer, has experienced their own anxiety in the past and may have a preconceived idea of how to treat this symptom. The therapist may start treatment assuming their experience was similar to what the client is experiencing now. What the therapist does not know is the client's anxiety stems from guilt of cheating on a test. The client, not wanting to disappoint the therapist (or have the therapist tell their parents), does not correct the therapist's misunderstanding. In this way, the client and therapist respond to one another, sometimes without even realizing it.

Thermostat Metaphor

Since it was designed, researchers have attempted to find the perfect metaphor to explain the concept of cybernetics. One of the most frequently referenced is that of the thermostat and thermometer. A thermostat is different from a thermometer. A thermometer simply reads the temperature of the room, but it does not influence it. A thermostat, on the other hand, reads the temperature of the room and, if it finds it unsatisfactory, signals a mechanism to change it. In the summer, a room can heat up quickly. If the room has a thermometer, all we would know for sure is that the room is getting hotter. However, if the room has a thermostat, the device can be set to have a comfortable range of temperature of a few degrees. If the room goes beyond that range, the thermostat will signal the appropriate technology to kickstart the air conditioner. The air conditioner will then bring the temperature of the room back down into the comfort zone. The air conditioner therefore responds to the thermostat's instruction of when to both turn on and, eventually, turn off. When the temperature drops, the thermostat signals the air conditioner that it does not need to continue running. The devices respond to one another.

While this may be a gross oversimplification, this metaphor demonstrates the key concept of cybernetic feedback. First-order cybernetics are the thermometer; it does not influence the system, or room. Second-order cybernetics

12 *Theoretical Overview*

are the thermostat; it both responds to and influences the room based on the system's needs. In particular, it responds to the need to be in that comfortable range. Families, similarly, tend to have a comfortable range, or a degree of change with which they can confidently cope (Watzlawick et al., 1974). Beyond that range, they often need assistance returning to balance or, as we see more often in therapy, finding a new balance. Of course, this does not account for all the variables that contribute to a family's metaphorical temperature.

In addition to this mathematical background, family systems theory considers social science theories of social psychology, learning theories, and behavior therapies.

Social Science Contributions

Social sciences are a branch of sociology seeking to understand human culture and relationships. A few of the social science theories contributed to and used GST, leading to application in family systems theory. These include structural functionalism, social exchange theory, self-regulating system model, and developmental task model.

Structural Functionalism

According to structural functionalism, society is a complex system whose parts work together to promote solidarity and stability. These are achieved through social rituals and norms. Society must decide on a broad level what behaviors are good, acceptable, unacceptable, or harmful. To instill these, society depends on social structures to enforce ethical standards and establish consequences when those are unfulfilled. Generally, structural functionalism asserts that people's lives are guided and shaped by social structures. Social structures include families, communities, religious organizations, and the like.

To promote solidarity and stability, system members must follow the *AGIL paradigm*, developed by American sociologist Talcott Parsons. It is part of a larger action theory that aims to make sense of human behavior based on what motivates people (Parsons, 1975). In this way, it connects to the previously mentioned systems theory and cybernetics. *AGIL* stands for adaption, goal attainment, integration, and latency. (See table on next page.)

To achieve these, people must consider internal, immediate social influences and external, communal influences. Immediate social influences could be family, schools, religious connections, media, and the like. These are the structures that directly influence the individual. External includes natural resources, commodity production, political offices, and social norms. These are larger scale influences that typically indirectly influence the individual. Social functions can be similarly instrumental (necessary to survival) or consummatory (necessary to for social regulation). Lastly, social functions can occur in manifest (as intended) or latency (unintended). That is to say, social norms can have unintended consequences to social functions.

History of Family Systems Theory 13

Structural functionalism relates to family systems theory in multiple ways. The two share an emphasis on stability and the actions people take to maintain it. They demonstrate desire to find and hold onto a norm. We see this at both a broad social level or within specific families. Lastly, both acknowledge the role of community to develop norms present in smaller systems, such as the family. In these ways, structural functionalism overlaps with family systems theory.

A	*Adaptation*	When interacting with the environment, people utilize the space and resources around them to create a functioning society. This includes using natural resources to create economic commodities. This is associated with cognitive ingenuity and resourcefulness.
G	*Goal Attainment*	Members of the social structure will set future-oriented goals and intentionally act to reach them. The assumption is that goals are not achieved by accident but require attentive decision-making by the individual and aided by the society. This is associated with expressive ingenuity and creativity to achieve these goals.
I	*Integration*	A social system is made up of several smaller systems, such as social groups and families in a wider community. These communities must be able to harmonize and, on some level, come together behind a shared unifier in the interest of maintaining the broader social structure. In this way, integration is associated with developing morality as grounds for human connection and collaboration.
L	*Latency*	This function applies integration across multiple generations. It is the assurance that one generation will pass their moral codes and social norms on to the next, mediating changes to those. Naturally there may be slight variations, but to truly overhaul the systemic functions is nearly impossible. This requires constitutive ingenuity, using power to keep a defined structural organization.

Social Exchange Theory

Broadly speaking, social exchange theory focuses on the phenomenon that people seek the most cost-efficient, desirable outcome in a situation. It aims to maximize one's reward or benefit and minimize the cost to achieve this. It considers both long- and short-term outcomes of the cost and benefit balance. If the perceived cost is higher than the perceived reward, people are less likely to pursue it. This cost/benefit analysis standard is individualized; it is up to each unique person to determine where the perceived threshold of cost-to-benefit balance shifts. It is also a central belief of social exchange theory that people behave in self-interest. This is not a bad thing; it means we act in a way that aims to assure our survival.

14 *Theoretical Overview*

Ivan Nye is a key researcher in social exchange theory. He focused on family relations and delinquent behavior, publishing a text by the same title (Nye, 1958. Specifically, he analyzed family structure and interactions, along with wider structures such as social class, as behavioral influencers. According to the National Council of Family Relations (2014), his work applying social exchange theory to families highlights the role of choice and how individuals make their choices based on a balance of their individual and communal needs. He could also be considered a major contributor to family systems theory in this way.

In addition to costs and benefits, exchange theories consider the role of *resources*. These can be physical/material/fiscal or emotional/symbolic commodities. Therefore, when considering cost and benefit, people must consider the resources they have to achieve their desired outcome, materially and emotionally. This includes *affect theory*, which looks at emotions in cost–benefit analysis and one's decision-making process. It also adds the concept of reciprocity, which considers the impact a decision will have on a relationship as part of the cost or benefit. Social exchange theory acknowledges the balance of self-interest and interdependence in decision-making and reward assessment. Lastly, social exchange theory considers equity and inequity, which considers the role of power and influence to other parties. When costs are equal from multiple parties, one must consider the benefits that may vary from party to party. This can relate to my sense of morality, developed by my social structures, including my family.

Core Tenets of Social Exchange Theory (Nye, 1978)

1   Individuals make a choice based on which option is likely to provide the most gain.
2   Cost being equal across options, people select the option likely to provide the greatest reward.
3   Reward being equal across options, people select the option with the lowest/fewest costs.
4   Immediate outcomes being equal, people select the option with the best long-term outcome, and vice versa.
5   Costs and rewards being equal, people select the option that...
   a   Yields the greatest social approval (or lowest social disapproval).
   b   Allows the most autonomy.
   c   Is least ambiguous.
   d   Offers the most security to them
6   Other costs and rewards being equal, people will choose to associate and build relationships with...
   i   Those whose values and opinions generally match their own.
   ii   Those they view as equals rather than those viewed as being above or below them (measured by one's status, abilities, and characteristics).

Social exchange theory overlaps prominently with ideas in family systems theory. Its attentiveness to the role of interactions and motivation is central to family systems concepts. Additionally, it identifies family as a relationship that influences an individual's decision-making process. Family is a source of bias in the cost–benefit balance. As mentioned earlier, our relationship with family impacts how we view costs and benefits. A person may greatly consider the impact their decisions have on their family. Examples could be deciding whether or not to stay in school or focus on employment during times of financial duress, or decisions around who and when to marry. Families influence these decisions. The exact nature of how they influence is where family systems theory is so relevant.

Self-Regulation Model

This applied theory of social behavior focuses on self-control, particularly regarding goal achievement (Baumeister et al., 2007). It theorizes that personal behaviors and thoughts strive to achieve a pre-established goal. It acknowledges personal role and responsibility to achieve those goals. As with the *AGIL paradigm*, goals are not achieved by accident. This can be applied to individuals or to systems. This system model includes four components, four elements, and three means of self-regulation.

The four components of self-regulating systems are (a) *standards of desirable behavior*, (b) *motivation to meet those standards*, (c) *monitoring for threats to that standard*, and (d) *willpower of the individual(s)*. Standards of desirable behavior can be defined systemically – community or family – or individually. Desire to meet those standards can also be personal or systemically motivated, depending on the cost or reward. Are you noticing the tendency for these theories to overlap? It's not a coincidence.

When it comes to systems, there are four steps to self-regulation.

1 Set system-wide goals. These tend to be hierarchically prioritized in order of importance. The system has this order embedded into their decision-making process to act in a way that aims to achieve those prioritized goals rather than those of lesser significance. This can be particularly challenging when the goals of lesser significance to the system may have greater significance to the individual.
2 Executive capacity. Even with input on the goal from multiple sources, one leader is responsible to reach decisions on behalf of the system about this goal. The rest of the system is expected to respect and act according to this decision. This can relate to hierarchical boundaries, which we will discuss later in this text.
3 Monitor the environment. Environment impacts decision-making and goal attainment.
4 Monitor the system. Monitoring the system – including self and one another – checks for the system's adherence to the established hierarchy. This attention to relationship can also influence decision-making, as we know from social exchange theory.

16 Theoretical Overview

Beyond the components and steps, there are three means of self-regulation. Self-regulation means sticking to the desired process and acceptance of the hierarchically defined goals. In this language, self-regulation could also be called obedience. The three means are coercion, negotiation, and induction. Coercion demands obedience through threat of punishment. Negotiation entails bartering loyalty, security, sense of belonging, approval, and status in exchange for adherence to the system's rules. Induction means the individual adopts the system's hierarchy as one's own through socialization or conversion. In other words, a person follows the goals because they genuinely believe that is what is best.

Here is a broad social example of this concept. Many world religions include desired behaviors and avoidance of certain contradictory behaviors. Faiths encourage respect to superiors and elders and being kind to one another while discouraging behaviors such as theft, murder, and idolatry of worldly possessions. To enforce these ideas, faith can use any of the means of self-regulation. Coercion would be threat of hellfire and eternal damnation. Negotiation states good behaviors in this life will result in rewards in the next life or afterlife. Induction results in good behaviors because a person genuinely believes it is simply the right thing to do. In this example, the goal of good behavior can be achieved through any of the three means.

In addition to goal achievement, self-regulation theory can also be applied to impulse control. Cognitive psychologist Albert Bandura (1991) designed a three-step process:

1 Self-observation or introspection.
2 Judgment or social comparative assessment.
3 Self-response, which includes rewarding or punishing oneself based on the success or failure to meet social standards, as judged in the previous step.

Overall, this cognitive psychology process led to the design of social cognitive and social learning theories.

Self-regulation theory also addresses the illusion of control (Fenton-O'Creevy et al., 2010). Sometimes we are so driven by internal goals that we begin to believe in the false ability to control parts of our external environment. Often this is a response to or result of desire to control chaos or distress around us. Like the work of Bandura, realistic assessment of one's locus of control stems from address one's introspective and judgment processes along with a new assessment of self-response that considers both willpower one's means of self-regulation (White, 2008).

As a cognitively based social theory, self-regulation theory relates to family systems theory in a multitude of ways (Jesser, 1975). The description of self-regulation is, by definition, cybernetics. It is self-maintenance to reach a desired goal. It also acknowledges three important variables:

- The role of the system in individual decision-making.
- The presence and role of hierarchy in a system.
- The role of interaction in goal-setting and decision-making.

Overall, this social theory may be one that most directly relates to the concepts of family systems theory that we will discuss in this text.

Developmental Task Theory

This model relates to the psychosocial theory of human development (Newman & Newman, 2018). It asserts that people are constantly developing and changing biologically, psychologically, and socially. Biologically includes genetic makeup and physiological maturity; one's psychology includes one's personal values, goals, and perception of the world; and social component includes one's culture and its values. Throughout one's whole life, your body, mind, and social circles are changing as you mature, build new skills, and have new experiences. Generally, one's life falls into certain stages, and there are typical events that occur in each stage based on age and cultural norms. These events can occur in individuals and systems. These events can also be called tasks, hence the name of the theory.

Introduced by Robert Havighurst (1972), a chemist and physicist, the theory has launched to include additional well-known social theorists such as Erik Erikson and his psychosocial stages. Erikson expanded Havighurst' six stages to nine, accounting for expanded life expectancy and nuanced differences in prepubescent and adult development. Research continues in this theory surrounding cultural norms and the roles they play in the developmental stages. For example, early versions of the stages of life assumed marriage and childrearing. Shifts in social norms now seek a more inclusive version of the stages that account for the increasing number of people that elect not to take these steps or take them in a different order.

One constant in this theory is emphasis on the role of adaptability to survival. The ability to adapt allows families to grow, but families must be mindful not to be so flexible that they lose their distinguishing familial identity. There are three forces influencing family adaptability. First is the evolving individual development of system members. Second, shifting norms of family member roles across life cycle stages. Lastly, changes in family structure and situation. All of these happen naturally over the course of life. Children shift from preschool to elementary school. Adults shift vocations and locations. Parents become "empty nesters." People individually mature while in relationships and seek to shift the relationship norms to accommodate that growth...and the relationship may or may not survive that shift. These are normal events, pleasant or unpleasant, that mandate adaptability.

This theory relates to family systems theory so much that an entire course of it is required by the Commission on Accreditation for Marriage and Family Therapy (COAMFTE) for training programs in marriage and family therapy. It gives attention to the role of adaptability to family health and how people change and develop throughout their whole lives. It is a constant responsibility of the individual to balance their growth with that of their family system. In this way, the developmental task theory is central to family systems theory.

18   *Theoretical Overview*

Key Researchers of Family Systems Theory

In addition to those listed earlier, several others have contributed to family systems theory as it is today. Sociologist Ernest Watson Burgess, for example, connected families to symbolic interactionism and provided information about how families are influenced by larger social constructs (LaRossa & Reitzes, 1993). This perspective further highlights the role of family interaction in family identity and functionality. Similarly, Burgess (1926) researched the role of family adaptivity in family happiness and stability. Broderick (1993) quoted him, "The family does not depend for its survival upon the harmonious relations of its members, nor does it necessarily disintegrate as a result of conflict among its members. The family lives as long as an interaction is taking place" (p. 27).

In the mid-twentieth century, a team came together that transitioned family systems theory to family systems therapy (Ray & Schlanger, 2008). The Palo Alto Team, or Bateson Project, was the early collaboration in Palo Alto, California. It included famed names such as Gregory Bateson, Jay Haley, Don D. Jackson, John Weakland, Paul Watzlawick, Virginia Satir, and Ivan Boszormenyi-Nagy, to name a few. These names would go on to create family therapy models such as strategic family therapy, structural family therapy, symbolic experiential therapy, and contextual family therapy, laying the foundation for countless other models. Strategic and structural family therapy techniques, in particular, are rooted in family systems theory concepts.

The team spent ten years together designing a unique theory of interaction and communication focused on the behaviors of family. The team's clinical supervisor, Don D. Jackson, founded the Mental Research Institute (MRI). The MRI was central to their discovery and long-term research of this philosophy of human behavior. Officially it included two groups, one of Bateson and his associates and another of Don Jackson and his colleagues. Membership between the groups and their research topics frequently overlapped.

Originally, the groups came together to study family systems theory as it applied to families coping with symptoms of schizophrenia. As a result of their research, the team proposed the concept of the double-bind in communication, which we look at more extensively in Chapter 5. The Palo Alto Team's article "Toward a Theory of Schizophrenia" (1956) was considered pivotal in family systems theory's understanding of familial interaction. This paper also introduced a perspective that mental illness, including severe mental illness like schizophrenia, is still treatable. Similarly, treatment does not have to be merely symptom management. The team's article focused on family interactions to alleviate symptoms, not just minimize them.

Each author of the article and member of the team contributed uniquely to family systems theory's development. All are pivotal and essential to our understanding of family functioning as we know it.

Gregory Bateson

Gregory Bateson was an English anthropologist, social scientist, and linguist. He was one of the early contributors to integrate cybernetics into social and behavioral sciences. He applied these concepts to ecological anthropology, observing systems to be simultaneously innately interdependent and in competition with one another (Bateson, 1963). He believed systems were self-correcting to achieve a concept called homeostasis, which we will explore in Chapter 9. Despite seemingly complex explanations of behavior, he viewed the world as full of simple relationships, frequently malfunctioning and seeking resolution, what he called the economics of flexibility (Bateson, 1972).

Don D. Jackson

The supervisor of the Palo Alto Team, Don Jackson, an American psychiatrist, is particularly credited for his contributions regarding homeostasis and family rules. He and *Richard Fisch* introduced a brevity to treatment that contradicted several of the psychoanalytical theories prominent in the mid-twentieth century. He is most famous as the first director of the Marriage and Family Institute, which was a central location to the development of family systems theory and its therapeutic practices. Jackson and Fisch collaborated to back the Brief Therapy Center, also in Palo Alto, along with John Weakland and Paul Watzlawick.

John Weakland

John Weakland began his career in chemical engineering but shifted to anthropology and sociology as a result of his friendship with Bateson. His research accentuated the importance of observable interactions instead of relying on inferences, which invite misunderstanding. He pioneered use of family systems therapy with individuals and marital therapy with aging couples. He reiterated the field's early emphasis on constructive reflection and centering on the basic focus on helping people in distress and aiding in invaluable relational change.

Paul Watzlawick

Paul Watzlawick assessed communication and how its many facets should be analyzed. He and his associates first proposed the understanding that communication can carry multiple messages. Similarly, they noted communication can be interpreted and evaluated in multiple ways. Their contribution to communication theory, especially as it pertains to family systems, is irreplaceable. Chapter 5 will explore this concept extensively. Watzlawick also explored the family systems theory idea that people's unsuccessful solution attempts can further the presence of the problem, which is explored in the concept of circular causality later in this book.

Milton Erickson

Psychiatrist and psychoanalyst Milton Erickson (not to be confused with the previously mentioned psychoanalyst Erik Erikson) pioneered extensive research on suggestion and hypnosis that differed from previous hypnosis methods. Per the Milton Erickson Foundation, where earlier approaches

20 *Theoretical Overview*

depended on a submissive patient, Erickson's method emphasized client resilience and engagement. His approach would come to be known as interactional therapy, and would be found on the American Society for Clinical Hypnosis.

Jay Haley

Jay Haley studied communication before being invited by Gregory Bateson to join him in California to be part of the Bateson Project. He contributed ideas about behavior as a product of interaction rather than individualized action. This interaction, he noted, included the participants' relationship with one another, even in the present moment. His emphasis on identifying problems, creating goals, and designing interventions around those goals was dubbed "problem-solving therapy," and was a radical approach at the time. He developed this approach alongside Bateson, Jackson, Milton Erickson, Weakland, and additional teammate *William "Bill" Fry*, who also studied the practice of humor in human interaction. Haley was also the founding editor of the family therapy journal *Family Process*, which has released countless significant works regarding family therapy.

Salvador Minuchin

Salvador Minuchin brought attention to hierarchies and boundaries in families. He designed training programs to correct dysfunctional dynamics in families, leading to the development of structural family therapy. Minuchin theorized families attempt to solve their problems through strictly behavioral changes. However, he believes lasting significant improvement requires a change in systemic interaction patterns. Minuchin specifically worked with families coping with anorexia nervosa, focusing on the familial contributions to maintained symptomology and family ability to contribute to healing, as well.

Virginia Satir

Virginia Satir theorized about the difference between the surface or presenting problem and the deeper issues clients may be coping with. Instead, she focused on how people coped with their problem as a part of its continuation. Attention to the present moment was essential in work by Satir and *Carl Whitaker*, who focused on the role of the therapist in familial change. They are considered founders of symbolic experiential methods of therapy. She is also considered a cofounder of the MRI.

Ivan Boszormenyi-Nagy

Ivan Boszormenyi-Nagy (1966) focused on the role of loyalty and relational ethics in family homeostasis, a sub-concept of how change occurs in a system according to family systems theory. He titled this model contextual family therapy. He also helped lead family therapy into international application.

The Ultimate Group Project

Befitting their theory, team members would say their accomplishments come from their combined efforts and contributions, not from their individual genius. It was in coming together that the group developed the unique scheme of double-bind in family systems theory that permeates throughout. As mentioned earlier, the double-bind highlights how mixed messages between members of a family result in feeling unable to win in a scenario. This was particularly prevalent between mothers and their schizophrenic children. Jay Haley and the rest of the team were among the first ever to see a family in therapy for conjoint treatment of the family rather than treating individual members. The MRI team's research included the therapeutic treatment of this interaction, which was foundational to the development of other systemic therapy models.

There have been innumerable contributors to the early development of family systems theory. These have included mathematicians, economists, anthropologists, sociologists, psychiatrists, and psychologists. In addition to the names mentioned earlier, there are also Murray Bowen and Monica McGoldrick. Murray Bowen, a medical doctor, explored on holism, boundaries, hierarchies, and interaction patterns across generations and within subsystems as the source of several problems within individuals and among relationships. He, too, designed a multigenerational model of family therapy as a result of his research. Monica McGoldrick expanded upon this in the study of gender and culture in family systems and genograms as a multigenerational intervention and assessment tool. Genograms are considered a central tool of Bowen's multigenerational family therapy approach.

In summary, the table below identifies the key names associated with the development of family systems theory, family systems therapy, and their contributions:

Key Researcher(s)	Key Contributions
Ludwig von Bertalanffy	Founder of general systems theory (GST)
Norbert Wiener	Originator of cybernetics theory in 1948
Talcott Parsons	Sociologist bringing structural functionalism to familial context
Ivan Nye	Sociologist bringing social exchange theory to familial context
Ernest Watson Burgess	Emphasized role of adaptability in family functioning
The Bateson Project & Palo Alto Team (Gregory Bateson, Don D. Jackson, Richard Fisch, John Weakland, Paul Watzlawick, Milton Erickson, Jay Haley, William Fry, Salvador Minuchin, Virginia Satir, Ivan Boszormenyi-Nagy)	The Bateson Project out of the Mental Research Institute (MRI) contributed essential research about family systems theory as a therapeutic approach with families
Paul Watzlawick	Major contributor to family systems theory (FST) communication theory
Murray Bowen	Originator of multigenerational family therapy

22 *Theoretical Overview*

This is far from an exhaustive list of contributors to the theory. Several others have made vital contributions to both the theory and practice of family systems therapy.

Overview of Key Terms

In Part II of this text, I will dive into the six key concepts of family systems theory: Wholeness, communicate, context, co-occurring systems, boundaries, and circular causality. Each of these concepts focus on patterns in individuals and families. The goal is to not only make sense of those patterns but to find what works better than what is happening right now. These are critical when understanding families and applying family systems theory in psychotherapy.

Psychotherapy includes primarily talk therapy that focuses on mental illness and emotional unwellness without prescribing medication. Psychotherapy provides the invaluable quality of confidentiality, or respectful privacy, to allow people to process through their troubles and build a greater understanding of life and self. According to the American Psychological Association (2016), about 75% of people who receive psychotherapy find it beneficial. This includes experiencing symptom relief and positive changes in the body and brain. Those trained in family systems theory, and family systems therapy, are uniquely prepared to work with individuals, families, romantic relationships, and groups. We have a specific approach that creates space for all concepts to which other methods of therapy may not be as attentive. But before going into these concepts in depth, let us review general information about defining theories versus models and clarify the role of the systemic therapist in psychotherapy.

2 Differentiating Therapeutic Theory and Clinical Modality

As I went through my therapy schooling, I noticed students and professionals alike would reference therapeutic *theories* and *modalities* interchangeably. They would treat the terms as synonymous. However, it is not always helpful or accurate to treat them as the same thing. This chapter is dedicated to providing clarification and how it applies to the remainder of this book.

Defining Therapeutic Theory

If we look strictly at a definition of theory, it's pretty mechanical: An idea that attempts to explain a concept, identifying general principles that sometimes could be empirically tested. You could almost call it a well-established hypothesis. Theories tend to be methodical and formulaic, seeking to create as little room for exceptions as possible. However, it all boils down to those first few words. A theory is an idea. It is an attempt to make sense of something. It serves the same purpose in the context of social and family theories.

Social Theory

Social theory is so multifaceted and complex, it could easily take up several books by itself. However, if we're strictly looking to define it as a concept, we can summarize it briefly. Social theory is an explanation of how social interactions and functioning work. Over the decades, many theories have been proposed, some explored in Chapter 1. A few familiar social theories include symbolic interactions theory, social learning theory, social exchange theory, conflict theory, and structural functionalism. Some of the social theories have hard science backgrounds, such as general systems theory and chaos theory. Social theories predominantly theorize how interactions impact ourselves, one another, the relationship between, and the influence on a wider social context, such as a community or government. These social dynamics can have personal and profound implications in establishing cultural norms. Of course, families are a specific and unique social dynamic and therefore require their own definition.

DOI: 10.4324/9781003088196-4

24   *Theoretical Overview*

Family Theory

Like other social theories, family theory focuses on influence of interactions. Specifically, it considers concepts like boundaries and feedback loops, both of which we will explore more thoroughly in the next section of the book.

Family theory differs from other social theories in four key ways. First, families uniquely combine intergenerational dynamics that other social dynamics rarely consider. Second, familial relationships last longer than most social groups, potentially an entire lifetime. This is the third key attribute; families entail two types of social relationships: Affinal and consanguineal. That means that we keep the relationship not just because we like our families (affinity) but due to a blood bond (consanguine). This is the fourth unique attribute of family social connections: They are bonded by blood, marriage, or kinship. As a result, there can be perceived obligation to one another to preserve the relationship even when affinity is absent. It is both a biological and social relationship, connected through time and commitment, maintained by heritage and devotion. Family, more than any other social relationships, contributes to personal and relational identity.

So, what does that mean for family therapy? It means assessing and addressing those relationships and recognizing they come with more complexities than we could possibly see on the surface. It means familial theories of interaction cannot always be empirically or quantifiably measured. There is so much more to them than that.

Theories seek to explain, interpret, and predict future action. Therapeutic theory, therefore, is an attempt to explain, interpret, and predict not only interaction patterns, but the meaning ascribed to those interactions. Theories do this by creating a conceptualization – a philosophy on why we do what we do. Beyond that, it is an attempt to assess for how we can intervene to maximize effective and beneficial interactions. Keep that phrasing in mind: Therapeutic theory is the idea, not the action. The action is the therapeutic model.

Defining Therapeutic Modality

Therapy models put therapy theories to practice. This includes specific interventions and techniques that the therapist uses to address their clients' problems and move them closer to completing treatment goals. However, there is more to a model than the interventions typically associated with it; it also has a theory of how change happens (Hubble et al., 1999). These treatment goals can be behaviorally focused or seek deeper change. In cybernetics, we called this the difference between first- and second-order change.

First-order change is behavioral change, frequently directed toward symptom management. These goals tend to take less time to achieve but risk being reversible. They explore connection between thoughts and behaviors without in-depth self-exploration. *Second-order change* is a philosophical shift in paradigm. It challenges previous assumptions about the world, oneself, and one's relationships. It may require more emotional engagement and potentially more intensive work. As a result of this shift in values or beliefs, behavioral changes follow. Therefore, this version of change still addresses presented problematic symptomology. In family systems theory, we focus more on second-order change because first-order thinking assumes a linear cause-and-effect that oversimplifies human interactions. First-order change can be limited when you add complications such as secondary gains, which insinuate something is achieved in maintaining the symptom (Fishbain, 1994). This could decrease a client's desire to change.

Within either, therapists utilize psychotherapeutic methods specific to their model, called interventions. These are predominantly talk therapy that enable people to cope with reality and make the necessary changes to reach a desired outcome, possibly with experiential attributes that help the client shift their perception of the problem and potential solution.

Examples in Family Therapy

Over the course of this book, I will identify several of the most common or popular family therapy models: Strategic family therapy, structural family therapy, Bowenian multigenerational therapy, and narrative therapy, to name a few. In each chapter of Part II, I will demonstrate how each use family systems theory concepts in their approaches. This demonstrates how all the models fall under the theoretical umbrella of family systems theory. It also demonstrates that the two terms – theory and model – are not, in fact, one and the same.

So How Are They Different?

There are a few ways to further clarify the difference between therapeutic theory and modality. As stated before, theory is the "what" while the model is the "how." Theory is the conceptualization; the model is the application. To speak metaphorically, theory is the map, and the model is the directions to get from one point to another. Therefore, the terms are not as interchangeable as some may believe. However, some theories have a model that directly utilizes its concepts. This can add to the confusion, but they remain separate things.

When the Differences Are Harder to Identify

It can get challenging when therapeutic theories have modalities that share their name. Common examples include person-centered therapy, gestalt therapy, psychoanalysis, and cognitive-behavioral therapy (CBT). These approaches are both conceptual and applicable; there is both gestalt theory and gestalt therapy. I will go over these four here instead of throughout Part II because their theories can be integrated with family systems theory in psychotherapy.

26 Theoretical Overview

Person-Centered Therapy

Person- or client-centered therapy is based on the works of Carl Rogers (1942). According to this theory, a client comes to counseling due to feeling anxious and vulnerable as a result of incongruence between their thoughts, behaviors, and emotions (Bott, 2002). It includes three core conditions for change to occur in therapy. First, a therapist must demonstrate congruence, or authenticity, in relationship with his or her clients. That is to say, the inner and outer personas of the therapist should be consistent. This demonstrates trustworthiness and models how to live an authentic self. The second core condition is well-known for what Rogers called *unconditional positive regard*.

Unconditional positive regard means the therapist always accepts the client as they are (Raskin & Rogers, 2005). This includes offering consistent non-judgmental empathy to the client. This is the third condition: Creating a non-judgmental space that believes the client's report of their reality, no matter how much it may disagree with another account, including the therapist's own. Accurate empathetic understanding accepts the client's story as truth and their experience as valid to their perception. That is not to say it blindly accepts unhealthy behavior and perspective, though. The theory is that offering acceptance and esteem for the client encourages them to be the version of themselves they aspire to be.

Person-centered theory has been used in several settings: Teaching, professional coaching, administration, and especially psychotherapy. It speaks to the natural human desire to be respected and cherished. This theory – respect invoking change – is highly applicable in a therapeutic setting. In this setting, it becomes a therapeutic model, not just a theory. It is now an action – a "how." Interventions of validating and reflecting enable clients to view their experiences in a new light, even changing their perception of themselves and others. This is applicable both in the client–therapist relationship, which will be explored extensively in the later chapter, and between members of a social system, particularly between members of a family.

Family systems theory and person-centered theory share many features, bringing out the best in one another through knowledge of interaction styles (O'Leary, 1999). For one, both theories highlight empathy as a pivotal tool toward change (Warner, 1989). They pay attention to relationships as central to lasting change (Bozarth & Shanks, 1989). Second, they acknowledge perception as subjective. What Rogers (1957) called "self-concept" can be applied as "family-concept," considering how either contribute to a person's identity both formatively and actualized. Third, both highlight the client's power to change their circumstance. Some theorists view experiential family therapy as a partnership of person-centered, humanistic, and family systems theories. Fourth, unconditional positive regard can be comparable to family systems theory's ideas of positive connotation; both strive to view their client in the best light. However, there are limits to these commonalities.

More than in person-centered theory, family systems theory presumes the therapist's knowledge and expertise will benefit the client. The assumption is the therapist knows more about healthy family dynamics (the theory) and how to get there (the model). For example, early family systems theory approaches included more instruction from the therapist. Strategic family therapy model includes forms of client injunction through paradoxical interventions or directive tasks that assume the therapist's expertise supersedes that of the client family. This contradicts person-centered theory, which prioritizes client knowledge in healing and its application. Lastly and significantly, Rogers did not endorse therapy for multiple people at once, acknowledging the challenge this poses to his core conditions for change. Rogers' writings include reference to familial influence of client-centered therapy but nothing about its application.

Gestalt Therapy

Gestalt theory was introduced to psychology by Max Wertheimer, a German psychologist who experimented with the *phi phenomenon*. Phi phenomenon perceives that humans use perception to make sense of things they do not understand or "fill in the blanks" when they do not have the full picture. *Gestalt* is a German word without direct English synonym. It can be loosely translated to a concept of structuring a whole using existing form and pattern. Paul Goodman and Fritz and Laura Perls designed the concept's therapeutic application (Stevenson, 2018b).

Gestalt therapy has a theory of change: The more a person tries to change, the more they stay the same. Instead, radical self-acceptance and ownership of one's life leads to the desired version of oneself (Frew, 2017). While seemingly paradoxical, it teaches a skill crucial to living more in the present. This is achieved through client insight toward "the myriad [of] threads" that contribute to a person's identity development (Fischer, 2017, p. 4). This relates to the family systems theory concept of context, which we will talk about in Part II. To achieve this insight, there tend to be specific interventions and processes. Even within these, the model encourages both the client and therapist to be creative in understanding problems and seeking solutions.

Like person-centered therapy, gestalt therapy emphasizes therapist respect and compassion as an intervention unto itself. Empathy and relentless curiosity seek to completely understand the client's experience, including the emotional repercussions in the moment. It does this without judgment or pathological implications, aiming only to understand and validate. For the client to truly feel invested in becomes a phenomenological experience for them, a profound representation of consciousness and experience blended together. It brings multiple levels of consciousness to the first-person present-tense through experience. That is to say, it brings both issues and healing into the here and now of therapy.

Gestalt therapy interventions stem from Virginia Satir's integration of systemic and experiential practices (Satir et al., 1976). These use the therapeutic space and time to create substantial interactions and, as a result, substantial change. Focus on the here and now is how the therapist helps the client avoid

28 Theoretical Overview

dwelling on the past or getting preoccupied on future unknowns. That is not to say it ignores or minimizes the past but talks about how it affects the present. This is called *processing*, or the recognition that there is more than the "stuff" clients present with in therapy, called *content*. Process explores the experience of the content or the experience of sharing that content with someone else, such as the therapist. Emphasis on process is another commonality between gestalt and family systems therapies (Lynch & Lynch, 2005).

Two specific interventions associated with gestalt therapy (though no model has exclusive "dibs" on any intervention) are the empty chair and exaggeration techniques. The empty chair technique has the client interact with another chair in the room, envisioning another part of themselves or another person to be sitting there, conversing. The client moves from one seat to the other, portraying the differing perspectives over certain issues. The purpose is to get the client to increase self-awareness, self-reflection, and self-validation (Perls, 1969). The exaggeration technique has the therapist draw attention to a nonverbal act, even something small, the client demonstrates that connects to their current feelings about the topic. The therapist asks them to repeat it exaggeratedly. This serves to increase client awareness of their emotions and how they express them. Both interventions practice identifying, naming, and addressing underlying internal problems and how they might be impacting a person, including their relationships.

Like client-centered therapy, gestalt therapy has both commonalities and contrasting qualities to family systems theory. It views rules and structures within the system as part of the system, treating the relationship like an additional person in the room. Gestalt therapy heavily emphasizes the influence of a person's context on their behaviors, decision-making processes, and identity. Lastly, both heavily emphasize process of therapy as influential to its outcome, potentially more so than therapy's content. Like family systems theory, gestalt therapy also confronts the challenge to simultaneously be mindful of the intrapsychic and interactions. However, the way it does this differs significantly from family systems theory.

Despite these similarities, there are also drastic differences between gestalt theory and practice and those of family systems. For one, gestalt therapy focuses heavily on individual work, perhaps witnessed by the partner or family member. The family may be invited to respond and react to what they witness, but the majority of emphasis is on individual development. Overall, gestalt therapy views the system as secondary to the individual. It is a philosophical difference that views the system as collection of individuals rather than parts of a whole.

Psychoanalysis

Gestalt and psychoanalysis are both humanistic psychological theories, believing in mankind's innate drive toward self-betterment (Ackerman, 2019). However, while client-centered therapy reflects on the client's expertise, psychoanalysis assumes expertise of the therapist. This insight-oriented theory began with the renowned Sigmund Freud in the nineteenth century. His theory of the mind considers the subconscious and unconscious depths of a person's identity. These depths contribute to a person's personality and ability to create and maintain meaningful relationships (Freud & Hall, 2019). The assumption is that one's past greatly contributes to that unconscious via transference.

Transference is when an individual places emotion toward one person and puts those on someone else. Freud's theory says emotional responses to childhood experiences can lead a person to make choices from those responses, even in other situations and with other people later in life. However, it is not just childhood relationships that are replicated; it is apparent in adult relationship transference, too. Transference can be expressed in anger, hostility, fear, romantic attraction, adoration/idealization, or even child-like or parental loving, along with a multitude of other intense feelings. For example, in therapy, sometimes a client will become enamored with a therapist who listens to them in a way no parent or partner has before. However, the client may not be consciously aware of this connection. Psychoanalytic, also sometimes referred to as psychodynamic, therapy seeks to bring that unconscious to the cognitive forefront (Dreikurs, 1967). This awareness is believed to be the catalyst to change away from problematic beliefs and behaviors (Fosshage, 2003).

Psychoanalytical therapy can require clients to meet with their therapist as many as three to five times per week. In those sessions, the client explores cognitive *free association*, letting the mind make connections and discussing these with the therapist. Unless the presenting problem is situation-specific, therapy can frequently last years. It takes this long because change happens very slowly in psychoanalytical therapy. In psychoanalysis, therapists try to change deeply engrained beliefs of an individual (Blumenthal & Notman, 2006). Psychoanalysis focuses exclusively on second-order change. It also acknowledges intrapsychic identity is formed by both interaction and perception (Rhodes, 1981). Therefore, it accepts a systemic understanding of the world (Larner, 2008).

Many types of therapy stem from classic psychoanalysis. Some models use self-reflection similarly but focus on fixing the present problem rather than dive as deeply into introspection. Family systems theory considers these past contributions, primarily focusing on how they apply to present relationships. The theories both focus on interactions. Freud acknowledged the unique and identity-defining dynamics between a mother and child, which the Bateson team also studied. Freud was one of the first to explore triadic family relationships, something family systems theory calls triangles. Erikson redefined Freud's psychosexual theory into psychosocial theory of development. This included numerous references to the impact of the family on individual development and the individual on family functioning (Bretherton, 1993). While the theories and modalities of psychanalytical and family systems theory are drastically different, it would be untrue to describe them as opposites. The same could be said with family systems and CBTs.

30 Theoretical Overview

Cognitive-Behavioral Therapy

CBT is born from the joining of behavioral and cognitive therapies. Pivotal theorists such as Albert Ellis and Aaron Beck brought the theories together to form what is now one of the most well-known and highly practice therapies in the western world. CBT theorizes psychological problems are founded in distorted and problematic patterns of thought and behavior (APA, 2020). According to CBT, positive change in one's thoughts will lead to positive change in behaviors, and vice versa. In theory, facing one's problems head-on will result in improved quality of life. In practice, this model uses self-reflection worksheets, roleplay, and mindfulness to recognize faulty thinking for what it is. This process includes specifying the belief's origin, identify alternative thoughts, and act on those instead. The model has the strongest efficacy working with anxiety disorders, somatoform disorders, and anger control problems, but it also has demonstrated effectiveness with depression, marital problems, and substance use treatment (Hoffman et al., 2012).

Dialectical behavioral therapy (DBT) is based on CBT, but with greater emphasis on emotional contributions to thoughts and behaviors, too (CMHA, 2015). DBT is more intentional to consider social implications in treatment, as well. It was designed specifically to work with people who are emotionally unstable, including those who self-harm and act out other unhealthy behaviors. It practices the same core principle as CBT. Many theories and models utilize similar philosophies: Emotions, cognitions, and behaviors do not function independently; they are integrated.

Family systems theory uses these concepts by different names. It looks at reality as a multiverse of perspectives to explain varied meaning-making of events. This meaning-making is what results in those distorted thoughts and mismanaged behaviors. A shift in that meaning-making is how change happens both individually and within a social system, including a family. This includes a therapeutic focus on modifying thoughts, emotions, and behaviors away from existing dysfunctional patterns. This can be accomplished in numerous ways, in numerous models of therapy. This is an example of how different theories can work together and how a single theory can result in multiple modality approaches of therapy. CBT is both a theory and a model that overlaps into several other theories and models.

Now, I acknowledge the controversy it may be for me to identify CBT as a theory and model without exploring more extensively how it applies to family systems theory in other chapters. As identified earlier, the approach has plenty to offer. It has so much to offer, CBT is widely accepted by insurances as the pinnacle of evidence-based practices. That means they believe it works best for clients and want practitioners to use it rather than other, less research-validated methods. Additionally, it averages approximately 8 to 12 sessions, which is considered relatively short-term, an additional appeal for insurance companies.

This is where we run back into that problem I mentioned back at the beginning of the chapter: Neither individual nor family health can be quantifiably measured. The best effort is to measure progress via behavioral outcomes. The problem is that behavioral outcomes (first-order thinking) do not necessarily indicate healthy mentality or sustained change (second-order thinking). That being said, we must recognize the limits of the world in which we live, along with the limits of the theories to which we adhere.

Key Limitations

Having addressed four examples of overlapping theories and modalities, it is only fair to recognize the limits of viewing therapy as dichotomous theory and model. Philosophically, there are limits to each on both a general level and as applied to family systems theory.

Philosophical Limitations of Theories

Renowned researchers Jaccard and Jacoby (2010) proposed ten questions to evaluate the quality of a theory:

1 Is there widespread acceptance and consensual validation of the theory?
2 Is it useful?
3 Is it logically consistent?
4 Is it agreeable with known data?
5 Is it testable?
6 Is it transferable to other scientists/sciences?
7 Is it uncomplicated?
8 Does it have breadth (a wide scope of potential applicability)?
9 Is it novel or creative? Does it offer new insight into a field or industry?
10 Does it generate research activity?

Family systems theory meets these criteria in abundance. It is, after all, a social application of general systems theory. However, there is some debate if it is uncomplicated or testable.

Limits of Family Systems Theory Specifically

Critics of family systems theory have specified three perceived shortcomings in family systems theory. First, family systems theory lacks a cohesive method of application. That is to say, it does not have a specific model. Second, the theory lacks internal consistency, reportedly making it difficult to learn because it is simultaneously too broad and too specific in how it can be used. Variations of the theory can be process-, structure-, or worldview-oriented in modality application. Unfortunately, each of these present as the correct version of family systems theory rather than working collaboratively. Lastly, there is a lack of predictability in family systems theory. There is neither a predictable process of theory application (interventions) nor specific desired outcome that would demonstrate successful completion of the theory's application. Another way of saying this is that there are too many variables to reliably predict the therapy's

32 *Theoretical Overview*

process or outcomes. However, while some critics consider this problematic, the founding theorists view this as a strong tenet of the theory. It is not a "one-size-fits-all" theory.

All this to say, family systems theory is imperfect, but to call this a flaw would be illogical. Philosopher Karl Popper (1963) stated potential falsifiability to be a key quality that separates scientific theory from pseudoscience or mere philosophy. In his perspective, this is more validating than verification because it does not rely on inductive reasoning. From this outlook, the very thing that others viewed as problematic is actually evidence of family systems theory's strength as both a theory and model.

Therefore, criticisms of family systems theory are not threatening to its current and future use in social sciences (Marchal, 1975; Merkel & Searight, 1992; Becvar & Becvar, 2018). Often, the criticisms can be met with paradoxes. Here are a few more examples:

1 **Criticism**: The theory heavily focuses on familial environment, possibly to the neglect of individual psychology.
   Paradox: This is a gross overgeneralization, and untrue. We'll talk about this in Chapter 10.
2 **Criticism**: Family systems theory does not give due diligence to other social systems outside the family, such as school or broader culture.
   Paradox: Due to the social role of families, they tend to be the most influential system, regardless of quantity or quality of interaction. Families teach people the most about what it means to be a functional human. Therefore, family systems theory does not ignore the context of other social settings; it recognizes them as secondary to the family.
3 **Criticism**: As mentioned earlier, family systems theory does not describe a precise mechanism of change.
   Paradox: Human change is not an exact science. It is going to look different in each family, each person, each system. This is not a shortcoming but a reality of the human experience.

Overall, family systems theory rejects reductionist theory, the belief that understanding each part will give us the information necessary to understand the whole. Modalities of family systems theory understand this in how they apply the core concepts in various ways.

Philosophical Limitations of Modalities

Despite how much time and energy is dedicated to learning models in therapy academic programs, a therapist's modality may not be a deciding factor in therapeutic success. Abundant research shows no one model has consistently demonstrated significantly better therapeutic outcomes than others. However, the model can provide structure for the therapist. Following this logic, the therapist's confidence in the therapeutic model may make a greater difference. This is especially true when we consider the sizeable role the therapeutic relationship plays in client change (Lambert, 1992). However, clients must "buy in" to a therapist's worldview regarding how to achieve the client's desired outcome. The therapist's worldview will be communicated in their modality/modalities of choice. Part of building a therapeutic alliance will include the therapist drawing a connection between their own worldview and that of the client to create common ground from which to move forward. But I'm getting ahead of myself on that subject, which we will cover in Chapter 3.

Summary

This chapter has served to differentiate a therapeutic theory from a therapeutic model. The former is the idea, the latter is the application of that idea. This chapter applies these concepts to family systems theory, considering its theory of origin, general systems theory. This included introducing the concept of first- and second-order change. The chapter goes on to look at theories that work alongside family systems theory in its counseling approaches: Person-centered therapy, gestalt therapy, psychoanalysis, and CBT. Having covered these, the chapter concludes in acknowledging the published criticisms and limitations of theories and, specifically, family systems theory. However, despite these, the theory remains a formidable approach to counseling individuals, families, groups, or other systems.

3 Roles and Responsibilities of the Therapist in Family Systems Theory

The exact role of a therapist can vary from one model to another. However, there are some consistent role qualities. There are also patterns of responsibilities of the therapist both in session with the client and out of session.

Role of the Therapist

In family systems theory, the role of the therapist looks a little different compared to psychoanalytical therapy. In Chapter 2, I described how psychodynamic therapy, akin to psychoanalysis, frequently uses the therapist as the expert informing the client of their subconscious needs or desires. The psychoanalytical therapist identifies these needs or desires by listening to the client over a prolonged period of time. The psychoanalytical therapist is specifically listening for patterns in the client's thoughts, actions, and emotions. These patterns reveal themselves through intense and extensive exploration of the client's past. As this information is shared, the therapist poses hypotheses of the inner meaning of those events and choices the client made. Both psychodynamic and systemic therapists use a client's history to provide context for the present, but appear to use it differently.

Systemic therapists explore the clients' histories selectively. Some approaches, like Bowen's multigenerational therapy, will explore the history of family generations before the client. Bowen believed those generations influence the client's experiences and beliefs in the present, not just the past (Bowen, 1978). The key idea is the client's process of self-exploration; the client is the one coming to the conclusions and solutions. Clients typically embrace ideas best when the idea is their own. Family systems theory therapists speak and work to encourage these self-revelations that may lead to individual and systemic change. Most significantly, systemic therapists do not believe a diagnosis is necessary to work with a client.

A Nondiagnosing Stance

While marriage and family therapists are trained to recognize diagnostic criteria and legally may diagnose clients, systemic therapists frequently choose

DOI: 10.4324/9781003088196-5

not to. This is because the practice of diagnosing can be contrary to our core belief of systemic problem origin. Early models of family therapy acknowledge the presence of diagnoses, such as schizophrenia in the famed article by Bateson, Jackson, Haley, and Weakland (1956). However, they did not view that diagnosis as the end-all, be-all. It doesn't show the whole picture. Problems start, they believe, in interaction patterns, and the diagnostic symptoms persist because of those perpetuated interaction patterns. By this design, the diagnosis does little more than label and limit one member of the system as the source of the problem.

This is a second reason diagnoses do not work well with systemic therapy. When working with families and romantic relationships, the systemic therapist views the relationship, not one patient, as the client. The fifth edition of the Diagnostic and Statistical Manual of Mental Health Disorders (DSM-5) includes V-codes, which identify relational problems. However, at the time of this publication, insurance companies do not accept V-codes as a primary (read: billable) diagnosis. Therefore, it is the duty of the therapist to use diagnostic codes responsibly and mindfully, if at all (Combrinck-Graham, 2013).

The exact nature of these roles will depend on if the therapist identifies as a modern or postmodern therapist. Please note, we will specifically look at how modern and postmodern thought influence therapeutic approach. I will not attempt to summarize the grander philosophical underpinnings of either modernism nor postmodernism.

Role of the Modern Therapist

Modern therapy can be affiliated with first-order cybernetics introduced in Chapter 1. In modern therapeutic approaches, the therapist is the expert not just of their industry, but when interpreting client behaviors, thoughts, and feelings. In modern approaches to therapy, the therapist can offer an explanation and ascribe meaning to events in the clients' lives for them. In modernistic therapy, the therapist can function as coach or guide, offering instruction and direction. This authoritative approach can be a good fit for clients who desire an objective explanation of their circumstance and offer a next-step plan of action for change. This is the second commonality between modern therapy and first-order change. The therapist makes drastic efforts to remain objective and distant from the emotional entanglements of the family system. The therapist does not become a part of the system.

Examples of Modern Family System Therapies

- Strategic family therapy
- Structural family therapy
- Bowenian multigenerational family therapy
- Gottman's couple therapy
- Trust-based relational intervention therapy

36 Theoretical Overview

The shift from modern to postmodern therapy is not a drastic leap. The skills and education of a modern therapist are still vital. What changes is how those are incorporated into therapy.

Role of the Postmodern Therapist

Postmodern therapy can align with second-order cybernetics (Frosh, 1995). The emphasis tends to be on symbolism and language creating or interpreting meaning in the client's life. This rejects the modernistic idea of a true or right way to interpret something. Instead, the client's personal meaning-making influences the narrative development of the client. The therapist's role is to explore these alongside the client in a collaborative relationship. They act as a consultant rather than the more instructive coach. The client is the expert on their life; the therapist is the expert in how to view narratives in new ways and notice client narratives that may be skewed or have been ignored or minimized. This is called *polyvocality*, inviting multiple perspectives as equally valid.

Postmodern therapy embraces other second-order cybernetic qualities, too. It acknowledges the impossibility of total objectivity. Postmodern therapists acknowledge that by treating the system, we become part of it, in a way. We are directly influential, no matter our therapeutic model, or extent or method of guidance. In this sense, total emotional distance is impossible, according to postmodern theory. Unfortunately, some misinterpret the postmodern impossibility of distance as a loss of interest in being objective.

For some, postmodernism's lack of direction and emphasis on subjectivity of reality is a source of criticism. Excessive attention to language and meaning-making does not necessarily expose any truth about the client. It may only be the version of themselves or their situation they want to present, like an online persona or character they play. In this way, postmodernity as a concept has been called shallow and superficial. In therapy, this has been equated to ineffective and irrational. While I may disagree with those conclusions, I would agree that modern and postmodern approaches are not opposites; they are siblings of thought. They consider one another and apply the ideas how they see fit, just as a client would. How these ideas are applied may vary from therapy model to model.

Examples of Postmodern Family System Therapies

- Contextual family therapy
- Narrative therapy
- Solution-focused therapy
- Symbolic experiential therapy
- Internal family systems therapy
- Emotion-focused therapy
- Acceptance-commitment therapy

Despite other differences between modern and postmodern therapies, both are intentional in their use of language. Language is an inevitable tool in family systems therapy. How it is understood and used also differentiates directive and nondirective therapists.

Role of the Directive Therapist

Modern systemic therapy models are frequently directive in nature. The therapist provides direction in the session and from one session to another. This can include assigning a specific intervention technique either in session or as an out-of-session task of the client. In this way, a directive therapist takes responsibility for the client's path toward progress. However, this is not the same as taking responsibility for the change that may occur. Responsibility is not the same as taking legal liability for it; where liability is enforced externally, responsibility is intrinsically motivated. This is why it can be so important for the client to take responsibility for themselves and their actions. There is some concern that the therapist proposing the actions decreases the client's responsibility for change through them. They might say, "Your idea didn't work," or something similar, disregarding their role in the lack of success. However, a directive therapist can offer behavioral instruction and follow-up exploring the client's cognitive and emotional experience of that instruction and its implementation.

Even among nondirective therapists, there are three occasions when directive therapy may be necessary. First, if the client is endangering their health or safety. Second, if the client is a risk to the health or safety of others. Third, directive therapy may be necessary (Anderson, 1946) if the client poses a significant inconvenience to others. Of course, the challenge of the latter is the subjective nature of the phrase "significant inconvenience." Additionally, highly individualistic, dominating, or oppositional clients may benefit more from directive therapy than nondirective. In all of these occasions, though, the client may be unaware of the extent of their influence or the meaning ascribed to their behavior. It is through exposure to that influence and learning that meaning that directive therapy hopes to both solve the presenting problem and provide insight to avoid the problem in the future.

Examples of Directive Family System Therapies

- Structural family systems therapy
- Contextual family therapy
- Internal family systems therapy
- Emotion-focused therapy

Role of the Nondirective Therapist

Nondirective therapy has origins with Carl Rogers's person-centered therapy. He believed the purpose of therapy was not to solve a particular problem

38 *Theoretical Overview*

but to grow within oneself. He further defines growth as a process of individuation and integration, taking that independent identity and placing it in social constructs and situations. This means therapy focuses on the session-by-session emphasis of the client – what they want to talk about that day. The client leads the session. They decide both the content and process of each meeting. Therefore, the role of the nondirective therapist is to be accepting of and allow the client to determine the direction of each therapy session. These are the defining characteristics of the approach.

In purist nondirective therapy, the therapist would avoid suggestive language that may be misconstrued by the client as advice or instruction. Harsher language might even call it coercive or dominating, disrespecting the client's autonomy. A key attribute of the nondirective therapist is acceptance of the client as they are. Rogers asserts that trying to force a certain socially determined range of acceptable behaviors and perspectives often results in feelings of rejection and shame. If any behavioral change occurs, it is from negative, self-condemning emotions rather than growth. It is, therefore, more likely to be temporary. Similarly, this attitude lends itself to what Rogers deems a dependent relationship between the therapist and client. If the therapist senses a dependent dynamic growing between themselves and the client, it may be helpful to shift to a greater focus on advocating for the client's independence and autonomy (Anderson, 2019).

Examples of Nondirective Family Systems Therapies

- Bowenian multigenerational therapy
- Narrative therapy
- Solution-focused therapy

What Do I Do with This Information?

So now that you know a bit about modern, postmodern, directive, and nondirective therapies, how do you pick which model is for you? Here are ten scales to consider when determining your model, based on those of Goodell, Sudderth, and Allan (2011). Reflect within yourself where you fall on the spectrums between these statements:

Lasting, meaningful change can occur abruptly	← – – – – – – – – – →	Meaningful change happens over a long time
Amazing change can occur in the therapy session and create change outside of it	← – – – – – – – – – →	Change happens predominantly outside of the therapy session
My clients know best what they need; I just walk alongside them to get there	← – – – – – – – – – →	I know what my client needs to feel better; I act as a coach to help them up to get there

The past gives a person meaning-making and we have the tools to help the client change theirs	← – – – – – – – – – →	It is not necessary to delve into a client's past to provide them the tools to live better now
As the educated professional, I can prescribe intervention techniques designed to make the client change	← – – – – – – – – →	As an educated professional, I can know what works in theory, but the client is ultimately the expert of their life
There is a designated hierarchy in which a family functions best	← – – – – – – – – – →	Each family has a hierarchy that works best just for them
Past generations continue to influence family roles today	← – – – – – – – – →	There is no point focusing on the past generations, just the present
I am a problem-solver	← – – – – – – – – →	I focus on the process of learning and growing
I am a to-the-point kind of person	← – – – – – – – – →	Being direct makes me uncomfortable
I am a quiet observer	← – – – – – – – – →	I am quick to speak up when I notice something

Even as we explore your identity as a modern, postmodern, directive, and nondirective therapist, there will be consistent qualities and responsibilities of the systemic therapist both in and out of session with clients.

Role of the Advocating Therapist

To be an advocate means to help a person or system help themselves. It is an extension of the therapeutic alliance (Bratter, 1976). The therapeutic alliance is the relationship between the client and therapist. In the alliance, the therapist must ensure the client feels heard, understood, and validated. This is true whether there is an individual client or a whole system. The therapist should build an alliance with every person in the therapy space to do the best work. A therapist can be an advocate for their client regardless of modern, postmodern, directive, or nondirective identities. Empathy is an essential characteristic of advocacy. Empathy is the ability to understand and share another person's feelings for what they not, not what you assume they are or based on your own experience. There are 12 examples of nonempathetic responses:

1 Ordering and directing. Specifically, directing with a tone of authority rather than directing in the pursuit of understanding, as a directive therapist would.
2 Warning or threatening. This includes heavily insinuating negative consequences, particularly in response to treatment noncompliance.

40 *Theoretical Overview*

3 Giving advice, making suggestions, and providing premature or unsolicited solutions. This does not respect client autonomy in advocating for their expertise in their own lives.

4 Persuade with logic, arguing, or lecturing. This can be construed as talking-down to the client.

5 Moralizing, preaching, or telling clients their duty. These include statements of what they "should" do. It similarly denies clients of their decision-making autonomy.

6 Judging, criticizing, disagreeing, or blaming. This implies the client is in the wrong and can include a tone of superior thinking. Criticism is not conducive to empathy.

7 Agreeing, approving, or praising. This one catches some people by surprise. However, these can also be obstacles in client autonomy because agreement can indicate a correct and incorrect action or line of thought. Though unintentional, this can be comparable to unsolicited advice.

8 Shaming, ridiculing, labeling, or name-calling. Blatant disappointment, including rude disappointment, communicates a sense of superiority of the therapist.

9 Interpreting or analyzing. This is a cognitive diversion away from empathy, moving toward psychoanalysis and being problem-centric.

10 Reassuring, sympathizing, or consoling. This act can tamper with the relationship hierarchy and create an attempted "otherness" of the therapist that can hinder therapeutic alliance.

11 Questioning or probing. We can ask questions to learn more about the client but not with the intention of uncovering a "right answer" to their problem. Additionally, if the questions are too numerous or intense, it can feel more like an interview than therapeutic.

12 Withdrawing, distracting, humoring, or changing the subject. This is a shift away from the client's discomfort to divert from your own. While humor can be a polite attempt to distract the client off emotionally distressing subjects, it can also distract from important emotional processing and can appear dismissive of the client's initial statements.

A lack of empathy can present in several ways. However, there is more to advocacy than empathy. There are practical and emotional skills, as well.

Practically, advocating for one's client can include many paths of action. It can be providing community resources and connecting to social services. It can be involvement in a treatment team with other medical professionals serving the client. It can be participation in operational and social public policies that works to improve the life-quality of our clients or potential clients.

Emotionally, it can be empowering the client through our own faith in their capacity for growth and positive change. We can offer this aspect of advocacy in session, sitting across from the client. Whether the client is marginalized or oppressed by external factors of their environment or by internal barriers of self-perceived limitations, the therapist has the ability to reiterate the client's ability to be more than those restrictions. We know there is so much more to the client than their struggles, and there are so many ways both in and out of session that we can remind them of that.

In-Session Responsibilities of the Therapist

While fulfilling their role as a therapist, there are certain responsibilities the therapist must accomplish, too. In session, the therapist is responsible for their actions and words. These include creating a safe space, demonstrating basic attending skills, multidirectional partiality, demonstrating flexibility, patience, and providing open curiosity about the client.

Creating a Safe Space

Before the content of therapy begins, the therapist is responsible to create an environment where the clients may feel safe to explore themselves and their relationships. This safety fosters a trusting relationship that will be essential for the client to be receptive to these other therapist responsibilities. A safe space includes both the physical and emotional space.

Physically, the room should include comfortable, age-appropriate furniture and soft, soothing colors. It helps to include something from nature, or something pretending to be, like a fake plant, artwork of a landscape, or wood walls, flooring, or furniture. Ideally, it would also include natural light and adjustable lighting to accommodate to a client's brightness comfort. However, the space should also be private to respect client confidentiality. Lastly, the space can include a personal touch, something that speaks to the therapist's personality. For example, a therapist may include their credentials or small objects without giving the appearance of clutter. This can also include small, positive distractions for the client's eyes or hands to mull over, particularly during intense conversation. These physical qualities set a mood for the interaction, one that safe words can further emphasize.

Creating an emotionally safe space is a significant responsibility of the therapist from the very beginning of the relationship. Important qualities include the following:

- Being nonjudgmental to what a client says.
- Express interest in what your client says and who they are.
- Invite authenticity by demonstrating authenticity.
- Acknowledge witnessed vulnerability and struggle.

It also does not hurt to verbalize the desire for therapy to be a safe space. But those words mean very little when not followed by action that nurtures that safety. Authenticity is the capacity to be oneself, wholly and honestly. A therapist can be themselves and remain professional, but this balance requires mindfulness of the therapist. That being said, clients are typically receptive to a therapist who appears comfortable and confident in themselves and their work. This can be communicated particularly in confidence providing basic attending skills.

42   *Theoretical Overview*

Basic Attending Skills

Attending skills are how the therapist demonstrates to the client that they are actively listening to the client. The four most common ways a therapist can demonstrate active listening is through eye-contact, body language, vocal qualities, and verbal tracking. The amount of appropriate eye-contact can culturally vary; even individually, certain people may be more comfortable with it than others. Generally, clients can be more comfortable with direct eye-contact when the therapist speaks but less eye-contact when they speak. Body language includes leaning toward the client slightly; keeping a relaxed, natural posture that remains attentive; and mirroring, or matching the client's facial expression and physical position. A therapist can also mirror a client's vocal qualities. These include vocal tone, inflection, pace, and volume.

Vocal qualities do not have to be mirrored; how they are used overall can be therapeutic. A therapist can intentionally even oppose the client's non-verbal communication to keep the space therapeutic. If a client is anxiously speaking rapidly and loudly, to mirror this may not be therapeutically beneficial. Instead, the therapist can speak softly, slowly, and evenly to ease the anxiety in the space. The therapist is attentive to the needs of the client in this way. The therapist can also communicate this through verbal tracking. Verbal tracking serves to assure the client you are following along with what they are saying. It includes restating what the client says; summarizing; and reflecting, or providing language for, their emotions as they spoke. With this, the therapist offers a verbal invitation for the clients to correct them if they are tracking incorrectly or misidentifying an expressed emotion.

Attending skills may be particularly relevant when working with couples or families who experience in-session conflict. Being able to manage conflict in session is a responsibility for systemic therapists, in particular. Part of managing conflict is not taking sides with one against member of a family system over the other.

Multidirectional Partiality

Some people believe the opposite of taking sides is neutrality. However, I suggest something different. Neutrality may feel like being on no one's side. Instead, multidirectional partiality is being on everyone's side. I want all of my clients to feel heard, understood, validated, and cared for. I want them all to know I appreciate what they bring to the relationship and bring to the therapy room. If all members of the family feel appreciated and heard, I notice they are more willing to listen, too. This is a tool to manage conflict in the therapy room. After all, conflict is often easier than the time and labor-intensive process to find harmony. Using attending skills, certainly, and making sure to offer those skills to all who are present, not just with the individual you may personally agree. Multidirectional partiality will also be important in model-specific interventions and techniques, making sure to offer consistent well-rounded empathy to the whole presenting family system. This may require some maneuverability and flexibility on the part of the therapist to meet the needs of each unique client system.

Flexibility and Patience

With time and experience, therapists frequently select a theory and model of therapy that matches their worldview. Within these models, there are specific interventions and techniques that serve as therapeutic tools. Though research does not show one model is innately better than another, modality consistency can be a positive experience for clients. The details of implementing intervention tools can appear straightforward in a textbook but feel like fishing during a hurricane in practice. Therefore, executing techniques may require some flexibility rather than strict technique adherence (Owen & Hilsenroth, 2014). Flexible technique adherence relates to better outcomes compared to those who are inflexible in their interventions. However, flexibility and eclecticism are not the same. Part of therapist competence is the ability to recognize when and to what extent to be flexible and to account for the intensity of the intervention tool/application. This is an ongoing process for learning therapists.

Flexibility overlaps with patience. Patience is an essential quality of a therapist. It can be tied to client resistance in treatment. Traditional individual therapies can assume resistance is unreadiness to change. However, I view it as an extension of feeling unsafe or unsure in the therapy space. Whenever a client is not following along with my intervention implementation, my assumption is not a shortcoming on their part. Instead, I assume I did not explain it well. If the client is not honest with me about something, my assumption is that I can do more to help them feel safe to be authentic and truthful in session. I will be flexible in my intervention approach to find a method to which they are receptive. This could include changing the way I introduce a new idea or phrase a particular thought in session. One way to do this is through genuine curiosity and interest in the client and desire to learn and understand them.

Curiosity

Conceptually, curiosity comes from a desire to know something. In therapy, it can be a desire to understand something or someone. It is also a desire to explore. There are three types of curiosity: curiosity for information, for play, and for meaning and possibility (Hill, 2020). The latter, he argues, is most helpful in therapy. When a client comes to therapy, they are in a mental state that affects them physically, emotionally, and spiritually. As a therapist, we can explore this state with them and, in the process, expose the client to other states of meaning and possibility. The therapist invites clients to consider alternative states using the not-knowing stance. I do not know the client's thoughts, experiences, or meaning-making; I can only guess until the client clarifies it for me. Offering this curiosity can allow the client to reflect on their experience too, asking, "Why did I think that or make that assumption?" Therefore, to be curious is not only to the benefit of the therapist seeking to

44 Theoretical Overview

understand the client, but creates opportunity for the client to better understand themselves.

Each of these qualities – creating a safe space, demonstrating basic attending skills, multidirectional partiality, demonstrating flexibility, patience, and providing open curiosity – is a therapist's ethical responsibility to provide the client. There are several other ethical expectations of the therapist, and this is not an exhaustive list of clinical responsibilities. Therapists have laws about case documentation, reporting, and training upkeep. With all these tasks, the therapist must be intentional to implement these practices; they do not happen by accident. Similarly, a therapist must be intentional in how they practice their out-of-session responsibilities, as well.

Out-of-Session Responsibilities of the Therapist

The out-of-session responsibilities of the therapist can be summarized as versions of mindfulness. Mindfulness is a cognitive and emotional practice of attentive self-awareness and *self-compassion* (Neff, 2011). Self-compassion is nonjudgmental self-awareness demonstrated through self-kindness, mindfulness, and a sense of shared humanity, which recognizes one's humanness without holding that against oneself. These concepts relate to the *person of the therapist.*

Person of the therapist is a person's natural tendencies and those intentionally developed to make oneself a better therapist. This includes skills in empathy, cultural awareness, ethical decision-making, and consideration of others as equal to yourself. It also includes natural listening skills you can hone into professional use: active listening, reflective statements, attending skills, use of open-ended and bias-free questions and statements, and the like. It's possible to improve all of these with practice and intentionality: How I think about and communicate empathic reflection, and becoming more attuned to ethical conundrums and cultural challenges of numerous populations. You achieve this through self-awareness and honest self-reflection, acknowledging where you need to grow, even in those natural abilities. There is always room for growth. There is always space to become a better therapist. Two important ways to do this is through self-reference and self-care.

Self-Reference

Intentional self-reflection is an out-of-session responsibility of a therapist. Maybe it sometimes happens abruptly by chance, but intentionality is key to consistent self-growth. A central part of self-reflection is self-reference. *Self-reference* is a systems theory concept introduced in the more recent years of research. It notices the impossibility of absolute objectivity and challenges therapists to be mindful of how they are subjective. Self-reference asks the therapist not only how are you subjective, but how does it impact one's therapeutic approach? It challenges therapists to be aware of their point of view and how that may come across to a client in therapy.

This being said, we cannot always know how our worldview impacts us. Sometimes we have blind-spots, where our worldview is so thickly "filtered," that we do not realize there are other valid perspectives, as well. This is where supervision and your own therapy can be quite helpful. Mental health professionals can assist one another, as they might a client, to see from new perspectives. Without this open-mindedness, we risk providing less helpful therapy and risk not taking steps to grow as a person. Even (especially!) as a therapist, we need to take care of ourselves. That can include being a therapy client ourselves, but it also includes so much more.

Self-Care

Conceptually, *self-care* is straightforward; it's taking care of yourself. In practice, though, it can be more complex. It primarily includes setting boundaries, personally and professionally. We will talk extensively about boundaries in Chapter 8. Here I will simply summarize them to be the extent to which we invite influence from others, physically and emotionally. Poor self-care typically aligns with poor boundary-setting; as a result, a person may feel overwhelmed by others' overinvolvement in their lives, or, at the other end of the boundary-setting spectrum, extreme isolation. Either extreme is considered unhealthy. In the middle there is a happier balance that accepts influence from others and recognizes when it is time to say, "no," and focus on oneself (Suppes, 2019).

In the culture of the United States, there seems to be a shift occurring that allows or encourages this balance. In some work environments, an older line of thought still reigns that discourages employees from taking time off to take care of themselves. Fortunately, a growing population recognizes how productivity is actually enhanced by balancing time in and away from work. No matter how much you love providing therapy, it is still work. It is emotionally taxing to sit across from people you care about and do those in-session responsibilities. Taking care of ourselves improves our ability to care for our clients, too. You can be your strongest advocate.

So, what is self-care, practically? Stereotypically, self-care is a spending-spree spa day. But some days the richest thing about me is the slice of cake I bought at the grocery store. Self-care is not about spending money. Self-care is doing what is in your best interest. Sometimes it's encouraging myself to eat the salad; other days it's indulging in something sweet. That is to say, sometimes self-care is perseverance; other days it is knowing when I need to slow down and rest. And I do not need to chastise myself for that. The choice not to reprimand myself and the decisions I make is part of self-care, too. Self-care is both a physical act and a state of mind. It's the way we talk to and about ourselves. The self-caring state of mind is one of self-compassion.

Self-Compassion

As mentioned before, self-care is the intersection of self-kindness, mindfulness, and a sense of shared humanity. This mindset allows you to see yourself

46 *Theoretical Overview*

more objectively than you previously have. It accepts the ways you are average, above-average, and flawed without judgment or self-loathing. Self-compassion creates space for self-growth by eliminating the punitive middleman of cognitive self-harm. Instead, it reviews one's thoughts, actions, and feelings in a validating, honest, and empathetic tone. It is not unlike the empathetic curiosity we offer our clients.

There are a few things you can do to help give yourself this mindset. First is intentionality and practice. Shifting into a self-compassionate mindset probably will not be a one-shot effort. There may be times when you find yourself speaking to yourself harshly. However, all we can do is (1) notice when we do it, and (2) offer ourselves compassion for it. Ask yourself, "Why might it make sense that I felt that way?" Giving myself understanding can decrease my self-judgment and allow me to move toward a compassionate response that will actually yield better outcomes than severely punishing myself mentally or physically.

Examples of Self-Care

Behaviorally, self-care can mean many different things. There are four types of self-care: physical, cognitive, emotional, and spiritual. Examples of physical self-care can be drinking plenty of water, eating healthy, exercising, meditating, or getting a massage. Examples of cognitive self-care are journaling; reading for pleasure; or individual creative hobbies such as painting, playing a musical instrument, working on cars, and cooking. Emotional self-care may be talking to friends, laughing, crying, and offering encouragement. Lastly, spiritual self-care examples include yoga, time spent in nature, or connecting to a spiritual community such as a church. Several of these examples can actually serve as multiple forms of self-care, such as meditation being good for you physically, mentally, and spiritually.

If the purpose of self-care is rejuvenation, sometimes self-care is giving yourself a break. Rest is a form of self-care. It might be a nap on a weekday, going to bed earlier, or letting yourself watch a movie instead of stressing over finishing a class reading assignment early. Self-care can also mean pushing yourself sometimes. Self-fulfillment is self-care. It might be waking up a little earlier to go for a jog because you know you feel better after you do. It might be pushing yourself to complete your notes after a long day because you know your mind will be more at ease when you get home if you do. I frequently ask myself, "What do I need *right now?*" and the answer is often quite telling. But I have to slow down long enough to ask the question and listen well enough to hear my internal response.

One of the most prominent things we can do is take time away from screens. Screens not only can physically hurt our eyes, but what we look at can be hurtful to our hearts and minds. Reengaging with nature by going for a walk or hike, gardening, or stepping outside and taking a few deep breaths can make a world of difference. For many people, this is a spiritual experience,

Role of the Therapist 47

recentering an individual on their higher power and life purpose. Clearly, there is much more to self-care than (temporarily) guilt-free spending.

What about When Self-Care Goes Wrong?

Ironically, in a field that frequently boasts the importance of self-care, it is not uncommon to meet therapists who do not practice what they preach. However, as a new generation of therapists begin, I hope they will understand why self-care is so important. It is important to our overall health and our ability to provide beneficial services to our clients. Poor self-care and boundaries can result in three problematic patterns in therapy: inappropriate self-disclosure, countertransference, and burnout.

1 *Inappropriate self-disclosure*
   Self-disclosure directly relates to boundaries in therapy. It is a discussion of the therapist's personal life and experience, often intended to relate to the client's situation. Sometimes it can be appropriate and helpful, as long as the focus remains on the client. However, when a therapist is exhausted and losing healthy boundaries, they may disclose inappropriately. The attention stays on the therapist and their experience rather than shift back to the client. The therapist may emotionally lose control and become increasingly reactive in session. Self-disclosure can be a powerful tool in therapy if used correctly, but should be used as a last resort. If there is another appropriate intervention, try that first. It would not be helpful to use self-disclosure and experience countertransference as a result.

2 *Countertransference*
   Earlier, transference was defined as emotions displaced by the client from one person on to another. This could include client emotions put onto the therapist that may have been originally associated with another authority figure, such as a parent or teacher. Countertransference is the same idea in the opposite direction. *Countertransference* is the therapist projecting emotions onto their clients that may have other origins.
   For example, I supervised a student therapist who saw a client that reportedly was resistant to treatment, frequently rebuffing the therapist's feedback using the phrase, "yea, but," and describing why their situation was impossible to overcome. The therapist became terse and frustrated with the client in session, presenting in-session as verbal brevity and lack of patience. It ultimately resulted in the client discontinuing therapy. Upon review in supervision, the student divulged that the client reminded her of an old friend who frequently used the same phrase. According to the therapist, that friendship had ended abruptly and on bad terms. The student acknowledged she had never processed the loss of that friendship and perceived rejection. As a supervisor, I encouraged the student to attend her own counseling to reflect on and heal from that experience.

48   *Theoretical Overview*

In this example, the student's countertransference had cost the relationship with that client. This was the result of the student not doing self-care surrounding her lost friendship. While this is a single case example, the final problematic pattern can be costly, even to a counselor's license and profession.

3   *Burnout*

Therapeutic *burnout* is marked by compassion fatigue. This results in indifference or outright dread of one's therapeutic work. Burnout comes from one or more of the following (Montero-Marin, Pardo-Abril, Demarzo, Garcia-Toro, & Garcia-Campayo, 2016):

a   Consistent overworking due to unattainable goals.
b   Understimulated and underchallenged in work assignments.
c   Overall exhaustion resulting in carelessness, stress, and feeling unappreciated.

When a therapist experiences high levels of burnout, they can become emotionally unstable and less ethical in their clinical services. This includes both direct contact with clients and indirect responsibilities like documentation. Therapists who experience burnout may be more likely to have inappropriate self-disclosure and countertransference. This is most likely when the therapist has not been practicing self-care. Learning to recognize early signs of burnout within oneself and manage them may be a recurring out-of-session responsibility of the therapist.

Summary

In conclusion, the role of the therapist will depend on their identity as a modern or postmodern therapist and their choice to be directive or nondirective in their techniques. The therapist's preferred therapeutic model will depend on their worldview of how to be an effective therapist. While research does not show one model to be outstandingly better than another, it does appear that a therapist's comfort and confidence in their model can make a difference. That comfort and confidence can be demonstrated in fulfilling the responsibilities of the therapist both in and out of session. Using these tools, a therapist can grow to better understand themselves and be mindful of how family systems theory applies to their own lives and those of their clients.

Part II

Theoretical Application

4 FST Concept I
Wholeness

Countless stories, romantic comedies, and craft-store sign templates glamorize finding your "other half." Being in a relationship is part of most fictional characters' happily ever after, and this is not entirely a concept of fantasy. Research has shown good, strong marriages are positively associated with good, strong physical and mental health (Kiecolt-Glaser & Newton, 2001). Research shows individuals in relationships, including marriage, experience greater life satisfaction and initially fewer depressive symptoms than those of the same age cohort who are single (Musick & Bumpass, 2012). Conversely, troubled marriages can be linked to heightened stress and depression and everything from increased cardiovascular activity, hormonal dysregulation, and changes in immune system functionality (Robles & Kiecolt-Glaser, 2003). However, this is different from saying someone is incomplete or not whole when not in a romantic relationship.

Connection between physical and mental health is not restricted to romantic partnerships. Relationships influence one's physiological and mental health both positively and negatively. Health influences satisfaction with a relationship, too. This includes friendships, mentorships, business colleagues, and family of origin, too. In all these types of relationships, each person contributes something different. There is a specific and unique role that person uniquely fills in the relationship that no other person can replicate exactly. In turn, the relationship, like each person contributing to it, is entirely unique. This is the notion of wholeness.

What Is Wholeness?

In the early twentieth century, decades before the Mental Research Institute (MRI) team would come together, Jan Christian Smuts (1926) proposed the concept of "holism." It incapsulates the idea that what each person brings to a relationship culminates into so much more than those individual skills and perspectives. Between each person's contributions, an existentially greater thing comes to exist. Smuts called this *creative synthesis*, allowing for dynamic evolution of a relationship. The evolution considers each person's past, present, and future alongside the past, present, and future of the relationship

DOI: 10.4324/9781003088196-7

52   *Theoretical Application*

itself. The relationship is, in some ways, a separate being interacting with the individuals in it. To use a term infamous in the field of marriage and family therapy, the whole is greater than the sum of its parts.

Holism, or wholeness, is viewing society and relationships as a system, like an organism. Holism suggests a system – whether that be romantic, friendly, professional, or familial – cannot be fully understood from the perspective of a single member. There are qualities that only emerge when other members of the system are present, too. Members of a system are not independent islands; they influence one another. The relationship is naturally reciprocal; neither a person nor a relationship can be fully understood without the context of the other.

Fritz Perls, a gestalt original theorist, applied holism to a cultural level. According to Perls, there is more to a person than their experiences. A person is more than their behaviors or what happens to them. Identity is not so passive or static. As events occur in one's life, we actively contribute to these and the way they will influence us moving forward. Even the concept of identity speaks of dynamic influence of thoughts, emotions, values, beliefs, and choice (Stevenson, 2018a). All these contribute to the sense of wholeness within oneself. Individuals in the relationship also contribute to the identity of the relationship – what makes it romantic, professional, friendship, mentoring, and the like. Wholeness exists both within individuals and between people.

The idea of individual holism, or wholeness, stems from Arthur Koestler's (1967) conceptualization of the holon. Simplified, a holon is something that is simultaneously an independently functioning entity and a part of another whole. In groups of people, we see individual identities – independently functional – working together to create a group identity. These groups can be brought together involuntarily, such as families, or voluntarily, such as friendships. Either way, these organizations can bond by a common identity or goal as a group.

Goal-Setting as a Family System

Social systems, including families, are goal-seeking. That is to say, there is something that would indicate the relationship has achieved something. There is a directive, or mission, the family bears. This could be anything from a simple task to the passing on of family ideology. Goal-setting includes a minimum of four features:

1   A means to identify a goal.
2   A means to identify and pursue a path toward that goal.
3   A means to identify when they deviate from that goal.
4   A means to return to the path toward that goal when they deviate.

These features require a decision-making process to identify and pursue a goal, but not all members of a system will have the same decision-making process.

Similarly, not all family members will have the same goals. Per family systems theory, though, there is a fifth feature:

5   Family goals are organized into hierarchies [of prioritization] .... Those of a higher prioritization are less likely to be revised or abandoned.

In other words, families come together, as a whole, to prioritize certain goals higher based on their needs. Some goals address basic need, and that goal must be achieved in order to physically stay alive. From there, goals are prioritized in a family based on their personal value systems. Some goals may be ongoing and inflexibly essential to family identity and family success. A notorious example of goal-setting in psychology is that of Maslow's hierarchy of needs.

Maslow's Hierarchy of Needs

Maslow's (1943) hierarchy of needs is a visual representation of the need for a secure foundation before more specialized desires are addressed. This pyramid describes the basic needs of human life – shelter, rest, and bodily sustenance of food and water – as primal and essential. It is considered a basic need, along with the need for security and safety. Once these are attained, a person or system may address psychological needs. First, a sense of belongingness and love, then self-esteem or personal vitality. Maslow added stages of cognitive and aesthetic needs, which require knowledge and understanding, meaning, curiosity, and an appreciation/search for balance and beauty. Only upon achieving these needs can a person even aim for the pyramid's peak of self-actualization. Self-actualization is marked by feelings of self-fulfillment. Finally, also added after his initial design, Maslow (1966) identifies the need for transcendence. Transcendence is participation in and contribution to a value that goes beyond oneself. This could be a systemic attribute of the otherwise individualized hierarchy, where one is given a sense of wholeness. This demonstrates the hierarchy of need, where one need scaffolds off the achievement of the previous needs. It also serves as an internal motivational tool. A person is naturally inclined to climb that pyramid and try to reach the peak.

How does this relate to family systems theory? Both individuals and systems strive to complete the hierarchy of needs. Even if an individual in a family has completed one level, until other members of that system also have that goal met, it can be difficult for the first to continue moving upward on the pyramid. Otherwise, the whole will be torn apart. Instead, systems thrive when members of the family seek healthy balance between their individual goals and the systemic goals. This is the innate struggle of the holon. It is made up of both an integrative part and a part that seeks autonomy. Per holism, there is also a third part: The relationship between the integrative and autonomous parts. All three of these are taken into consideration when an individual makes a choice. Will it be in their personal interest? The family interest? Or in the interest in their relationship with the family? They may be prioritized differently based on the needs of the moment.

54 *Theoretical Application*

Are Families Always Goal-Seeking?

Families as goal-seeking systems is contradicted by the Rapoport model of reflexive spirals. Anatol Rapoport and William Horvath (1960) designed a mathematically based social network analysis. They noticed trends in how ideas and information are spread at various speeds. Those speeds often depend on variables such as race, gender, socioeconomic status, kinship, and proximity. This is linked with the social observation of biased networks, in which people are more likely to share ideas and even physical space with individuals with whom they have more in common. This is called the *preferential attachment mechanism.*

Rapoport (1968) would also say that families routinely participate in activities and patterns of interaction that have nothing to do with values or goals of any family member or the united family identity. Therefore, he may disagree that families are necessarily goal-seeking systems. Instead, he identifies the continued importance of seeking out wholeness for optimal functioning. Perhaps this pursuit of wholeness could be considered a goal and further evidence of general systems theory's application to human behavior. However, sometimes goals are difficult to pursue when different system members have conflicting goals. This can occur based on the individual system members' roles.

Family Roles

In the introduction, I gave a general definition of family roles, specifically saying that different family roles will have different responsibilities and types of influence on the system as a whole. To reach systemic goals, individuals tend to take on specific roles within their system. These roles provide a bridge between the individual and their setting, including their family system. It gives them a part to play.

Per social roles theory, the roles can be reciprocal to others in the system: To be a parent, there must be a child; to be a teacher, there must be a student, and so on. Roles tend to have relatively scripted parts to play; this provides some predictability. There are some common roles people play in their families. While their original research was done in the context of addiction, it is widely applicable. Over the years, other researchers have added to her ideas or changed some of the terminology, but certain themes remain consistent:

- **Scapegoat** or **black sheep**: This person is frequently viewed as the problem in a family system. When a family comes to therapy, there can often be a consensus of other family members that if this one person could pull themselves together, the whole family would be fixed and problem-free! To fill this role, the black sheep may bear the most obvious symptoms of dysfunction such as being aggressive or demonstrating a particular mental health diagnosis. However, this person also tends to be more in touch with their feelings than other roles, even if they do not express those feelings in appropriate or healthy ways. This person also tends to be more honest and have a strong sense of humor that have helped them persevere this vilified persona.

- **Hero**: The good and responsible person in the family, the hero tends to be high achieving. This can be viewed as overcompensation to balance the black sheep's lack of apparent achievement. They can be highly goal-oriented and self-disciplined. However, heroes can also be rigid rule-followers and have a hard time being flexible when necessary. Their desire to do right can struggle when they are faced with a world that is not as black-and-white as they would like it to be.
- **Rescuer**: The rescuer tends to be the family problem-solver. They want to help others, often at the neglect of their own needs. However, this can result in taking unnecessary responsibility to resolve conflicts in which they are not involved or do whatever is necessary to hasten a solution rather than necessarily create a lasting resolution. Rescuers can often be quite anxious and struggle with guilt over past perceived failures.
- **Mediator**: Generally speaking, the mediator is a buffer between members of the family and the problem. Often, they take on the emotional work of the conflict so that others will not have to. This role can appear in multiple ways. It can be similar to a rescuer, striving to find answers as quickly or smoothly as possible. It could be a nurturer, someone who strives to take care of others to help them feel safe and heard. They may strive to be objective, but might minimize the importance of emotions in decision-making. Unfortunately, this role is often taken at the cost of their own safety and mental balance.
- **Lost child**: This is a low-key role, so to speak. They seek to minimize personal attention and may be particularly subservient and passive to achieve this. They may be flexible to a fault as they strive to avoid the problem as much as possible. Regrettably, this lack of attention to their own needs can leave a lost child feeling aimless, avoid proactive decision-making, and follow instructions without question, even to their own detriment.
- **Clown** or **mascot**: This role frequently relies on humor in attempt to dissipate tension or give the illusion that things are not really so bad. Their talent for lightening the mood can come at the cost of their own ability to explore their true feelings because those depths may defy the "take it easy" attitude they are expected to personify. Therefore, clowns may end up stifling their own emotions to help others feel more comfortable.
- **Cheerleader**: The primary purpose of this role is to offer support. This can come at the cost of this person's individuality and can appear as enabling or minimizing of the problem. Their goal is to support others to reach a resolution in the hope that doing so will make the problem go away.

It is important to keep in mind that all of these roles contribute to the family's sense of being whole. Without any one of them, the family may not feel complete anymore or not know how to function. However, not all roles will be present in the system at the same time; for example, there will not always be somebody being a cheerleader or lost child. Depending on the size of the

56 *Theoretical Application*

system, it is common for people to fill more than one role at a time. Similarly, the role we fill may change depending on the situation.

Sometimes, we return to old, familiar roles when entering new systems. If I identified as a black sheep in my family, I may not feel a sense of belonging in other settings, too. I may identify as a loner in school or not initiate friendships with coworkers when I'm older. I might assume other people don't like me, which could affect my pursuit of a romantic relationship, if I wanted one. I return to this role because I know how to fill it. People like the familiar and will often keep a familiar dysfunctional role before they try to learn something new and unfamiliar. This is part of what keeps some dysfunctional family patterns around even when they do not work.

Criticism of Holism

Clinton Jesser, a social theorist, argued against holism as a natural state. He created the concept of *nominalism*, where society is a collection of parts pursuing *order* rather than parts unified as a whole pursuing *balance*. However, the pursuit of balance is essential to family systems theory to understand why systems behave as they do. These two theories identify vast differences between order and balance, though so often they may appear so similar. Order does not assume balance, but balance can create order. In either case, consideration of the whole is essential to create both balance and order.

Applicable Therapeutic Models

Applying wholeness to family therapy depends on one family systems theory assumption: Changing a part of a system will inevitably change the system as a whole. That means even small changes in a single individual can ripple outward to influence other system members and potentially lead to the desired overall change. However, it also forces the client to recognize what they are able to change or influence and what is beyond their control.

Being a marriage and family therapist – or systemic therapist – does not mean you cannot work with individuals. We just need to recognize that when we see individuals in therapy, we are not getting the whole picture. That being said, even when we see families or couples, we are only getting a slightly larger piece of the grand picture. We are still only seeing them in one relationship bond and setting. However, the family is one of the most influential settings for personal growth and identity development.

The concept of wholeness appears in every systemic therapy model. Here are four examples of how different models use the concept in similar but unique ways:

Bowen's Multigenerational Therapy

One of the first assessment tools a Bowenian therapist uses is the *genogram*. Comparable to a family tree, the genogram draws out family history in great detail. The genogram can include information about addictions, careers, geographic locations, significant dates, family names, physical health, mental health, and many others. Most prominently, it provides a space to visually depict relationship dynamics through vertical and horizontal relationships. These dynamics communicate closeness, distance, cut-offs, distress, and even abuse. This assessment tool dually serves as an intervention technique. The insight gained in the process of building the genogram can spark change all by itself. It typically includes a minimum of three generations.

The genogram paints a picture of the whole family. More than just the people present for therapy, this tool encourages going back multiple generations to learn whatever possible about one's ancestry. These individuals can continue to shape and influence us, even from beyond the grave. My parents' parents were taught about the world by their parents. This, in turn, influences my parents' worldviews. Their worldview impacted their parenting. Their parenting impacted me in more ways than I can name. In this way, people I may have never met influenced me.

This can be both positive and negative. If a generation is taught to be optimistic about the world and the people in it, that can influence the worldview of an individual who goes on to inspire hope in countless other settings. On the other hand, if a generation experiences abuse by an elder generation, they are more likely to perpetuate that with future generations. Earlier I stated that the individuals of a system contribute to the identity of the whole. In these ways, the whole can contribute to its parts, too.

Bowen multigeneration therapy greatly acknowledges the importance of family holism in its emphasis in therapy on balancing familial and individual identities (Bowen & Kerr, 2009). He calls these togetherness and differentiation of self. He would reiterate that we cannot erase family influence, but we can choose what to do with that influence or to what extent it will propel or hinder us. This model, maybe more than others, emphasizes the importance of achieving personal healing by reflecting on the whole family's past, not just one's own.

Structural Family Therapy

Structural family therapy also has an assessment tool similar to the Bowenian genogram. This pictorial representation of the family, called the *family map*, particularly highlights the closeness and emotional distance of the family members. It focuses on the present more than on the past. Unlike the genogram, this version particularly focuses on how power is spread or held in a family. Is there one person for whom theirs is always the final word? Is there someone whose contributions are consistently minimized or silenced? Are there situations, such as the crisis that brings the client to therapy, that bring out this dynamic more prominently than normal? The family map addresses these types of questions. It also allows for a bit more flexibility to who is considered a family member. It identifies subsystems, which will be a topic in Chapter 7. For now, we will simply state that subsystems include smaller, closer-knit members of a whole family. A family map can be a helpful tool to

58 *Theoretical Application*

identify these subsystems and, more importantly, discuss the fallout of these to the overall family connection.

A core tenant of structural therapy is that families, as a whole, develop a normal pattern of interaction and a functionality around that norm. That functionality particularly includes focus on how the family is organized. A family can become accustomed to this norm, even when it is not healthy or does not achieve the family's goals of healthy living and raising children to be independent, functional adults. Family members fall into the roles identified earlier and avoid the conflict essential to rebalance the hierarchy to its healthier version. Only one person in the family needs to change to bring about a change in the whole system. All it takes is one person to face the discomfort of potential conflict. This is done in the interest of improving the whole family, creating a more stable norm. This theory greatly recognizes how, when each person is able to bring their best, the whole truly is greater than the sum of its parts.

Narrative Family Therapy

It is a basic tenant of narrative therapy that we are born into what they call stories. These could also be called the narratives of certain systems. For example, there is often a dominant narrative, a story assumed to be the truth. This may be associated with one's race, sex, or religion; typically, a larger whole of which we are part. The assumption is your membership in this whole system means this dominant narrative is accurate to your experience. Similarly, we may make sense of our experiences through the lens of that narrative. This is similar to how individuals in a system contribute to the identity of the whole, but the identity of the whole also contributes to the identities of the individuals within it.

However, people often find this dominant narrative does not match their experience. There are other versions of the story, called alternative narratives. One therapeutic intervention in this model is to identify those alternative stories and use them as scaffolding a better understanding of self and their relationships. This can be called crafting or writing their story.

Narrative therapy also utilizes a technique called *externalization*. In this model, the person is not the problem; the problem is the problem. Too often problems are assigned to specific members of the family, such as the black sheep or scapegoat. Externalizing the problem does two things: It depersonalizes it from the person previously held solely responsible and takes the power away from the problem as it is deconstructed objectively instead. This allows the symptom bearer to be something other than the problem; they can now contribute to the solution, too (Pitts, 2019). Externalizing is not limited to problems. By viewing something as separate from the people it involves, therapists create language to appreciate how the relationship contributes to the whole picture. All together – the individuals and their relationships with one another – more accurately portray the family as a whole.

Internal Family Systems Therapy

Internal family systems (IFS) therapy epitomizes how even an individual is the whole of a collection of parts. According to this model, people consist of several interacting internal parts. Each part serves a role to help the individual's functionality. When working together, serving their roles properly, they function ideally as a whole. These roles can look very much like those introduced earlier: A hero who strives to make the individual look good, the mediator who wants to avoid emotional outbursts in public, the rejected part that is blamed when things go wrong and the individual has a bad day. But just like the extreme versions of these in other people, the hero can be too harsh and easily stressed, the mediator can get overwhelmed when it buries the difficult emotions too long, and the rejected part has more to offer than what is allowed of it. These parts are led by a core Self, a natural leader with the delegating skills that allow each part to shine in their unique areas of expertise. Just like with family therapy, IFS strives to find balance between these parts and create a sense of holism.

The parts crave being part of a whole. They desire that second and third level of Maslow's hierarchy of needs: security, safety, and a sense of belonging. These are things no human can achieve entirely independently. We need to belong to a bigger picture and have a bigger purpose. We crave being a part of a whole. IFS therapy explores how experiencing holism within ourselves with our own parts contributes to feeling whole in relationships with other people, too. We no longer ask others to complete us because we feel complete within ourselves. In this way, IFS demonstrates individual wholeness and describes how to achieve this through therapeutic intervention.

Case Study: Candice's School Anxiety

Candice, a 16-year-old girl, has lived alone with her mother, Angie, since her parents divorced when she was ten. On the rare occasions Candice's parents talk, Angie and Rick only talk about Candice's school events and social plans. They are able to do so quite amicably. Candice would describe her relationship with her mother as "good," though both are quite busy independently. Candice says her relationship with her father is "fine, I guess," noting that he routinely calls and texts her but the conversations are brief and surface-level.

At school, Candice is a star student. As a junior in high school, she is taking several advanced-placement classes. She also is in an honor society and choir, which participates in year-round competitions. She intends to apply to colleges and is currently considering several well-ranked universities. She has not yet picked a major, saying, "I still have time to figure that out." Candice has a close-knit small group of friends that she has known since freshman year who are also in choir. None of them have committed to a university for next year, either.

60   *Theoretical Application*

Candice's mother has been dating Paul for the past two years. Candice has met Paul and describes him as "a pretty cool guy, I guess." She says he treats her mother well and likes that he "tries to be funny." Paul has been divorced for about four years. He also has a sixteen-year-old daughter named Jessica. Her parents share custody, and she stays with Paul about every other week. Jessica goes to the same school as Candice. She is also in choir (though she is in a different section) and several of Candice's classes. Despite being outwardly similar, Candice describes Jessica as "kind of a bully" and irritably reports Jessica does not have to work hard to get good grades in school. Even though their parents are dating, the pair have acted indifferent toward one another. They rarely interact at school and spoke minimally during the few "family dinners" their parents required they attend at various points over the past two years.

Candice's mom recently approached her to let her know Paul intended to ask Angie to marry him. He would be moving in with them the summer before Candice's senior year. Since that conversation, Angie has noticed changes in Candice. She no longer gets up early and often misses the bus to school. She has missed her first-period class several times in the past few weeks. Angie recently received a notice from one of Candice's teachers that she has not been turning in her homework and seems "out of it" during class. At home, Candice has demonstrated increased irritability toward her mother, resistance to complete chores, states she no longer cares about going to college, and has spent more time alone in her bedroom. Her mother recently confronted her about this change, to which Candice tearfully burst out that she was overwhelmed and "just [doesn't] care anymore." This conversation prompted Angie to schedule a session for Candice with a therapist.

Treating with Bowenian Multigenerational Therapy

Interpretation of the Problem

Two core intervention goals of Bowenian therapy are decreasing anxiety and increasing self-differentiation (Gilbert, 1992). It is likely that Candice's school stress overlaps with her relationship changes at home. According to Bowen's theory, Candice may be experiencing relationship anxiety from several angles. She may feel a lack of fulfillment in her relationships with her biological parents. She may feel disconnected from them. She may also feel anxious about her impending stage-of-life transitions, including her mother remarrying and the possibility of herself leaving the home. The latter could also overlap with self-differentiation as she takes a significant step to establish herself as an independent mind and being from her family of origin. Her role as an only child and hero are being challenged. Candice's sense of wholeness may be challenged right now.

FST Concept I 61

Anticipated Solution

While creating a genogram, the therapist might learn more about how Candice's family history has prioritized and measured academic or vocational success. This may contribute to pressure the client feels, particularly if there is a new competitive perception with her stepsister. Part of this will also be perceived consequences of not following those family expectations and how this impacts the client individually and the family as a whole. It is possible she felt required to do well in school and attend college based on family expectation, even if her vocational desires are elsewhere or unclear. Allowing her to explore these thoughts and feelings could be important to increase her level of differentiation.

The therapist could also look for possible patterns of divorce and remarriage in the genogram. Candice may be experiencing role confusion shifting from an only child of a single mother to roles of stepsister, stepdaughter, and self-identifying more as an adult as she shifts to roles of greater independence. Generally, the focus would be on identifying Candice's source of anxiety and taking steps to minimize those. This can be accomplished through increased connection with her family – including her mother, biological father, and new stepfather and stepsister – to avoid perceptions of abandonment or isolation. It can also be accomplished individually as she explores the difference between family expectations, the development of personal goals, and the balance between these.

Example Questions

1   "It sounds like you have gotten comfortable with how things were between you and your mom, but bringing Paul into the family will bring some big changes. What feelings come up for you when you think of those big changes?"
2   "I see your family has a history of being high achievers. What do you think they would say if you decided not to go to college? What is it like for you for them to believe those things?"
3   "I see divorce is not very common in your family. How did you and your mother cope with this deviation from the family norm when you were younger?"
4   "What would your dad say if you reached out to him instead of waiting for him to contact you?"
5   "It sounds like you and Jessica haven't gotten along very well, but also that you don't know each other well. What do you think Paul would say about that?"

Treating with Structural Family Therapy

Interpretation of the Problem

Structural therapy places emphasis on hierarchy and power in families. In healthy families, children will not hold power over their parents because this

62   *Theoretical Application*

dynamic rarely fosters healthy emotional development. In this family dynamic, it appears Candice claimed prominent power after her parents' divorce. Their interactions appear to be on her terms, even when she is not present. However, she has been mostly responsible with this power, until this situation. She has attended school on her own volition, done well in academics, and maintained peer friendships. However, she may have done these out of her role as a mediator or peace-keeper between her parents. In Structural therapy, this would be called *triangulation*. Candice also appears to be sensitive to others' power, including Jessica's. This is evident in Candice's identification of Jessica as a bully, a role that innately steals power from others.

Candice is also experiencing a power shift as Paul and Jessica are introduced into a new family system. Angie also has made her decision to marry Paul without getting approval from Candice first. While this is a normal and healthy power dyad between a parent and child, it may feel unfamiliar or abnormal for Candice. She may also be uncertain about how power will be divided among the new family system and what the hierarchy will look like. Any time two families come together to form one, power will be redistributed to create a new norm, and where there were once two hierarchies there will now be one. One person who was previously at the top of their hierarchy will have to step down. Candice likely feels uneasy about these changes.

Anticipated Solution

The therapist may use a family map to learn about the emotional closeness and distance as it currently stands but also to learn how the client would like the closeness to be between herself and her biological parents and new family members. The same intervention could be applied to other family members as well. Candice, Angie, Paul, and Jessica could all learn what the others want their family dynamic to look like.

This conversation could overlap with conversations about family rules that would keep the two teenagers on the same level of the hierarchy. Jessica and Candice will both still need their boundaries respected, and in exchange will respect the boundaries of the other family members. Feeling disrespected can often result in the opposite of the desired goal as family members function in opposition to one another rather than as a whole unit. The change will require patience and persistence. This includes recognizing the challenges that come with change and anticipating resistance. In fact, the symptoms that brought Candice into therapy could be symptoms of difficulty coping with the change.

Addressing power and hierarchy in a family does not have to be a harsh, forceful conversation. The structural family therapist can still prioritize joining and demonstrate basic therapeutic skills of reflecting and reframing. Reframing describes a situation from a new perspective, shifting from problem-focused language to opportunity for constructive change. This could be essential to Candice's situation as the therapist can explore what new opportunities and relationships can be gained and built as she shifts her role in the family. Rather than being a hero or mediator, she can focus on her personal goals as she grows into an independent adult. She can relieve herself of the responsibilities that come with holding power and leadership and shift to cope with the normal life stage experiences of an early adolescent. She can also observe how her mother and Paul balance and maneuver this change without interfering or stepping in, learning to allow them to be mature adults, too.

Example Questions

1   "What do you think the step-sister relationship should be like? Whose help do you need to make that happen?"
2   "It is important for the parenting team to function together, united. Angie, what would you like to see from Paul that would help you feel like a united front when working with the girls? Paul, what would you like to see from Angie?"
3   "Candice, I can tell you have worked a long time to take care of your mom. What would be different for you if you knew she could take care of herself?"
4   "Making new family norms can be hard. Candice, what are some family norms between you and your mom that you would like to keep, if possible? Jessica, what about between you and your dad?"

Treating with Narrative Family Therapy

Interpretation of the Problem

Candice appears to be experiencing a few drastic shifts happening around the same time in her life. Not only is she possibly moving out of her childhood home into a life of increased independence, her identity as an only child and her mother's primary family member is about to change. In narrative therapy, we give careful attention to the identities we fill and what we believe those say about us. Candice might identify herself as a hard-worker and finds it distressing when someone so outwardly similar to her has similar levels of success with less effort. Additionally, her identity as her mother's family is now changing as new family members are being introduced: Paul and Jessica. This, along with the stage of life transition toward independence typical of her age, may have her questioning how her relationship with her mother is about to change. Candice appears to feel overwhelmed with the changes, resulting in feelings of emotional exhaustion and hopelessness that led to her mother prompting therapy.

Anticipated Solution

Two significant narrative therapy interventions come to mind to address this systemic problem involving Candice. First is called reauthoring, or rewriting one's perception of a situation (Carey & Russell, 2003). For Candice, this could

64 *Theoretical Application*

be to redefine family. This can overlap with language of exception-seeking or what narrative therapy refers to as sparkling moments. This challenges the client to consider previous occasions she and her mother managed to maintain their identity as family despite other challenges, such as her parents' initial divorce. The client had to redefine family at that time, too.

Reauthoring can also explore how she can maintain her unique relationship with her mother despite the multiple changes happening around them, such as exploring the option of private phone calls or time spent together with just the two of them. It will likely be hard for the client to imagine coming home from college for holidays and experiencing home so differently with new people there. The therapist can normalize this and explore how Candice can hold onto happy memories, mourn a version of the future that she imagined but is no longer going to happen, and allow change to happen nonthreateningly. Lastly, reauthoring can discuss how she imagines a friendship looks between a woman and her adult daughter, considering how this will appear specifically in her relationship with her daughter.

A second intervention option is to externalize the problem that Candice is experiencing rather than identifying Candice as the problem. The client gets to name the externalized problem. Sometimes it is given a noun for a name ("the monster" or "the slave," for example), but it could also be named after an emotion ("the anger" or "the anxiety" are common). Candace might call her externalized problem something like "the overwhelming feeling" or "the stress." Separating the problem reminds both Candice and her mother that there is more to her than the problematic behavior. It also reiterates that Candice can assist in identifying and taking part in creating a solution.

Example Questions

1   "What do you think is the difference between a father and step-father?"
2   "It sounds like you feel pretty stressed. What can your mother do to help the stress go away?"
3   "From what your mom described, you've been quite the hard-worker and achiever at school. What do you think that says about you?"
4   "What do you remember about the first time your family experienced a big change, when your mom and dad split up? How do you remember changing your view of family when that happened?"
5   "How do you think being able to come together as a family against this problem could make a difference?"

Treating Using Internal Family Systems Therapy

Interpretation of the Problem

IFS can be a great therapeutic option for people who already use parts language: "A part of me feels one way, but another part feels totally different." In Candice's case, this could be, "A part of me wants my mom to stay single,

FST Concept I   65

but I know that's super selfish." Another example for her could be, "It drives me crazy that Jessica gets as good of grades as me when she doesn't work as hard. It's so unfair. But I can't do anything about it." These examples are a little subtler than the first sentence, but we see the necessary pieces to use parts language with her. She has conflicting perspectives and feels like she has to pick one. In reality, both can be true at the same time. Candice can want her mom to stay single because it is what she is used to, and she can also recognize that it is an unrealistic, even selfish, thing to ask her mother to stay that way for Candice's own comfort.

From the short case summary, we see four of Candice's parts:

- *The Hard-worker.* This part has helped Candice succeed in school and remain attentive to multiple extracurricular activities. In IFS, this part would be a manager. It gives her purpose and helps her feel accomplished. The problem comes when this part works itself ragged or feels unappreciated. This part is acutely aware that Candice's success is what keeps her parents connected, even distantly, and takes responsibility for that. There is also pressure to continue performing at high levels, and if this part doubts itself, it may have an "all-or-nothing" attitude resulting in Candace's abrupt lack of interest in continuing school. This perception may be worsened or invalidated by the similar successes Jessica has apparently without the same required effort.
- *The Daughter.* Candice appears distressed by her relationship with her mother potentially changing. This change is due to her potentially moving out and her mother potentially marrying. This part probably appears with the maturity of a girl around age ten, since that was when her parents divorced. At that time, her relationship with her primary caregiver, her mother, was very important. This is the part that desires for her mother to not remarry out of childish self-interest. This desire likely comes from a desire to be more connected to her mother, not due to ill-will toward her mother. This part might be an exile if Candice feels she is too old to feel this way or feels rejected by her mother in the choice to remarry and "inherit" a new daughter, Jessica.
- *The Firefighter.* This part, named for the role it shares in IFS, exists to counter the negative beliefs the Daughter appears to carry about Candice: That she is replaceable or unimportant. These are also the beliefs that the Hard-worker is striving to prove wrong. This firefighter is what comes up when those feelings are triggered in Candice. She might lose motivation or appear lazy, but really she is needing comfort and validation in herself and the difficulty of coping with change.
- *The Critic.* Many people have critical parts that lead them to feel their thoughts or feelings are unacceptable or that they are not handling a stressor the right way. This part is a manager, attempting to control Candice's response to her stressors by essentially telling her, "Get over it." Her inability to do this (because it is not actually a logical process) further triggers her firefighter into action.

66 *Theoretical Application*

Of course, in IFS, we would allow the client to name their parts, not unlike the externalizing names described in narrative therapy. The key difference is that "the stress" described there would here be understood to be a part of Candice, not something to get rid of.

Anticipated Solution

IFS has two key interventions, both of which could be used in this case. The first is increased Self-leadership. Aside from the parts of a person, there is a constant central presence that leads the parts like the director of an orchestra called the core Self. This presence is a source of compassion, curiosity, and the natural leader of the internal system. Distress appears when a part attempts to fill the Self's leadership role. In Candice's case, her Hard-worker has likely stepped into this role unnecessarily to cope with the constant demands of academia. Candice's core Self can work with the therapist to regain the parts' trust as a leader by demonstrating its ability to do so. Stepping back into this role allows the system to function more optimally as a whole rather than just a collection of parts.

The second intervention is called unburdening. Oftentimes our parts have healthy levels of functionality but become dysfunctional when they over-work themselves. If Candice's Hard-worker has come to believe Candice has nothing to offer if she is not outwardly successful, it may work itself into an overdrive and exhaust itself. In this case, it appears the part feels it has worked hard for nothing if it is comparing itself to Jessica's seemingly effortless success in school. Unburdening is a meditative intervention in which Candice's core Self interacts with the parts and allows them to feel heard and understood. Doing so offers those parts the validation and support they crave while redirecting motivation through nonjudgmental encourage-ment that the Critic lacks.

Example Questions

As mentioned earlier, IFS can be a meditative, self-reflective approach to therapy. We can talk about the parts, or we can "go inside" and interact with them directly. Meaningful change is more likely to occur with the latter, but even increasing our understanding of our parts on a cognitive level can increase our empathy toward them.

1   "Tell me about how the Hard-worker got its job."
2   "What would happen if the Hard-worker stopped doing its job?"
3   "Where is the Daughter in your body? Where do you feel it?"
4   "How do you feel toward the Firefighter right now?" (This question is to gage if the client is currently perceiving their parts from Self or from another part. If the client does not approach the Hard-worker with com-passion, curiosity, and connectedness, they are not viewing it from the

FST Concept I 67

Self. In that case, we would ask the current part to step aside and allow the Self to view the Hard-worker instead.)

5   "What else do you want me to know about you, Daughter?"

Reader Reflection

1   Thinking back on your childhood, how did wholeness present itself in your family, if at all? If not, how might its absence have impacted you?

2   If the whole person is more than their experiences and behaviors, what else do you think contributes to a person's identity?

3   Thinking back on your own childhood, what was a value your family had? How did they live out that value as a whole family?

4   Thinking back on your own childhood, what family role did you tend to fall into? What would it look like for a therapist to fill that role?

5   Bowen talks about a whole person including a balance of individuality and togetherness with one's family. What does that balance look like for you? How would you want it to look? ·

6   How do you think family hierarchy contributes to wholeness? How does it make it more complicated? Easier? Better? Harder?

7   Look at the four modality examples. Which one matches your worldview best? How so?

Think over how you have answered any of these. Your answers reflect possible biases or assumptions you may not realize you have about families and what is normal. These will go on to impact you as a therapist, unless you are intentionally mindful to think outside your biases. Remember, all people have biases! They are not innately evil! Biases are only problematic when we do not recognize them as one option of many equally valid perceptions.

5 FST Concept II
You Cannot Not Communicate

When I was taking classes for my degree in marriage and family therapy, one of my professors commented that the majority of clients who present for couple's therapy initially report they want to work on their communication. They assumed if they just changed the way they talked to each other, their problems would go away. However, over the course of treatment, it often would come out that the clients were not attentive to nonverbal communication and frequently held underlying beliefs that restricted the couple from reaching the desired version of themselves.

The importance of healthy communication between people has gone from a professional endeavor to a phenomenon of the public. Blogs and bookstores alike dedicate sections to effective communication tactics in professional and personal settings. Communication theory is abundant and multifaceted. This includes its purpose and application to family therapy. Communication theorists Berger and Chaffee (1987) established communication as understanding the creation, meaning-making, and implications of symbols and signals. Family therapy takes this theory and applies it practically. It asks how those symbols and signals influence family interactions and relationships. While communication theory includes both mass and interpersonal communications, we will focus almost exclusively on the latter.

Communication is more complicated than a yes or no question of whether or not someone does it well. It requires its own concept definition. There are multiple types of communication to consider, including verbal and nonverbal. There are also rules or principles of communication that surmise underlying beliefs. In addition to these, one's style of communication can influence relationships, along with one's interpretation of others' words and actions. All of these are points in the web of communication that happens between two people, and it grows more complex as more people are included.

Communication is the imparting or exchange of information. This definition includes several key attributes:

1 Communication is both given (imparted) and received (exchanged).
2 Communication passes *information*, which can be broadly defined as what is conveyed or represented by a particular arrangement of things.

DOI: 10.4324/9781003088196-8

(Both of these definitions are amalgamations of those provided by Oxford and Merriam-Webster Dictionaries.)

3. Communication and information include both symbols and signals. Symbols can be images or objects that represent something else. This includes pictorial representation, gestures, and other culturally developed depictions. It can also include letters on a page that come together to form a word that represents a thing or idea (Segal & Beavin Bavelas, 1983).
4. The definition of communication indirectly speaks to the means or types of communication, digital and analog.

Types of Communication

Communication is frequently broken down into two groups: digital and analog. *Digital* includes the words themselves. It can also be called the report. Whether those are presented verbally or written, the exact word choice demonstrates the digital communications. *Analog* includes the nonverbal communication. Nonverbal communication includes body language, facial expressions, tone, inflections, and gestures.

Consider the following sentence: *I have no money.*

Digitally, this is four words. The information states simply the speaker does not have money. However, the analog can speak volumes:

- How does the sentence communicate something different if you imagine the speaker has their hands on their hips versus in their lap?
- How does the sentence communication change if the person shouts, whispers, or speaks at a normal volume?
- What changes if the person speaking has a sneering lip raised when talking? Compared to when they speak with wide, averted eyes? Or if they roll their eyes when they made the statement?
- How does having eye contact with the speaker impact the sentence's interpretation?
- How does it impact the reader to imagine the speaker waving their hand in dismissal when they say these words? How does this compare to someone fidgeting their hands while talking, or spreading their arms open wide?
- Say the sentence four times; each time, put an inflection on one of the four words. How could this change the meaning of the speaker's words?

Many of these minute differences are dependent on the relationship of the speaker to the listener. This relates to another form of analog/nonverbal communication: *metacommunication*. Metacommunication could be called communication about communication. It provides cues for how information should be interpreted by the audience. It is impacted by one's context (the subject of Chapter 6) such as the relationship between the individuals speaking, the

70 *Theoretical Application*

physical setting and surroundings, the situation. These undertones will impact how people interpret their verbal and nonverbal interactions.

Let's use the same sentence as stated earlier (*I have no money*). How could it impact one's receiving this information if:

> ...it comes from a friend, parent, boss at work, or homeless stranger on the street?
>
> ...it comes in a one-on-one meeting versus as a public announcement?
>
> ...it comes after a known financial struggle versus by surprise?

These are just a few examples of metacommunication. Depending on who is speaking, what they say can communicate the hierarchy of the relationship, such as if it is between equals or power imbalance.

Bateson and his team were among the first to observe that an exchange of information has two qualities: The message and metamessage. The *message* could be the digital, the *metamessage* would be the analog. It is the relationship-defining attribute underneath the interaction. The metamessage establishes the rules and limits of the communication and the relationship, regardless of what is said. It is part of the context. When the interpersonal relationship is under review, such as in therapy, analog communication is frequently given more importance. Digital communication – the exact words used – becomes almost meaningless. However, per the principles of communication, it can never be entirely insignificant.

Principles of Communication

In addition to the notions of the message and metamessage, Bateson and his colleagues developed three core principles of communication:

- It is impossible to not communicate.
- It is impossible not to behave.
- Meaning ascribed is not always meaning meant.

One Cannot Not Communicate

This double-negative is to say that we are always communicating. Digital, analog, message, metamessage; some kind of communication is in every shared space. Even in silence, we communicate. Take the example of two strangers in line at the bank. The pair may never speak to each other, but as they silently stand apart, they communicate. They offer the culturally deemed appropriate personal space and do not initiate conversation. The metamessage communicates a lack of direct contact, and the business setting allows this to be normal. Think how silence communicates differently if the pair made eye-contact, one smiled politely, and the other turned away without returning the gesture. Even when electing not to return the smile, the person is communicating through their behavior.

One Cannot Not Behave

Behavior is a type of communication. Just as we always communicate, people always behave. We are always doing something. Just like silence is a form of communication, stillness is a behavior. Behavior can communicate when we do not have words; just ask anyone who has been in a traffic jam and received an unkind hand gesture or honk of a horn from a nearby vehicle. Behavior often communicates emotions for which the speaker may be unwilling or otherwise unaware of how to express (Pacer Center, 2015). Additionally, behavior can mirror our thoughts and emotions; they all influence one another.

For example, when I am in a good mood, I am likely to behave in a way that reflects this: I smile more, laugh more, am more willing to socialize, and more open to new ideas. Conversely, if someone else's behavior is potentially harmful to me, this can put me in a bad mood. To feel better, I must be intentional to behave and think positively to pull out of that negative headspace. I must communicate differently through my actions.

Meaning Given Is Not Always Meaning Meant

The meaning a person gives something is a subjective product. It is rarely (if ever) the true, perfectly matched meaning of the originator. Oftentimes, what someone says is interpreted differently than intended. This can be based on the communicators' relationship and assumptions they make about one another and what is said verbally or nonverbally. This also describes the Bateson team's observation that the message sent is not always the message received.

In elementary school, my peers would sometimes play a game they called telephone. To play this game, the participants sit in a circle. A person is designated the starter; they make-up a sentence and whisper it in the ear of the person next to them. Hearing the message, the listener passes it on to the person on their other side. That person continues it to the individual next to them. One by one, the message is passed around the circle until it loops back to the original speaker. The last person states what they heard, and the starter states the original message. In my years of playing and observing this game, never has the starting sentence matched the message at the end. The game is meant to dissuade gossip and rumor-mongering, but it demonstrates more than this. If a strictly digital message can be so easily mangled, imagine the complexity when we add analog communication components.

How we interpret communication from others has a circular impact with the meaning of the words themselves:

- The way I feel about the person speaking will influence how I interpret what they say.
- The way I interpret about what the person says will influence how I feel about the person speaking.

72 *Theoretical Application*

We interpret the communication given to us, making meaning of it. This interpretation includes three components: Syntactic, semantic, and pragmatic.

Watzlawick's Interpretation of Communication

In his forward for the second edition of Watzlawick et al. (2011) groundbreaking text on human communication, Bill O'Hanlon describes a story he had heard of when Paul Watzlawick went to interview a psychiatrist who specialized in working with patients with schizophrenia. When Watzlawick arrived to the meeting, he briefly introduced himself to the psychiatrist's secretary. He stated, "I am Watzlawick." Confused by his Austrian accent, not knowing who he was, and not seeing the name on the psychiatrist's appointment book, the secretary interpreted his statement as, "I am not Slavic." She responded, "I never said you were." Puzzled and mildly annoyed, he replied, "But I am."

The pair's mutual confusion and disagreement increased in volume and tenacity until the psychiatrist came out of his office. He questioned, "Paul, why are you yelling at my secretary?" and asked the secretary, "Why are you yelling at Dr. Watzlawick?" In this sentence, he provided Watzlawick with identifiers that clarified the situation: A full name and a title. Watzlawick used this misunderstanding as an example in his book of how simple assumptions can result in vast miscommunications. Prime among this is the assumption that what one says is heard and understood in the same way it was intended. However, Watzlawick identifies three components of communication, in all of which there is room for error: Syntactic, semantic, and pragmatic.

1   *Syntactic communication*

Syntactic communication entails the details of digital communication. Is the message using the correct and accurate word choice the originator hopes to convey? A radio metaphor could be appropriate for this type of communication: Is there static or noise getting in the way of the message sending accurately? Are the correct channels being used? Does the speaker have the capacity to reach their intended audience? Is there redundancy that interferes with the message? These coding interpretation details have less to do with the listener's meaning-making and are more factual, not audience-specific.

2. *Semantic communication*

This is the meaning-making of communication. In order for communication to be successful, both the originator and receiver must have an agreed understanding of the terminology involved. Earlier, I provided some introductory vocabulary in the preface. Even in this chapter, I offered definitions of key terms *communication* and *information*. I do this to try and ensure I successfully convey my thoughts and share my ideas in a way that is understandable to the reader. It is necessary to be in mutual understanding – colloquially "on the same page" – to be an effective speaker or listener.

Imagine receiving an invitation to a vet appreciation event. You want to attend, but you wonder if your veterinarian would let you bring your dog to the celebration. When you call the RSVP phone number to ask, they ask if your dog is a service animal, stating only service animals for the veterans would be allowed. Both of these identifiers – veterinarian and veteran – can be abbreviated syntactically as *vet*. Only the semantics and context can indicate which one the invitation meant.

3. *Pragmatic communication*

The pragmatic, or practical aspects, of behavior can be tied to non-verbal communication. This includes behaviors such as body language, facial expressions, tone, inflections, and gestures. It would not include context or metacommunication. In the example stated earlier, the tone of the person on the phone taking your RSVP may dissuade you from attending the gathering based on this miscommunication. Alternatively, their tone could be empathetic or humorous, stating you were not the first to ask that question. Even without seeing body language or facial expressions, the pragmatics of voice inflections communicate tone and ultimately can influence whether or not you feel comfortable attending the event.

While each of these is defined and described individually, they inevitably occur interdependently. This influences interpretation. Sometimes this is done humorously, such as using sarcasm playfully. However, when syntactic, semantic, and pragmatic messages do not match, the inconsistency can be confusing and damaging to the intended message. Interpretation also depends on the relationship of the communicators. Remember, the more intimate the relationship is between the originator and receiver, the more communication relies on semantic and pragmatic communications. This can be further emphasized in styles of communication, too.

Styles of Communication

There are three styles of communication: Symmetrical, complementary, and parallel. Neither symmetrical nor complementary are innately functional or dysfunctional. An appropriate balance of the two, parallel communication, could be considered ideal.

Symmetrical Communication

Symmetrical communication is distinguished by the mirroring styles between individuals. Both partners may be equally brief or verbose in their language. When one person becomes loud or quiet, so does the other. Both may gesture gregariously during conversation. These relationships can become volatile as the pair feed off one another's energy and passion, building higher and higher, more and more tense. Feeding off one another's style can also go the other, more reserved way. When one partner withdraws from a conversation,

74   *Theoretical Application*

the other does not pursue them. As a result, the individuals isolate. They do not reach a resolution. However, there are occasions when symmetrical relationships can be good and healthy. When one person approaches the other with calm, it is easier for the second person to reciprocate this.

Having symmetrical styles does not mean they experience the same semantic communication. One may speak tersely because they are stressed; the other may respond similarly concise because they personalize what is said. The latter may assume they are the source of their other's stress. In fact, having the same communication style can include assumptions that the other person thinks the same way you do or gives the same meaning to those communication components.

Complementary Communication

Complementary communication is marked by differences in communication patterns between interacting people. When one person becomes loud, the other becomes quiet. While one may be long-winded in explanations, the other may be brief and concise. Some models of therapy, such as emotion-focused therapy (EFT), use an example dynamic of the pursuer and withdrawer in a relationship. In this model, during times of distress, a complementary relationship will see one person physically or emotionally chase after the other, seeking assurance and resolution to the problem. The other person, likely overwhelmed or exhausted, may pull away physically or emotionally, creating space that makes their partner fearful for the relationship's attachment.

At extremes, neither of these styles is ideal. They can foster miscommunication and confusion within the relationship as people misinterpret the communication style of the other. For example, for some people, loud speech is intimidating and harsh, regardless of other communication cues such as what words are being said. Therefore, when a loved one speaks loudly to them, they might shrink away, no matter the conversation topic or environment. In different situations, depending on topic or environment, one style may be more appropriate than the other. A person may interpret this situation and deem which type is more constructive to their conversational goal – what they want to communicate. This is called *parallel communication*. It includes consideration of context to determine the appropriate communication style, which we will discuss in Chapter 6.

When Communication Fails

Inevitably, there will be situations when communication falls short. There is an informational theory behind this called the noisy-channel coding theorem, or Shannon's theorem (1949). This theory describes the role of disruptive noise in their strong code model. The strong code model is a linear model focusing on how information travels through imperfect channels. This could be literal external noise – children chattering, traffic sounds, static over a phone – or emotional noise, such as existing beliefs about the speaker that influences how we hear their message. It is worth noting that Claude Shannon, the originator and for whom the theory is named, worked for Bell Telephone Laboratories. He literally looked at how communication was interrupted or made impossible.

Earlier I mentioned the childhood game of telephone, where participants sit in a circle and pass a message around, whispering what was heard from one person to the next. The game is riff with opportunity for noise and inaccurate communication. There are two potential points of inaccurate communication: Semantic and effectiveness. *Semantic problems* are in the creation and interpretation of the message itself, such as using the incorrect word in a sentence. In telephone, my peer might have whispered the word "element" in my ear, but I thought she said "elephant," so that is the word I would pass on to the person on my other side. *Effectiveness problems* are interferences based on the relationship between the originator and audience. The audience may be more likely to misinterpret the intention of the originator if there is a mistrusting or absent relationship there. In the telephone game, if the peer I sat next to was someone who previously bullied me, I might assume that they are intentionally changing the message in the telephone game to make me look like a bad listener. This preexisting belief about my peer will impact the way I hear the message they whisper in my ear.

Shannon also describes communication failures based on interpretation, or coding. He says failures are a result of either (1) incompetent coding, (2) incompetent decoding, or (3) "noise" degrading the quality of the signal. This means coding problems come from miscommunicated intent (saying something incorrect), miscommunicated interpretation (understanding something incorrectly), miscommunication due to interference (inability to hear), and the all-encompassing intersubjectivity of communication. Clearly, there are many places things can go wrong in communication.

Part of this potential for miscommunication, as I mentioned earlier, lies in the relationship between the speaker and listener. This is especially impactful within the family.

Communication in the Family

In many ways, our family is the first place we learn to communicate. This can be a space to learn helpful communication tools – like the alphabet, how and when to say please and thank you, and how to answer the phone. (I once knew a small child who would answer their toy phone saying, "Yellow!" since this was how their father answered his cellphone. It was quite endearing.) This is also where we first learn our senses of humor and how or when to use it. The family is also where we learn how to listen and make sense of others' communication (Fitzpatrick & Ritchie, 1993). This can be helpful but is also a perfect opportunity to make assumptions of meaning-making based on previous experience. Unfortunately, these can be quite inaccurate. If my family believes using curse words is an unacceptable form of self-expression, it may be jarring to be in environments where this form of speech is normalized. If I observed that such words were used only with extreme anger, I might believe that other

76 *Theoretical Application*

people who curse are also angry. It can be particularly confusing when their nonverbal cues do not indicate anger. As a result, I might not know how to respond. This inconsistency is an example of the double-bind theory.

The Double-Bind Theory

A prominent discovery of the Palo Alto Team is the communication double-bind. It is a subconcept of communication. The double-bind was a central feature of the team's leading work "Toward a Theory of Schizophrenia," a paper that redefined family therapy in 1956. At its core, the double-bind is a no-win situation. It occurs when a person receives mixed messages and their subsequent illogical attempts to make sense of it. Extreme double-binds can result in persistent detrimental symptomology, even when the family states a desire to decrease symptoms present, which can seem paradoxical (Massey, 2017). The six criteria of a double-bind can be found on the table on the next page.

Imagine being a young adult who has learned the following social rules from their parent:

- If you do not question authority, you are weak.
- It is rude and disrespectful to question a parents' authority, so don't.

If both of those are true, it likely would feel like a no-win situation. No matter what happens, it's the wrong thing to do. You are either weak or rude. Not only that, but either way, the parent is the exception to the rule. The double-bind is associated with prominent helplessness or hopelessness. This example shows why. It is impossible to select a winning option; all of the options are equally logical and simultaneously illogical when combined. Falling into a double-bind often results in defensiveness because a person must justify their choice, fully aware that no choice was the right one to make. If this is confusing to read about, imagine the confusion of being in such a bind. It could feel like quite the paradox.

The double-bind has six criteria:

1 Two or more people, often delineated by the symptom-bearer and a system member, typically a family member.
2 A recurring experience or theme resulting in an established expectation of response.
3 A primary negative injunction, or an identified punishment for a behavior. This punishment may typically be overt anger or withholding love.
4 A secondary injunction that contradicts the first, typically communicated nonverbally. These may indirectly communicate that the punishment is not, in fact, a punishment or that the speaker is

not a punishing person. There can also be tones that give conflicting instruction with the original message.

5 A tertiary negative injunction forbids the symptom-bearer from escaping. This reinforces the above entrapment. This can be especially present if there is a hovering hope for reward if the symptom-bearer finds a way to manage the double-bind in their favor (which is pretty much impossible).

6 After repeated exposure, all five of the above do not have to be present for the pattern to persist. Any single part will be sufficient to initiate feelings of anxiety and panic associated with the theme.

Paradox and Counter-paradox

In 1971, the Milan Center for Family Studies released a text about paradoxes and counterparadoxes in the family structure that theorizes in tandem with the Palo Alto Team. The double-bind could be considered a *paradox*; it is the illogical sequence of behavior resulting in a certain outcome (Selvini Palazzoli et al., 1971). *Counter-paradox*, on the other hand, introduces a juxtaposing paradox, such as the response to the original paradox. That is to say, something does not make sense, but it works. It is meant to provoke change. Paradoxes and counter-paradoxes can be used as clinical interventions. Psychologist Klaus Deissler (2013) provides the practical example of his grandfather offering him money if he could hiccup ten times in a row, a task he often failed as a child. However, this resulted in the greater end goal; he no longer had the hiccups. Therapists can offer similar interventions, depending on the model of therapy they use, to counter double-binds that may be present among client systems.

Applicable Therapeutic Models

Strategic Family Therapy

Strategic family therapy came directly out of the Palo Alto Team's work with communication in family relationships. Watzlawick was a member of the Palo Alto Team and a central contributor to the early works of the Mental Research Institute. They were among the first to notice the unstoppable nature of communication – that *you cannot not communicate*. Strategic family therapy was also one of the first to apply paradoxical interventions, particularly among a family, and draw attention to the double-bind present in family that inhibits symptom alleviation.

More prominent than paradoxical interventions, strategic family therapy introduced an intervention called reframing. Reframing is the communication skill of shifting one's view on a situation. Verbally, it is the ability to use different words to describe a situation in a new way. This technique can be used to create optimism and hope, challenging existing narrow views of a problem

78 *Theoretical Application*

or problematic interaction. It also can be central to humor, which can also be therapeutic and an emotionally healthy perspective shift. This emotional shift is the mark of the reframe intervention; the new perspective brings new emotional connotations with it. This is the power of second-order change that makes it potentially more lasting than the exclusively behavioral shift of first-order change. A reframe does not change the facts that are present; it changes the meaning attributed to those facts and, therefore, the consequences of them. This is the power of language in communication. It can shift our interpretation of facts through tools like reframing.

Symbolic Experiential Therapy

Virginia Satir is sometimes referred to as the mother of family therapy. Her research particularly focused on the power of in-session transformative experiences. She noticed four types of dysfunctional communication styles:

1 The *Blamer* tends to be highly critical and often speaks in generalizations, rarely taking responsibility for its contribution to a problem. However, the Blamer also can be deeply lonely and afraid of being unlovable. It both fears and anticipates rejection; as a result, they stay emotionally distant to keep emotionally safe. In this way, the Blamer attempts to feel in control when in reality, they feel very out of control and vulnerable.

2 The *Placater* tends to have a go-with-the-flow facade that focuses on other people's comfort and happiness, even at the cost of their own. This can appear as a push-over or highly apologetic personality. This communication persona wants external peace, even if the cost is internal turmoil. They may struggle to express authentic emotions, good or bad, and instead take cues from those around them for what emotions are safe to express.

3 The *Super-reasonable* may seem similar to the Placater. They also "go with the flow," but do so from a place of emotional disconnect. They tend to appear highly logical, making choices from the head rather than the heart. They have a hard time admitting mistakes because it entails flawed logic. They shift blame for errors to other people or processes. The super-reasonable person may view emotions as problematic. As a result, they deny themselves emotionality and are uncomfortable around others' emotions. Despite a cold exterior, this communication type is attentive to fairness and desires love and acceptance.

4. The *Distractor*, or irrelevant, type tends to appear unfocused and talkative. They might appear lighthearted and humorous. They may struggle to be direct in their speech or behavior, such as avoiding eye-contact or outright intimacy. People might assume their unfocused nature to mean they are purposeless or evasive. However, this person fears the discomfort of confrontation and views it as unnecessarily risky. This can also result in shallow relationships despite a deep craving for connection.

As you can see, all four communication styles stem from low self-worth and interfere with a person's ability to connect authentically with those around them, including their families (Davies, 2019).

So how do we heal from these styles? This is in the shift into the fifth style, the *Leveler*. The Leveler is able to express itself without falling into the communication traps of the other four. It speaks authentically without being harsh, managing problems from a nonjudgmental perspective that is honest about its feelings, desires, and intentions. To reach this perspective in session, Satir would call this a part and invite the client to view it as an internal resource in need of strengthening. Once the therapist demonstrates this acceptance is possible, the client may put it to practice for themselves.

Solution-Focused Therapy

Solution-focused therapy is a strengths-based approach. It prefers to focus on the goals for the future rather than the problem or the past. In it, the therapist intentionally phrases questions and thoughts to highlight the client's assets and internal resources that allow them to overcome a problem (Lipchik, 2002). This model places emphasis on the client taking personal ownership not just in the problem's current status but in their ability to create meaningful, lasting change.

Solution-focused therapy does this through specific types of questions that deliberately use communication to lead the client to see their situation and goals from a different point of view. These include:

- The miracle question, which asks about the client's preferred future.
- Exception-seeking questions, which seek to learn how the preferred future is already minorly present or has been present previously.
- Presuppositional questions, which consider how things will be different once the change has been made.
- Scaling questions, which help quantify progress and recognize the power of small changes.

Solution-focused therapy is also intentional to avoid bias in its language. Its founder, Insoo Kim Berg, would exclaim, "Wow!" in response to a client's stories in session. She did this because it communicates listening and investment in the client without preferential terminology that suggests a client should act a certain way. This is an example of avoiding praise in order to foster client autonomy. Remember, solution-focused therapy does not aim to provide solutions from the therapist but to allow the client to identify their solution. Along with the therapist, they explore how they can make steps toward it or even how they already are.

Contextual Family Therapy

Like strategic family therapy, contextual family therapy came out of the Palo Alto Team and the Mental Research Institute. Per Hargrave and Pfitzer (2003),

80 *Theoretical Application*

it emphasizes trust and how it is communicated in families. The model is unique in its attention to and language of relational ethics. These are the roles of loyalty, legacy, guilt, and connectedness within a system. It looks at how these qualities control a family and the individual decision-making processes of family members. Contextual family therapy focuses on how families promote fairness and growth of its members through *constructive entitlement*, which encourages forwarding the gifts you have been given from person to person or generation to generation. Forwarding gifts are not just physical items; it can be taking care of a person after they take care of you. This is described in language of ledgers and loyalties to identify what motivates people in their interactions.

Ledgers are the invisible interpersonal balance of entitlement, or what is owed and earned, and indebtedness, or what someone owes someone else. These can be overt, like keeping score, or covert, like assuming someone's compliance without clearly stated reason. Ideally, the ledger will be symmetrical and balanced; this would be the healthiest option. Unfortunately, we know that is not how it always goes.

Similarly, the concept of loyalty is a sense of indebtedness to one's family. It can be healthy to recognize how they helped you achieve in life, but it can also overtake individual identity. It can leave someone feeling like a pawn. In cases of divorce, a person may feel split in their loyalties, choosing one at the detriment of the other. Consider the double-bind concept, and imagine how that could leave someone feeling trapped by a family member, unable to escape their confusing double-message around love and personal value. This is the power of communication in contextual family therapy. The model uses *circular questioning* to learn one another's perception of one another's actions. This also seeks clarification of those covert assumptions, bringing them to the forefront for mutual understanding.

As with the concepts that came before this one, this is not an exhaustive list of models that consider communication. These four highlight the role of communication and the various ways it can be used both to understand a situation and to instill constructive change.

Case Study – *Cassie and Dan's Disconnect*

Cassie and Dan are in their early-to-mid-twenties. They married about two years ago when Cassie became pregnant a year into their dating relationship. Since then, they have lived with Cassie's mother, Helen. Helen is the caretaker to their child, Jaime, while the couple both work full-time and when the pair comes to therapy.

In session, Cassie and Dan report unhappiness with their romantic connection, feeling "in a rut," focusing more on their individual work and their roles as parents rather than partners. Dan describes Cassie as "hardworking but can be critical." Cassie says Dan is "sweet but lazy," giving the example of having the same job since high school without apparent interest in entering management or shifting to a different job where he would make more money. Both acknowledge the other as a good parent to Jaime. They say they would like to "get back to feeling in love." Cassie has also said she is worried Dan is attending therapy just to "appease her," stating, "I want him to want to do better for me and for us. Not because someone tells him to."

Despite these issues, Cassie spends most sessions talking about her dissatisfaction with their living situation. She describes feeling grateful for her mother's willingness to help with their toddler but does not like the way Helen talks around the child, including using profanity and loudly talking over the TV. Cassie also says she does not appreciate her mother commenting frequently about being the caretaker, making statements such as, "Good thing you have me, otherwise you'd be screwed and that college I paid for would be for nothing," and insinuating Cassie will "make it up to her" by caring for her in old age instead of "putting her in a home." Dan also expresses dissatisfaction with their living situation, but more so because he dislikes Helen "as a person," calling her "not very clean and an all-around nasty woman." Cassie does not disagree with him, but reiterates that they should be appreciative for the help Helen provides.

Helen refuses to join them in therapy, denying her role in their problems, and reminding them, "Who else would look after the baby while you guys figure your lives out?"

Treating with Strategic Family Therapy

Interpretation of the Problem

This family system demonstrates the influence of language in communication. All adult members of the system are contributing to the communication patterns, often through indecision and inaction. However, we now know inaction is still an action. This is particularly relevant in the relationship between Helen and Dan.

We see the power of language in how the couple talk to and about one another. Both members of the couple describe each other with both positive and negative traits: Sweet and lazy; hardworking and critical. This is also how Cassie talks about her mother: Helpful but profane and loud. The pair can fairly recognize the good and bad each person offers, but there seems to be greater emphasis placed on the negative. When we focus excessively on the negative, we risk making assumptions. This includes assumptions about others' motives or assuming other people communicate the same way we do. Cassie may be struggling with others in her life having a different communication style. Where Cassie seems to prefer the quiet, her mother likes noise. When Cassie pursues change, Dan withdraws, such as when they talk about his employment. Unintentionally, Cassie appears to be discouraging the very

82 *Theoretical Application*

change that she desires by making these assumptions. This is also part of communication paradoxes.

All system members (except Jaime) appear to use paradoxical language and logic. If Cassie believes Dan only changes to appease her, she is not allowing him to authentically change; she assumes his motives are skewed. She similarly assumes his compliance is based on instruction, not intrinsic effort to be a better partner. This limits his potential capacity for change and, in all probability, influences his willingness to make changes. We also hear Cassie describe that she wants to work on couple's issues but talks a lot about her mother; this speaks to a significant source of anxiety beyond her presenting issue. Helen uses paradoxical language that shames Cassie for depending on her but also emphasizes how much they need her to stay. She communicates her actions as debt to be repaid, which is further paradoxical about trusting her daughter to take care of her while not entrusting Cassie with her own child. These paradoxes get in the way of clear communication, intention, and action.

Though it isn't specified, Jaime plays a role in communication and interaction patterns in this family, too. The child can certainly play a role in reframing, which we will describe below.

Anticipated Solution

In strategic family therapy, paradoxical family interventions are an option. An example would be an assignment for Cassie and Dan specifically. They could set aside 15 minutes every day to spend time as a couple – away from others in the house – to complain about Helen. During those minutes, neither Cassie nor Dan may defend Helen; this is a time dedicated exclusively to airing complaints. They may not skim time; they must find things to complain about every single day, for the full 15 minutes, including something new each day. After the 15 minutes, the couple should spend at least 45 minutes as a couple, uninterrupted – talking, having sex, or going out as a pair. The couple may not talk about Helen during those 45 minutes.

This intervention is paradoxical because it unexpectedly assigns a negative attribute into the relationship – complaining. Often with paradoxical interventions, there may be initial concern about how helpful this will be. Is complaining really the behavior we want to encourage? However, the intervention goes beyond the immediate action; the outcome will reach beyond that quarter of an hour. Chances are, they will get bored of this after a while, lose interest, or run out of things to complain about. There are also potential positive exchanges since they will be given almost an hour where they do not talk about Helen and can focus elsewhere, preferably on each other. Chances are they would also rather do the fun things as a couple and, after the assignment ends, hopefully continue. Planning spontaneity as a couple is not as intimidating as it may initially sound – schedule the date but do not necessarily plan ahead what to do with that time. Allow that to be the surprise. Lastly, they may also be increasingly motivated to change their living arrangement to not be in the same home as Helen. Overall, this demonstrates the purpose of

FST Concept II   83

a paradoxical intervention: To shift perspective on what is actually wrong in interactions rather than identifying a specific person as the problem.

In addition or alternative to the paradoxical intervention, the therapist can use reframing. This also helps the clients view their situation differently through language changes. We can use this with all three adults. Cassie wants the couple to get better and reconnect; she has not checked out of the relationship. She's still in it, even when stressed. Dan's job history demonstrates consistency and loyalty; he and his job demonstrate his desire for stability. Helen wants them to "figure their lives out" because she wants the couple to succeed. Additionally, childcare may give Helen purpose in life and a place in the family. Reframing offers a new perspective into the family's longstanding issues.

Lastly, the therapist may dive deep into the principles of communication, particularly the power of both words and nonverbals. They can discuss how they interact with one another, or choose not to interact, such as between Dan and Helen, still communicates something. Finally, the therapist can talk over assumptions the clients are making in what is both heard and said between one another. For example, Cassie appears to be making assumptions about Helen in her use of profanity and volume in her verbal communications. By having a better understanding of communication as a concept along with its practical applications, the clients can also better understand how they influence one another moving toward positive change.

Example Questions

1   "Cassie, what difference does it make to think of Dan as a steadfast, consistent employee at his job?"
2   "I wonder if Helen finds purpose in getting to be so involved in raising Jaime. What do you think about that?"
3   In the meeting after the paradoxical intervention is presented, the therapist could ask, "What was it like each day to finish the complaint time and get to move into meaningful time spent together?"
4   "How could it be helpful to talk to Helen as a united front, as a couple and as Jaime's parents, about her profanity in front of the child?"

Treating with Symbolic Experiential Therapy

Interpretation of the Problem

First, we can see that all three adults in this system demonstrate one of Satir's problematic communication patterns:

- Cassie appears to function as super-reasonable. She seems aware of her emotions but rejects them in preference for logic. For example, she is frustrated with her mother but rejects this; in her perspective, to be frustrated means she is unappreciative of the help Helen provides.

84 *Theoretical Application*

Additionally, she does not identify her own contributions to the problem, possibly out of guilt or discomfort acknowledging her own flaws.

- Dan seems to be a placater. He initiates very little change and prefers to go with the flow. Cassie even identifies this with concern that any change he makes will only be to go with the flow of therapy. He is seen to be avoidant of Helen, avoiding direct confrontation in the interest of that external peace of the family. However, he was willing to match Cassie's verbalized problems with her mother when she expressed them, taking her cue that it was safe to do so.

- Though we haven't met her, Helen appears to function as a blamer. She appears to hold Cassie responsible for having a child but may view her has irresponsible for it, too. Helen seems to use this to justify her role as care-giver. She demonstrates speaking in generalizations and deflects personal responsibility in the family's dysfunctional dynamics. She is quick to point out the couple's dysfunction to keep the attention off herself. However, Helen may be struggling with feeling out of control in other areas of her life and may fear being rejected or lonely.

Throughout the system, we see a lack of emotional honesty, frequently evidenced in their communication. This is particularly true of Cassie, who appears to feel she is not allowed to be upset with her mother. Is there resentment or another emotion from Helen going unspoken? What feelings are between Cassie and Dan surrounding Helen's presence in the home? Around her self-claimed identifier as the primary caregiver to Jaime? The emotions may squeak out as time goes on and pressure to keep them down remains unyielding. In that case, the emotion may come out in an outpouring of hurtful expression, resulting in greater emotional distance and distrust rather than productivity.

Lastly, there is a presence of a double-bind. What is Cassie communicating to Dan when she asserts her belief that he only would change because someone told him to rather than through his personal volition? Overall, the system will need a reframe of both words and the emotions behind the words, creating second-order change.

Anticipated Solution

According to Satir, positive change happens in a system when everyone's basic needs or yearnings are fulfilled. This requires direct communication and improved understanding of one's context. She uses the metaphor of icebergs: "Like icebergs, we show only part of ourselves. Much of our experience lies beneath the surface" (Satir et al., 1991, p. 34). So much of who we are as people is unseen; sometimes we do not even realize the depth of our inner being. To address this in therapy, the therapist will focus on learning family dynamics and patterns. This can be achieved through a genogram, like in Bowenian therapy, or other sequences of questions. The goal is to increase awareness of how each person learned to behave and how they learned what is normal. This includes communication styles, expectations, acceptable types of emotions and means of emotional expression, rules of secret-keeping, and other perceived typical family roles and rules. With this improved understanding of one another's contexts, we can better understand and communicate with one another.

For this system specifically, this will include finding out how Cassie and Dan learned what is "normal" and how they are "supposed" to deal with problems. The therapist will use the language of "the problem" without identifying outright or who what that is. They would not talk about Helen as just a problem or source of stress because there is so much more to her than that identifier. This model of therapy takes careful consideration to the power of language.

In the process of listening to others' contexts and perspectives, clients increase presence of leveler-style communication. In listening, they can also learn how to better express their own needs by having examples of effective language provided to them by the therapist and others in the system. This is a version of the emotional reframe, too. The clients will practice speaking directly to one another about one's perspective and unmet needs. Satir places emphasis on the relationship between people and the affect they offer one another, often tied to previous experience and emotional connection.

Satir uses "I value you" statements, where the members of the system specifically identify how their relationship with one another enriches their lives. These can also be classically connected to I statements: "I feel [emotion] when [event] because [context and meaning-making]." Once one client makes this statement without interruption from other system members present, the other person repeats back what is heard until repeated back correctly. Afterward, the first person follows up, "What I need is [request]." This offers direct answer to the other person for what they can do that would be most helpful. Satir called this an increased connection to one's yearnings, or the desire to be understood, accepted, and loved. This is often connected to a person's sense of self-worth, which therapy will aim to improve by decreasing feelings of shame or fear from past events and helping the client mindfully live more in the present. This can include developing new rules and roles, connected to self-empowerment of the client. In this way, the experiential model uses direct verbal communication to create emotional connection in nonverbals. Lastly, Satir values mindfulness of being present-focused and helping clients have in-session breakthroughs in their relationships. This is why it could be helpful for both Cassie and Doug as a couple and, ideally, for Helen to join in the future.

Example Questions

Many of these questions can be asked to any of the system members present. In this case, that would be Cassie or Dan. However, should a time come when Helen comes, too, we can ask her similar questions.

1 "How do you hope my being involved will help?"
2 "Who does the problem bother the most in the family? How can you tell?"
3 "How does each person contribute to the problem sticking around?"

86 *Theoretical Application*

4   "How do you think the family will change once the problem is gone?"
5   "It sounds like Helen plays a pretty central role in how you two interact with one another. What do you think?"

Treating with Solution-Focused Therapy

Interpretation of the Problem

According to solution-focused therapy, the biggest problem in this system's communication pattern is problem-centric language and focus. They describe seeming to be overwhelmed by life circumstances both individually and as a family. However, despite these feelings, they seem aware that their problems are not insurmountable. There are many strengths the therapist will be able to highlight. On one hand, a person has been identified as the problem (Helen) rather than the relationship with that person. On the other hand, the couple are able to view the problem between them as a problem with their communication, not a problem in one or the other. Additionally, positive descriptive language of one another is phrased conditionally: "hardworking *but* critical," "sweet *but* lazy." The problem seems to rest in their feeling stuck in their current environment – both in their relationship and living situation. This is a common starting point in solution-focused therapy, one from which this system can easily work through.

Anticipated Solution

First, the therapist will need to determine the clients' motivation levels. In solution-focused therapy, clients will be visitors, complainers, or customers, depending on their willingness to identify a problem and take part in solution-driven change. In this case, Cassie is a customer; she has identified goals and would like to actively work toward them. She will likely need assistance, though, in phrasing those goals in terms of increasing desirable life attributes rather than simply eliminating the problem. That is to say, there is more to the solution than the absence of a problem. Dan appears to be a complainer; he wants help but may lack clarity of his abilities to contribute to the change. The case summary does not have him identify his desired outcome of therapy; however, when given space to, he may prove himself to be more of a ready-to-make-things-happen customer. Though she is not physically present, the therapist may guess that Helen is a visitor. She is not looking for help herself and denies her role in the systemic problem. Until she acknowledges her role, her positive influence in session may be limited.

Between Cassie and Dan, the anticipated solution will be to assist them to identify the preferred future rather than ruminate on present distress. The therapist can encourage client autonomy by allowing them to identify the preferred future rather than the therapist telling them what it is. Once the preferred future has been identified by each person – both partners are to be given time and space to answer each question in therapy – the therapist can begin to learn the little ways those positives are already present or have been for brief periods. The therapist will allow the client to be the expert on their lives, but the therapist can help the client to focus on how they have already started taking meaningful action. For example, even attendance to therapy demonstrates a willingness to move toward change.

As mentioned earlier, communication tactics are very important in solution-focused therapy. The therapist is not meant to minimize or ignore the past or present problems; we just do not want to get stuck in it. Instead, future orientation means recognizing how the past contributes to the present and how it might be holding the client back from the preferred future. Sometimes talking about the past and present can be incredibly helpful, so the goal is not to avoid talking about that. Instead, the goal is to ask the client how it is helpful to talk about parts of their life. After, it is equally important to reflect with the client over what feels different or better having done that. For example, Cassie and Dan can talk about their frustrations with Helen, but it can be good to explore with them how it is helpful to do so. This couple appears to be in high need of hope for a better future. Fortunately, that is something a therapist can eagerly provide!

Example Questions

1 "Let's imagine you go to sleep tonight, everything seems normal. Then while you are sleeping, a miracle happens, and all of the sudden, the problem no longer exists. Poof! It disappeared during the night. Cassie, when you wake up the next day, what is the first thing you would notice was different that would show you the problem was gone?"
[This is an example of how to ask the miracle question. From here, the client can continue drawing details out about that imaginary problem-free day. The purpose here is to highlight that the solution is more than the absence of the problem and solutions to the problem include actions that can begin now. For example, Cassie might say that she notices right away that the TV in the next room is not loudly playing a morning talk show her mother watches. That's not to say that her mother is absent, but that the TV's volume and content might be setting a rough tone for the morning. From there, other questions can include those similar to what is below.]

2 "Dan, in your problem-free day after the miracle happens, you described that you and Cassie would have your own apartment, no longer living with Helen. What difference do you think that would make for your relationship with your wife, to not live with her mother?"

3 "Dan, you mentioned earlier that you want to feel more loved and supported by Cassie. Tell me about a time when you felt loved and supported by her, even just a little bit or for a little while."

4 "Cassie, earlier I asked how frustrated you were with your mother, on a scale of 1–10 where one was not at all and ten was as frustrated as

88 *Theoretical Application*

humanly possible. You said you were at a seven. Tell me what would be different if you were at six."

5. [In continuation of the scale above] "How do you keep yourself from being at nine?"

Treating with Contextual Family Therapy

Interpretation of the Problem

As mentioned earlier, contextual family therapy focuses on communicating trust in a family. In this family, there seems to be moderate levels of trust, but it is conditional and inconsistently communicated. Cassie and Dan trust one another to be good parents to Jamie; they even trust Helen in this regard. Their trust is limited with Helen, though, in her identifying as a primary caregiver while they are each working full time. Both partners also use conditional language in how they describe one another, restricting the value of positive qualities with negative ones. Overall, limitations in trust are likely due to the uncommunicated rules around loyalty and entitlement, kept track via personally monitored ledgers.

In addition to limited trust, this family seems to struggle with imbalanced ledgers. In the short case study, we do not get details about Cassie's past relationship with her mother. Part of treatment will be learning more about this past. For now, it is evident that Helen perceives the ledger to lean in her favor. Her statements assume Cassie will take care of her in old age; this asserts her perceived entitlement to that care. Similarly, Cassie and Dan may have questions of about what Helen has the right to do in their home, considering her role as a caregiver to Jaime. They seem to be questioning what they are allowed to ask of her considering she is doing them a favor by taking care of Jaime while they work. This may be particularly true of Cassie, since it is her mother, with whom she has a lifetime of communication and ledger-balancing. She may feel she has split loyalties, too. It seems like Cassie feels like she has to pick one person, or one system, to whom she is most loyal: Her family-of-origin represented by Helen, or her new nuclear family, Dan and Jaime. She may be asking herself, which takes precedence, loyalty to her mother or her marriage? Right now, these thoughts are only suspicions of the therapist. Treatment will include asking these types of questions outright, confronting silent assumptions and fears in the family roles and rules.

Anticipated Solution

Treating this family with contextual family therapy will have great emphasis on relational ethics: The roles of loyalty, legacy, guilt and connectedness within a system. Treatment is going to include overt discussion of assumptions of ledgers – Who thinks they are owed what? Therapy will challenge unhealthy roles and rules that are currently being communicated through silence and assumptions. Additionally, therapy will identify each person's desired balance, or what they believe healthy family dynamics looks like. What does trust look like? How would you know when you can trust someone? This overlaps with the need to address unresolved family-of-origin issues. What expectations were placed on Cassie that may not have been outright clarified? How are those still present, even now that she is an adult and a parent herself? These are a few questions that could potentially be asked in treatment.

Example Questions

Circular questioning is particularly common in contextual family therapy. Circular questions are a tool to learn about interaction patterns and to understand the rules of the family, particularly previously unspoken rules. Circular questions will have one system member answer questions about how someone else in the system views the situation. This includes their perception of the other person's meaning-making process. Circular questions enlighten the system to how each person perceives one another.

1 "Cassie, what do you think Dan thinks about his job situation?"
2 "Dan, what do you think Cassie believes makes a good parent?"
3 "Cassie, what do you think Helen likes most about the current living situation?"
4 "Cassie, how will you know when you can trust Dan?"
5 "Dan, why do you think Cassie is so quick to defend Helen?"

Reader Reflection

1 Do I think there is a better or best way to communicate? What is that? How did I come to those conclusions?
2 Are there ways in which I prefer to communicate? What are those and why?
3 To what types of communication am I most sensitive? What do I notice first, and what has the largest initial impact on me?
4 What style of communication do I tend to do? Often this varies based on the type of relationship with the person with whom one is communicating. What style do I think an effective therapist should have?
5 How do I feel about the prospect of using paradoxical interventions with clients?
6 How might my delivery of a controversial therapeutic intervention influence its outcome?
7 What role does communication play in strengths-based language?

6 FST Concept III
Context Is Key

"CONTEXT IS EVERYTHING."

My professor in graduate school had us repeat this statement several times throughout my years of study. He wanted to highlight how all actions, thoughts, and feelings can make sense in context. When we understand what is happening in the space around someone, we better understand how the outside world influences a person's decision-making process.

Definition and Description of Context

I mentioned context in Chapter 5 as part of analog communication. It is the analog communication that is not conversation-specific. It is the big picture, including the physical and emotional setting of the communication. These two work together to provide additional meaning and understanding to the verbal and nonverbal communication.

Physical Surroundings

The physical context is the communication space and what fills it (Davies, 2018). It is what we can experience through the five senses: Touch, see, hear, smell, or taste. These can be experienced in several spectrums such as indoor to outdoor, natural to manmade, public to private, and isolated to crowded. These setting types co-occur, happening and influencing simultaneously.

Indoor to Outdoor

Indoors and outdoors are differentiated by the presence of walls, floor, and ceiling. Along with these, indoors can provide protection, such as weather resistance and temperature management. Indoors can also offer perceived increased security or privacy. Sometimes indoors can feel restrictive and formal while the outdoors represent freedom and the possibilities of options. There can often be individual interpretation. While this may seem cut-and-dry and more like an either-or than a spectrum, there is some variance. Indoors can still include open windows to the outdoors. Outdoors can include some of

DOI: 10.4324/9781003088196-9

the amenities that make indoors appealing, such as a patio. You can also have indoors among the outdoors, such as in a tent or vehicle. A parking garage could be halfway between indoor and outdoor.

Natural to Manmade

Though there is some overlap with indoor/outdoor, nature/manmade looks slightly different. Natural surroundings entail the presence of features that originate without mankind's assistance, such as trees, dirt, rocks, and water. These can be found indoors or outdoors. Ecopsychology studies how exposure to nature can have a healing effect and reduce stress (Robbins, 2020). Time in nature can help combat feelings of loneliness or isolation, promotes a sense of calm, and can improve one's mood (Pieters et al., 2018). Spending two hours a week in nature has been associated with better health and well-being (White et al., 2019). This is why so many indoor spaces have increasingly included natural elements, such as use of natural light, natural colors and textures in décor, and using nature-based sound effects and scents in the background. Even indoors, the presence of these can be soothing.

Manmade, on the other hand, includes more synthetic or industrial structures. This can include vehicles, cement, electric lighting, and plastics. Manmade objects and places frequently provide convenience and ease. However, some people experience manmade surroundings as restrictive or inauthentic. Consider the difference between the average busy city street corner compared to stepping into an open park. One provides potential safety from inclement weather while the other does not. One is associated with noise and pollution; the other is not. Either has their potential benefit. For some people, this can include separation of publicity and privacy.

Public to Private

This range indicates who is in or allowed in the space. At the private extreme, we think of places that may only have one or two people present: A bathroom, a changing stall in a store, or a spa, for example. Extreme examples of public spaces include a mall, concert or sports venues, and stores (department, grocery, etc.). There may be pockets of privacy in public settings, such as a store bathroom. While technically still public, they have a perception of being more private. There are many spaces in between these extremes, though, such as a doctor's office.

Public and private can also be separated by the relationship with the individuals with which one is sharing the space. When you are surrounded by strangers, even a theoretically private place, such as someone's home, can feel public. An example of this might be attending a baby shower. On the other hand, public spaces you share with loved ones can feel more private. Hospital rooms could be an example of this. Interestingly, attending a wedding can go either way, depending on how well you know the people who are there. This can also be differentiated by the number of people present, which separates isolation from crowded.

92   *Theoretical Application*

Isolated to Crowded

This range is indicative of people and items taking up space in the setting. The immediate image associated with the extremes of this scale is being alone to being shoulder-to-shoulder with others. Crowds tend to include many people, whereas isolation is indicative of only a few people, if any. However, this spectrum is not exclusive to people. It can relate to items, too. Clutter is another form of feeling crowded. This can be particularly true if the clutter is disorganized or dirty. For example, a garage can feel isolated if it is sparsely filled with systematically placed items, but can feel crowded if filled with clutter, dust, or debris. It can feel crowded even when you are the only person in the room because the room still feels full.

Isolation and crowdedness can also be measured by sound. Crowded space is frequently associated with an abundance of sound. This could be music, verbal interactions, and movement. Movement could be anything from glasses clinking together, people high-fiving, squeaky furniture, or a slamming door. When gathered together, building off one another, these noises can get quite loud. Loudness is like auditory denseness. For some, it can quickly become overstimulating and be associated with negative feelings.

People often have feelings associated with isolation and crowdedness. Isolation is frequently associated with quiet and privacy; it can feel more secure due to an increased perception of control in the environment. However, isolation can also be perceived as targeting, lonely, or abandonment. It can be a scary context in some cases. Crowds can also be scary or unpleasant. They can be overstimulating, lacking in privacy, security, or control. They are chaos embodied. On the other hand, crowds can also indicate a place of good times; it is where many people want to be. People attend events such as concerts and sports games because there is a comradery and sense of shared experience with those around you, even if they are strangers. Crowds can be a source of excitement and energy. People can frequently be sensitive to the energy of those around them, for better or for worse.

In addition to these spectrums, there are other factors of the physical surroundings: Climate, time of day, light, textures, sounds, and others. Like the spectrums, these contribute to a person's comfort in the space. People have opinions about these contextual attributes. Some people dislike crowds, noise, dark, or climate attributes like heat or humidity. The presence of these can affect their mood and, as a result, the emotional context. An additional part of the context is the relationship with the people who share the space. The relationship with a person is part of the emotional environment of the communication context.

Emotional Environment

As mentioned earlier, the physical setting contributes to the emotional environment. People experience different levels of comfort based on their surroundings. How comfortable a person feels will impact their ability to interact authentically in communication with others. The emotional environment will also depend on the nature of the relationship between the communicators. Before a word is spoken, people in communication already have an expectation based on their relationship. This expectation will influence how verbal and nonverbal communication is interpreted. Expectations include social roles and social rules; they also are based on previous and future interactions.

Social Roles

According to social roles theory, people fill a variety of roles throughout life. These are often in conjunction with another role, such as a teacher and student or parent and child. Our ability to fill a role and complete its fullest potential may seem dependent on the other to also fulfill their role to its maximum potential. That is to say, we have expectations of how we behave based on the roles we fill and how we perceive others should fill theirs.

For example, I communicate differently with my father than I do with a coworker based solely on their different roles in my life. I might use more humor with one than the other, speak more or less eloquently, sigh more, and be more relaxed. I may even be more comfortable with silence in one relationship over the other. I behave differently based on the role I fill with the person (child versus peer) and the hierarchy distinctly within those. I behave as an equal with a coworker, but if they have been at the job or industry longer than me, I will be respectful and listen to their expertise. Similarly, even now as an adult, I will always be my father's child and will respect his role's authority. However, I can say that because in my life, my father has not given me a significant reason to believe his authority is unearned or poorly managed. This personal relationship history is also part of the emotional environment.

In both relationships, I behave in a way that communicates how I believe it is appropriate to act given my role with them. But I also think differently based on how I believe the other person's role should behave. If I view my father's role as a nurturer and supporter, I am more likely to approach him with emotional vulnerability because I anticipate that he will offer me relief and compassion. However, if I view my father's role as primarily a disciplinarian and lesson-giver, I may be more likely to restrict our communication in subject and frequency, wanting to avoid appearing incapable or lazy. This sort of meaning-making is highly relevant in communication interaction patterns, or feedback loops, that assume a person perceives their communication (including their context) the same way others perceive it. These ideas will be touched on in both Chapters 7 and 10 of this book.

It is important to remember, though, that not all roles are clearly defined or directly connected with another person in another role. We can take on roles as general attributes of oneself. For example, if I am a people-pleaser, it may not matter who the other person is. I just don't want them to feel uncomfortable and will go far out of my way to avoid that for them. This role overlaps

94 *Theoretical Application*

with the social rule of discouraging acting in a way that leads to discomfort in others. Social roles and rules frequently overlap in this way.

Social Rules

Social rules can be family-specific or wider, applying to a whole culture. These can be rules about how you treat someone. Sometimes these rules are based on the person's station or their relation to you. Sometimes they are meant to be applied generally, often associated with ethics, integrity, and morality. For example, different people believe different rules about respect. Some believe it must be earned. Others believe all people should be respected, regardless of station or history. Still others believe respect is automatically received but can be lost based on poor behavior. Even with all these perceptions, there is a consistent finding that one cannot force or demand respect. This is a social rule: You cannot mandate emotion, and something given freely is more meaningful than when it is required.

Similarly, based on someone's relationship, certain emotions may be expected or discouraged. In the paternal example stated earlier, the authoritarian parent likely would not witness their child's more vulnerable emotions of sadness, fear, or even fragile happiness. Instead, only specific emotions are permissible; even these may be minimized to try and create an illusion of objectivity. Unfortunately, some families view all emotion as innately instable and therefore are to be discouraged. However, some families function under the rule that all emotions are allowed within the home, but outside the home, they must be quelled. For these families, the acceptability of the emotion is dependent on the setting as well as the relationship.

Rules can also be about what is allowed in one setting versus another. These could be rules about behavior, speech, or emotions. Frequently, context can provide clues to the rules and vice versa; the rules can provide context for the communication. Certain behaviors are allowed in certain physical settings, such as, "No running indoors!" or "Please be quiet in the library." However, behaviors can also be restricted by relationship: "Don't speak that way to your mother," or "Is yelling really the best way to get what you want from a partner?" Rules can also vary by age; certain behaviors and speech patterns that are permissible among children feel out of place when an adult says or does those things (Rivera Walter, 2017).

There are also several rules about emotions. Rules dictate what emotions are allowed in what settings, for how long, and to what extent. You can be happy, but not *too* happy, and not for *too* long before it starts annoying your peers, right? You can mourn the death of a loved one, but you need to be able to return to your job and your regular level of productivity within a specified time frame, right? Anger is never acceptable...unless it is fueling efficiency. Unfortunately, in western culture, the emphasis on efficiency has labeled emotions as the scenic route to failure. They take too long, get too big, and are too hard to work with. Therefore, social rules often decide it is more immediately beneficial to minimize emotion, even if this can result in tumultuous long-term corrective work in years to come. For some people, pressure to adhere to all these rules can actually be a source of distress as they believe there are more rules they do not know and are unwittingly breaking or following incorrectly. This anxiety can be particularly present if it has been a problem in past interactions.

Context of Past, Present, and Future Interactions

People can have strong feelings based on past interactions. They can also feel the need to behave and communicate a certain way to meet current expectations or perceived demands. Lastly, people communicate with future interactions and relationships in mind.

Context of Past Interactions

People behave based on previous interactions. The tendency is for people to replicate behaviors and speech that they find fits the setting, including the other people present. Growing up in a church environment, I learned appropriate behaviors for that setting. Now, when I go back to a church setting, I instinctively return to that version of communication. Past interactions can be with physical settings or relationships.

How people respond to a behavior or communication method depends on past interactions. For example, a person may decide to maintain a friendship assessed by a perceived level of empathy: Support and acceptance. The likelihood of the other person(s) offering empathy is often based in whether or not that have displayed that trait in past interactions. If they have not, a person may elect to terminate that friendship. The emotional state of the individual entering that dialogue will depend on how the friend has dealt with previous difficult conversations. Therefore, someone's mood and attitude toward another person can be based on their previous interactions with that person.

However, past interactions could also include past interactions over a timespan. The previous paragraph gives the example of past interactions with a single person determining their relationship. But the general interactions a person has throughout their day can also contribute to their attitude entering a conversation with anyone. If I started my day having missed my alarm; feeling rushed to get ready in the morning; not having breakfast; hitting traffic on the way to work; not having time to prepare for a meeting and not presenting as professionally as I would like; receiving a difficult phone call just before leaving to go home; knowing there would be more traffic and that I needed to go to the bank, go pick up a prescription, and prepare dinner before finally getting off my feet for the day... You can bet if that was how my day went, it makes of a context of physical and emotional exhaustion when I get home. This day's past interactions with fellow drivers, coworkers, bank and store employees have contributed to that exhaustion, one interaction at a time. From that exhaustion, I may not be as ready for an end-of-day conversation with my partner

96 *Theoretical Application*

as I would like. The past interactions have provided a context to which my partner did not contribute but must now reap the benefit.

These are the two ways past interactions influence the emotional context: Past interactions with the individual with whom I am interacting, and past interactions of my day which set the emotional tone for my next interaction in the present.

Context of Current Interactions

To assess current interactions, we are asking ourselves, "What does this interaction demand of me? What does it hope to accomplish?" We assess the immediate and long-term needs of the individuals and the relationship itself – the whole is still greater than the sum of its parts. This can include monitoring for opportunities, constraints, resources, and competing needs based in the current context.

Opportunities include how the context could improve the interaction, such as being comfortable in one's setting, private versus public, or even in one's attire. When someone is dressed professionally and in a professional environment, both the clothes and setting contribute to the context and give opportunity to better understand the role of the speaker. Constraints can mean what gets in the way in the context, such as contending sensory demands like background noise or physical comfort. Examples could be if someone is standing or sitting in an uncomfortable chair. Resources consider the physical/material/fiscal or emotional/symbolic commodities, to use the social exchange theory terminology. In therapy, a child might struggle to speak directly with the therapist, but when the therapist uses their resources of toys and games, the child can find more creative self-expression. Competing needs can include competing loyalties or ideas, related to the social exchange theory concept of equity versus inequity and independence versus interdependence. On a more literal level, it can also include restraints such as if someone needs to use the restroom or is hungry during the current interaction, which can interfere with clear communication.

Context of Future Interactions

People behave in ways that communicate our hope for the future of the relationship. If someone does not care about the future of the relationship, they are more likely to behave and speak in an uncaring manner. However, there is also the context of one's integrity as it influences behavior. We want to communicate in the present in a way that accurately reflects how we want others to remember or view us in the future. For example, if I as a therapist do not care how others perceive me, I may be rude or harsh to clients. As a result, they may never come back; they may refuse to attend therapy ever again based on a bad experience with a therapist. However, instead, I could behave in a way that keeps the relationship and the future in mind. When someone feels heard, respected, and valued, they are more likely to hear, respect, and value others.

They are more likely to be open to change. They are more likely to come back. They are more likely to refer other potential clients to me. All based on an interaction that was mindful the present and future.

Clearly, a context includes the physical space and the relationship with the people in that space. For example, both a person and a place can contribute to a person feeling safe or unsafe. This feeling of safety will be the context for their interpretation of the situation and any communication that takes place in that context. If a child has been bullied by a peer at school, they may have negative feelings about either the physical building or the bully, regardless of if the other is present. They might feel anxious about going to school even when the bully is not there. They might feel anxious to interact with the bully off school property, too. Either attribute of the context contributes to that feeling of distress.

As straightforward as this may seem, interpreting context can be incredibly challenging. There are so many variables to attempt to consider! Each of these can be interpreted in a multitude of ways. Often, this is where miscommunication can happen. There is not necessarily a mistake, simply different interpretations of the same context. Reflect on Chapter 5's section about where communication goes wrong: Communication intent, communication interpretation, or communication interference. All these come together with the risk of intersubjectivity in communication. How do you think the context contributes to the possibility of something being misunderstood? Having intense conversations in lighthearted public spaces can be confusing because it sends mixed messages about the intensity of the subject. Having a happy-go-lucky attitude at a funeral can be perceived as disrespectful to the grievers and the mourning process. Social constructs dictate a funeral to offer a dichotomic celebration of life and expression of sorrow at the person's death. It is simultaneously private and public, especially considering some social norm about when it is acceptable or unacceptable to cry in front of others. All by itself, a funeral presents a difficult context for grief.

Often, people will have preferences of their contexts. There may be attributes of their physical environment that allows them to feel more comfortable. A common example of this is introverted people versus extroverted people. Introverted people notoriously prefer to be alone or in places surrounding by people and things that do not demand an abundance of energy dedicated to them. Extroverted people may feel more comfortable in places with other people and excitement. They collect energy from their surroundings and activities.

More often than not, a person will sometimes be more introverted or extroverted depending on their situation. If they have had a full week of professional and personal demands on their time, it may feel better to withdraw into a private space and spend time alone doing something they enjoy, such as gardening outdoors or reading a good book in their home. On the other hand, that same person may want to be with loved ones after a hectic week, taking solace in the ability to be mentally present during the task at hand, whether it be something quiet, like watching a movie, or loud like going to a restaurant

98 *Theoretical Application*

or playing a board game. Most people are not purely introverted or extroverted. Much like their physical and emotional setting, they are somewhere on the scale between the two extremes. And they learn to function based on where they are, what they need, and what is being asked of them, at the time.

Inevitability of Context

In Chapter 5, I stated it is impossible to not communicate. Context is a form of communication. Therefore, there is always context. Everywhere we are, each person with whom we share space or interact are part of our context. When we are aware of how these contribute to our behaviors, thoughts, and emotions in the moment, we have a greater understanding of why we do, think, and feel the way we do. It also helps provide understanding for how others behave, think, and feel. I call this *emotional logic*: All things make sense in context.

That being said, saying something makes sense in context is not the same as saying something is healthy, helpful, or excusable based on context. We see this in specific families all the way up to context on a social level. A person's context contributes to how one interprets other things. This includes the development of personal biases. Personal biases, like context, are inevitable. We develop them based on our experiences and information given to us by others. Having biases is part of being human. Biases are how people pick a favorite food, find activities they enjoy, and make friends. Biases can be sources of hope, such as believing in the goodness of people or that things find a way to work out well. However, biases can also be problematic. On a societal level, it is how people justify things like racism, sexism, and ageism. Biases can be unhealthy and inaccurate. Problematic biases are the interpretations of context of which therapists will want to be mindful.

Part of therapy can include enlightening people to the influence of their context on their behaviors and internal processes. It can also include highlighting where the interpretation of one's context is causing more harm than good. This goes for the therapist, as well; we must be mindful to intentionally minimize our biases in therapy. This will help us better understand the contexts of our clients rather than assume they share in our understanding of contexts.

Family systems theory believes it is impossible to remove people from their contexts. We can influence the current context. We can shift from one context to another. We can even change how we perceive the present context. But there will always be a context. Therefore, therapists cannot help a client achieve sustainable change without considering the continued influence of their context. An unhealthy context will lend itself to unhealthy behaviors, thoughts, and emotions. Part of family systems theory will inevitably include how communication and context contribute to problems being perpetuated. All the other family systems theory concepts – from wholeness to individual psychology – fall under this source of influence. Context is more than just being mindful of one's environment or a conversation of "nature versus nurture." Context is an ongoing source of influence even *during* the process of change. Recognizing the reach of its influence is essential to promoting insight and healthy change.

Context and Constructivism

One reason we cannot remove context is because it is a big part of how we make sense of the world around us. Our perspective is based on past experiences and what we believe about how the world works. Remember the social theories from Chapter 1; those are all efforts to understand why people do what they do. As I mentioned earlier, people are incapable of entirely removing their perspective or being completely objective. That's because these attributes help create one's reality. *Fluid reality* means everyone has their own interpretation of objective truth. This can also be called *constructivism* because people construct their own reality. As a result, there can be multiple truths at the same time. In fact, because everyone has their own interpretation, it is impossible to know the objective truth. There is some debate whether objective truth exists at all.

In therapy, I have a collection of picture frames that are empty, but each pain of glass is coated in a different color of serein wrap. I will have clients look through those, and when they do, I hold up a blank white piece of paper. I ask them what color it is when they look through the frame. Their answers will change based on which frame they are holding up. I call the different colors of serein wrap a filter. Because of this filter, they perceive the blank paper to be different colors. They may have a cognitive awareness that the paper is white, but when viewed in a certain perspective – through the different frames – it appears different. I can also compare it to filters on a social media app; they influence anything from colors to proportion to inventing attributes that were entirely absent originally (like animal ears or a sparkly border or caption). They change enough about the picture that we may not be able to see things as they originally were. We can only guess. These personal filters, our fluid experience of reality, impact how we see ourselves, our environment, our relationships, our problems, and even our potential solutions.

Coexisting Realities

Because multiple perspectives happen at the same time, multiple realities occur at the same time, too. These multiple realities can coexist with varying degrees of cohesion; sometimes they are difficult to overlap because the interpretations of an event are so different. The extent to which two or more realities can coexist is called *structural determinism*. This may allow for some variations in truth, and a system may shift their perceptions to accommodate within that variation window. However, our filters may assert some versions of reality are impossible, which can influence what we believe about other people and how we interact with them.

As a result of our personal filters, two people can experience the same thing in very different ways. We may remember it differently based on the emotional

100 *Theoretical Application*

context it brings forward. In the end, one's perception is one's experience, regardless of objectivity or the original intent of the message sender. Have you ever had someone say or do something meant to be a joke, but it ends up being hurtful? Few things are as invalidating as hearing, "I meant it as a joke; why are you making it something serious?" or, "Well I'm sorry you feel that way." The latter refuses to take responsibility for their contributions to the hurt and places blame on the person for misinterpreting them. Really, the receiver did not misinterpret the message (action or words), they simply interpreted it differently. This differentiates interpretations as options rather than a right-or-wrong judgment.

That being said, it can be challenging when one person's report drastically strays from that of others. Outright lying or intentionally twisting reality extensively to meet an agenda is not as harmless as interpreting something differently. This relates to biases that become overtly dangerous or damaging. This differs from ignorance. Being ignorant is not the same as lying; those twists in reality are based on blind-spots. Theoretically, upon new insight and understanding, those blind-spots can be diminished or eliminated.

One's unique interpretation of context is based on one's unique interpretation of reality. For some, there is not a purist record of events that exists; even when people report facts, they use language that can inadvertently communicate their biases regarding the situation.

Co-constructing Reality

In therapy, it is not uncommon for therapists to attempt to make peace between multiple perspectives by highlighting how both can be true. We accomplish this by noting where there are consistencies between the two and by speaking to how individual contexts contribute to our perceptions. Together, we can help a systemic client – such as a couple or family presenting to therapy – co-construct a reality with mutual understanding. In this, the clients may come to view a situation in the same way. When people have a shared view of something, this is called a *consensual domain*. When there is a continued shared reality between multiple people, impacting the way they interact with each other and those outside the system, this is called *second-order consensual domain*. That is to say, clients can come in with coexisting realities, but through exploration and intervention, may come to co-construct a single reality instead.

It is worth reminding that the therapist will be doing all this from our own perception, too. We are approaching the situation based on our own context: Our own history and our own ideas of what makes a relationship healthy or unhealthy. We can try to be cognizant of our biases and minimize them, but they are still going to be there. We want to be mindful of how our structurally determined reality is our context, and it will not necessarily match that of our clients. However, it is not our responsibility to inflict our perceptions onto the client. We want to be mindful of this as we consider the contexts of our clients, too.

Why Context Matters

Context matters for three significant reasons. First, context matters because it provides the cognitive and emotional logic to why people do what they do. It can help even the most seemingly illogical choices people make seem sensible. We call this contextualizing. When we understand a person's context, we are more likely to be empathetic to them. We can use statements that communicate recognition of the context in their decision-making:

- "I can see how that made sense at the time."
- "Given where you were and what was going on, it seems like you did what felt right."
- "It sounds like a solid reasoning process in that situation."
- "That appears consistent with what was happening and what you've done before."

When we validate the decision-making process, we are not necessarily validating the decision. We validate the context and the extent of power it carries.

Second, context matters because it can light a path toward insight when someone is distressed about their decisions. It can be upsetting when someone behaves in a way they find inconsistent with their value system. They may come to therapy asking, "Why did I do this? It isn't like me." It can be disturbing for someone when their context does not match their emotional needs. If they believe a parent's social role should behave in a certain way, but their living example does not do this, it can be troubling. This inequity is part of their context. It provides insight to how someone behaves in search or plea for equity. It also connects to the third reason context matters. It is another way to recognize the limits of what we can change versus what we cannot.

Third, recognizing the limits of change is essential to healthy progress. When I talk to clients about change, this overlaps with conversations about control versus influence. We can influence how we interpret a context and how powerful its influence may be. We can change our behaviors, thought patterns, and emotional responses. We cannot change how others perceive a context. We cannot directly change their behaviors, thoughts, or emotions; we can influence, but not change. We will go into greater detail about this in Chapter 11.

Applicable Therapeutic Models

"From a social constructionist perspective, a primary goal of therapy is to deconstruct so-called facts by delineating the assumptions, values, and ideologies upon which they rest" (Becvar & Becvar, 2018, p. 9). When we talk to our clients, they will bring their interpretations of facts. Part of therapy will potentially include identifying overt definitions in relationships and "meaning-making" of parts of our context. Clients (and therapists) may have covert assumptions and biases we may not even realize are not factual. Therefore,

102 *Theoretical Application*

we must explore these assumptions, a part of the client's context, and the meanings they are ascribed. This overlaps with a concept called *epistemology of participation*. This asserts life and its qualities are given meaning through participation with it. Therefore, therapy becomes a space to potentially create new meaning (also new context and new reality) through new experiences. Several therapeutic models discuss and consider context in their approach. Some models even approach it in similar ways. The four therapies below share in those overlaps.

Narrative Family Therapy

A core belief of narrative therapy is attention to influence of context. The model calls this context the dominant story. The dominant story provides assumptions about how to behave, think, and feel in certain contexts. People make decisions about how to act or what to believe based on that dominant narrative. In this way, narrative therapy avoids blaming language on the client, instead recognizing the extent of the context's influence. The dominant story is frequently filled with biases and can feel restrictive and ominous. But initially, the assumption is that the dominant story is the truth. Therapy using narrative therapy explores alternative interpretations of context, often with the therapeutic intervention reframing. Reframing looks at a situation, person, or relationship – all attributes of context – and challenges the assumed meaning given to those. In this way, narrative therapy challenges the person's interpretation of a context and the possibilities that context allows or discourages. The model also calls this deconstructing the problem, being specific instead of generalizing about the context (White, 1992). This is how narrative therapists develop an alternative discourse that is not saturated with problem-centric language (Eron & Lund, 1996).

Contextual Family Therapy

Contextual therapy, like Bowen's family therapy model, places high emphasis on multigenerational influence. Family is a huge part of our context and contributes significantly to biases we develop in childhood. Some of those biases include what contextual therapy calls family rules of reciprocity and fairness. It is often up to the family context to decide what fair looks like. The family creates unwritten ledgers that track a balance of entitlement and indebtedness between family members or between individuals and society as a whole. The family can create a list of expectations for specific family members in effort to bring that balance to equilibrium. These can be overt (like keeping score) or covert (assumed compliance). This is an example of how family provides context by having behavioral expectations, sometimes expectations that are never specifically identified.

The ledgers of contextual family therapy are part of relational ethics, a dimension of relational reality. Relational ethics are the presence of loyalty, legacies, guilt, and connectedness within a system. A legacy is a multigenerational pattern, including behaviors or beliefs and attitudes. Relational ethics provide a context of what is expected in a family between its members. According to this therapy model, we behave in light of what we are taught to be expected and acceptable, based on family rules that are passed down over generations. These rules are the context behind the decisions we make and actions we take. These rules often dictate value systems of the family and discourage individual value systems beyond those.

Acceptance and Commitment Therapy

Acceptance and commitment therapy (ACT) also places prominent emphasis on one's value system. According to ACT, distress occurs when a person is behaving incongruent to their value system (Gilmore, 2016). Regardless of symptomology, this model postulates individual and relational peace can be experienced in identifying shared values and mindfully seeking to live those out each day. Each choice would ideally be based in the context of that value system. The model uses mindfulness-based interventions to offer oneself acceptance and kindness via its six central processes, called the hexaflex: (1) Being present-focused; (2) identifying one's values; (3) commitment to pursue those values; (4) defusion, or being objective about one's thoughts; (5) accepting and being willing to explore one's difficult thoughts, and (6) self as context. The final one is obviously quite relevant to this chapter.

Self as context means taking a step back and observing yourself. It is a meta-awareness of yourself; you now witness your thoughts, feelings, and behaviors rather than having or doing them. In this separation of awareness and experience, a person becomes more capable of viewing themselves without judgment, in a more realistic self-context. It considers one's consistent self, unchanged by time or experience. As in internal family systems (IFS) therapy, the Self is the natural centered, consistent, compassionate, curious leader of the other parts. It is able to assess one's context and its influence in a more objective, less judgmental, reflection (Fisher, 2017). It helps us be able to say to ourselves, "That makes sense why I did that, in that context." This is significant part of the "acceptance" aspect of ACT.

Emotion-Focused Therapy

Emotion-focused therapy (EFT) formed as a therapeutic approach for couples to address broken emotional connections that influence their ability to solve problems together as a joined unit (Johnson, 2004). Romantic relationships depend on a foundation of trust and healthy attachment, attributes that may have been broken in a person's family of origin or in previous relationships. As mentioned in our conversation around the context of past interactions, previous experiences of trust and mistrust influence future relationships. EFT places emphasis on creating a safe environment for people to be honest and vulnerable with one another, trusting that the other will be attentive to those

104 *Theoretical Application*

emotions and respectful of their context, or source. This safe environment includes the physical and emotional context for the partners.

EFT is divided into nine steps that over three stages. In the first stage, the therapist is becoming familiar with the clients' contexts and perceptions of reality. This includes their relationship cycle, which looks at how the two impact one another, building off the existing context, often creating an unsafe emotional context that does not foster shared vulnerability. This first stage is also a time of de-escalation as the pair increases awareness of the other's context and potentially begin to validate this other perspective. The latter is particularly important in the second stage, where clients overtly identify past attachment wounds that provide the context for their current understanding of reality. They might tell stories of feeling unloved, forgotten, or invalidated by parents, mentors, peers, or previous partners. In response, the client's partner would practice validating this context and how it influences the speaker's perception of reality.

Also in the second stage, the client and therapist strive to create a new interpretation of reality that validates previous experiences but allows the present relationship to be different. It creates opportunity for the partners to turn toward one another in times of hardship, finding support rather than despair. This invites the clients to perceive one another in a new way and creates a new reality around the romantic relationship. With the new understanding of one another, the third stage strives to put to practice a new way of viewing the other person.

While this model was designed with couples in mind, it can also work with families, forming those early attachment bonds. They seek to build secure attachments early in a person's life to enable them to have a healthy emotional context from the beginning.

Case Study – Jimiyu's Big Move

Tawney was a missionary in Kenya from the United States. While in Kenya, she met her husband, Atticus, and they adopted an infant boy named Jimiyu from a young member of their church. They lived together for five years in Kenya but when Tawney got word of her father's untimely death, she wanted to return to the States to take care of her mother. Due to complications with their immigration documents, Atticus was not able to go with her, but she was able to bring Jimiyu. That was about six months ago.

Since returning to the States, Tawney has struggled in her transition: She lives with her mother, whose health is worse than she realized; she missed her father's funeral due to travel complication; and she has not been able to find a consistent source of employment except through her host church as a child caretaker. Being separate from Atticus has also been a prominent source of stress as they have continued attempting to get him a spousal visa to bring him to the States. Recently, adding to her stress, Jimiyu has been acting out at home. Seemingly randomly, he will start to scream, stomp his feet, throw his toys, and bang cabinet doors. He has resisted continuing to learn English, which he had been moderately exposed to while in Africa. Tawney initially attempted to enroll him in preschool, but outbursts several days in a row – including hitting peers on multiple occasions – resulted in his removal. She has continued seeing these behaviors at her childcare services for church members' children, as well. At this point, he appears to prefer to play by himself, which Tawney encourages since he is sometimes able to do this quietly.

Tawney has come to individual therapy stating she is "at the end of her rope." She says she wants to return home, meaning Kenya, but feels she cannot while her mother is still alive. She tearfully reports feeling "completely overwhelmed" by the behavior changes in Jimiyu, who she described as a "playful, social boy" when they were in Kenya. She says she is worried he is acting out because she is not attentive enough to him but feels exhausted all the time: "I never expected to be a single mom, but that's how I feel now."

Contexts to Consider in this Study

In addition to physical contexts, this example case dives into cultural and familial contexts. Both of these are unofficial subclasses of emotional context. Along with these, there are still other contexts, such as legal and individual contexts. They significantly contribute to a person's distress levels, anxiety tolerance, and movement toward meaningful change.

Physical Context

- International shift: Moving from Kenya to the United States
- Living with mother as an adult
- Away from "home"
- Away from husband

Cultural Context

- Religious influence – As a missionary, Tawney likely has religious convictions that influence her identity
- Cultural differences between Tawney's and Atticus' history
- Cultural shift in social norms from Kenya to the United States
- Child needing to learn new native language for social interaction

Familial Context

- Married, long distance
- Child, adopted from known parent with personal connection

106   Theoretical Application

- Father died unexpectedly, missed funeral
- Mother's failing health, perceived obligation for mother's care
- Child behavioral outbursts and social isolation

Other Contexts to Consider

- Legally adopted child internationally
- Immigration status distress
- Unstable employment status
- Personal self-doubt, likely with relevant history
- Personal identity as a 'single mother,' emotional implications

These are all attributes to be considered during treatment, regardless of therapeutic modality.

Treating with Narrative Therapy

Interpretation of the Problem

First, regardless of therapeutic model, let's acknowledge the remarkable amount of distress Tawney is currently experiencing. Between her identified stressors, no wonder she feels exhausted! She has provided us with abundant examples of where her stress is coming from; all of these are part of her context.

Narrative therapy would focus on the points in her context that contribute to her socially constructed identity, or story: Her changing roles in the church and family, and her self-identification as a single mother, given her current situation. According to narrative therapy, the dominant narrative from society may be shaming her in her roles, including the social judgment that may fall on single mothers, particularly from conservative faiths. The dominant narratives are impacting how Tawney makes meaning of those experiences and, in turn, her self-perception. Treatment, therefore, will focus on challenging those dominant stories and identifying versions view her experiences in a way that highlights her strengths and unique resiliencies.

Anticipated Solution

Tawney may feel better over time as she finds a new way to live out her identity. Currently, she may be placing a great amount of emphasis on aspects of her identity that are outside her control. Her dominant story includes a very negative self-perception. Narrative therapy may have her focus on aspects of her identity that she can influence: Loving mother and daughter, for example. The therapist can assist her to explore how to be a loving long-distance wife, accepting that this is not how she wants things to be but her limited capacity to change it. Additionally, the model would place emphasis on the present and hope for the future, respecting the past without being stuck in it. For example, therapy will likely include grief work around her father's passing and missing the funeral.

Specific interventions that the therapist could use include externalizing the problem, unique outcomes, and reauthoring. Externalizing the problem includes referencing the problem to be outside Tawney, her mother, or her son. Jimiyu's behavior can be a problem without viewing him as a problem. This intervention seeks to depersonalize the problem, check for assumptions clients make about the problem, and deconstruct how different system members contribute to the problem perpetuating. Unique outcomes, or sparkling moments, seek occasions when the problem was not as prominent or defining in the client's life. For Tawney, this could be exploring times when she handling child outbursts at her job or how she handled the visa process when leaving the States for Kenya. Lastly, Tawney has the opportunity to place emphasis on alternative views of the dominant narrative to make it less pessimistic. This is the process of reauthoring, or rewriting one's perspective. Tawney can use this to reflect on her personal strengths and, since her faith is likely a source of strength for her, how her higher power has been a moving force and source of hope for her. In these ways, Tawney will hopefully refocus her life to experience more hope and remember there is more to her than her circumstances.

Example Questions

1   "It sounds like you give a lot of meaning to the idea of being a single mother. Where do you think those come from?"
2   "What do you believe makes someone a good wife?"
3   "What assumptions might we be making about Jimiyu's behaviors?"
4   "Tell me about a time when you felt better after praying and connecting to God."
5   "Tell me about a time when your father showed you how to be a good parent."

Treating with Contextual Therapy

Compared to narrative therapy, contextual therapy would give greater attention to Tawney's family of origin. This model looks at how the context in her childhood contribute to her attitudes and behaviors as an adult. In the current relational ethics, there is evidence of loyalty, legacies, guilt, and connectedness in Tawney's family of origin leading into her nuclear family.

Interpretation of the Problem

Said simply, Tawney's problem is being overwhelmed, specifically with perceived responsibilities. These include responsibilities to her child, husband, mother, and deceased father, and possibly also her church family. From the sound of it, she may even feel solely responsible in many cases. She identifies as a single mother because Atticus is unavailable to assist her in disciplining

108　*Theoretical Application*

or redirecting Jimiyu. Both Atticus and Tawney are limited in their ability to legally advocate for him, but as the United States citizen, Tawney may feel responsible to lead through the process using State-side resource that are unavailable internationally. No siblings are identified to share responsibility for caring for Tawney's mother. Additionally, Tawney seems to carry excessive guilt for missing her father's funeral and may feel the need to make up for this perceived failure.

Feeling all this responsibility for all these is understandably overwhelming! According to this therapy model, it is important for the therapist to first remember that the client is doing the best she knows how to do given their situation and the tools that are available. Those tools are frequently learned in their family of origin. Tawney likely learned earlier in her life the tendency to take on excessive responsibility and what that responsibility entailed. She learned tools of determination, perseverance, and tenacity. However, she may not have learned appropriate limits to those qualities or what to do when she has reached maximum capacity of stress. This could be the mission of therapy with Tawney.

Anticipated Solution

Contextual family therapy will give particular attention to how Tawney learned responsibilities as a mother, wife, and daughter. What does she believe her responsibilities are? What was she owed as a child, teenager, young adult, and now as an adult? What does she believe she owes her parents? What did her upbringing teach her she owes her husband and child? What meaning does she give to falling short in those responsibilities? Remember, this sense of indebtedness is not innately flawed; families can have a "pay it forward" reciprocity across generations, too. To do so is a sign of respect. Therefore, Tawney may reflect on her upbringing and want to raise Jimiyu with similar or greater love, depending on her perception of her past. These are parts of the contextual model's emphasis on relational ethics, or the sense of loyalty and fairness from family member to member.

With this increased understanding of her relational context, Tawney can take the opportunity to reassess those responsibilities and gauge what she is humanly able to provide to both her nuclear family and family of origin. This is part of multidirectional impartiality, or the therapist's ability to reflect on each person's roles and responsibilities. Key interventions of multidirectional partiality are: (1) Offer empathy, (2) give credit to the trustworthiness and love that lead up to this point and in the moments of heaviness or unfairness, (3) acknowledge efforts and contributions to take care of meaningful relationships, and (4) identify shared accountability among family members for occasions when they have gotten stuck in problematic beliefs and their individual capacities to shift those responsibilities to balance. Working with a therapist, Tawney can do all these things. They are all part of her process to redefine balance in her relationships and reevaluate how her values in her roles are being communicated in her actions. For example, if compassion is a prominent component of motherhood for her, the therapist can work with her to explore how she, too, is worthy of compassion, and look at how she shows compassion to herself and her son.

Treatment will also include what the family of origin has taught Tawney about how to grieve. It is likely her family demonstrated early in her life how to cope with grief, or how to avoid it. Additionally, it sounds like Tawney feels torn as a multigenerational caregiver, possibly granting very little time for her personal health, including her emotional health and grief. Her faith will also impact her perception of the grief process, toward which the therapist must be respectful.

Example Questions

1 "What did you parents teach you are the responsibilities of a mother?"
2 "How did you know that your family loved you?"
3 "What does your faith tell you your role is toward your mom?"
4 "How will you begin to show Jimiyu that things will get better in a way he will understand?"
5 "Tell me about a time when you saw either of your parents grieve. What was that situation? What did it look like? What was it like for you to observe that?"

Treating with Acceptance Commitment Therapy

ACT places great emphasis on one's self in context. It reflects on one's thoughts, feelings, and behaviors as part of one's context, both contributing and responding to one's physical and emotional contexts. ACT calls this observing self, a meta-awareness of both one's inner and outer world. This is part of problem interpretation and potential solutions.

Interpretation of the Problem

According to ACT, a central problem for Tawney is her lack of mindfulness and self as context. Below are some key things for the therapist to look out for that let us know how present Tawney is in her self-concept:

1 *Is she overly personalizing?* – This is similar to how contextual therapy looks at how Tawney overwhelms herself with responsibility. She appears to take personal and exclusive responsibility for helping others. She may even view the situations as a personal shortcoming. This is where you might hear a client say, "If I had done more, things would be different," or taking sole blame for something not going as planned.
2 *Has she accepted reality as it is?* – Tawney appears to accept reality rather than being lost in wishful thinking or "what ifs?" However, she seems disappointed in reality. This likely overlaps with unaddressed grief.
3 *Does she avoid the emotions and experiences of the present moment?* – Tawney appears to be aware of her emotions but may not feel permission

110   *Theoretical Application*

to feel them. They are not of a high priority for her among busy day after day. Being in the present moment can be difficult for people; when it feels unpleasant, there may also be minimal desire to sit in the discomfort. As a result, Tawney may be avoiding the emotional depth of her experiences right now, deeming them "too much to handle with everything going on."

4   *Does she have a stable sense of self?* – The case summary did not address this in full, but her identity as wife, mother, daughter, Christian, etc. appear consistent and important to her. Her identities as a missionary or professional caretaker may be more temporary. Therapy will potentially explore the differences between those.

5   *Is she aware there is more to her than her thoughts, feelings, perceptions and memories, and behaviors?* – This is likely a central theme that will come up in treatment. In a time of life when getting through each moment seems to demand your full attention, it can be challenging to think beyond that. For Tawney, this seems to be the case. The demands of each day seem to leave little time for attention to her overall spirit. This lack of self-care could lead to greater feelings of being overwhelmed, too.

Emotions, thoughts, perceptions, memories, and behaviors all change frequently and do not offer identity consistency. Improving awareness of one's consistencies and the unchanging qualities of one's identity, called the transcendent self, is central to ACT interventions.

Anticipated Solution

ACT's self-in-context is a form of mindfulness that will be central to the therapeutic process. Over all, there are six goals to ACT therapy as part of the hexaflex: (1) Be present-focused, (2) identify values, (3) how can he pursue those values, (4) be objective in self-reflection, (5) willingness to explore own difficult thoughts, and (6) self as context. Therapy with Tawney could focus on the final one; however, each of these goals overlap with one another substantially. Within self as context work, there are five parts, each of which Tawney may explore: (a) To facilitate defusion, especially from the conceptualized self; (b) to facilitate acceptance of reality and self; (c) to facilitate flexible contact with the present moment; (d) to access a stable sense of self; and (e) to access a transcendent sense of self (Harris, 2017).

Tawney would likely greatly benefit from exploration of her transcendent self. This matches with the final question asked in previous section: *Is she aware there is more to her than her thoughts, feelings, perceptions and memories, and behaviors?* Similarly, *to what extent is she aware of herself beyond her circumstance?* Tawney may benefit from recentering around her values and identifying where and how those are still present along with how she can increase their presence in her life. It will be important to identify these practical application questions beyond abstractly identifying values. This will overlap with noticing current events to begin being present-focused and highlighting context. Improving self-in-context also overlaps with improved self-acceptance and recognition of one's human limits. Hopefully, as an outcome, she will remember the joys of motherhood along with its challenges, engage with a peer group that could emotionally support her, and interact with her mother in a way that finds delight in her company. Tawney has demonstrated repeatedly in her life that she is a capable, overcoming woman; ACT therapy would strive to highlight this and make sure she knows it, too.

Example Questions

1 "Tell me about a time when you felt consumed by your thoughts, noticed it, then managed to pull yourself out of that."
2 "When you think about being a single mother, what feelings do you have in your body? What memories come to mind?"
3 "What are some things in your life that didn't change after coming back from Haiti?"
4 "As we talk about Jimiyu's behavior, what thoughts and feelings do you notice having?"
5 "Tell me about a time when you felt you did a good job at something."

Treating with Emotion-Focused Therapy

While EFT was formed with couples in mind, its application has broadened to include families and individuals, too. This means it can be applied to Tawney independently or alongside her mother, son, or other loved one. Either way, the emphasis will be on developing healthy attachments based in one's family of origin and applied to one's nuclear family moving forward.

Interpretation of the Problem

Successful, well-connected relationships are founded in trust and secure attachment. These transfer from family-of-origin to the nuclear family. For Tawney, this is dually important as she mirrors her trust dynamics between her mother and herself in how she parents Jimiyu. As her mother's current care-taker, she may be reflecting on how she was raised. As a result, she seems aware that the international shift and her own emotional distress are likely affecting Jimiyu, as she is his current family-of-origin. She knows this could impact his ability to form healthy and meaningful relationships both in the present and future. This is further evidenced in her mixed feelings about his elective social isolation.

To address any of these, EFT may have Tawney identify her interaction cycle with other people, or, alternatively, with herself. What are her cognitive, emotional, and behavioral interaction patterns? What has happened in her history, in relationship with that other person, that lead to that pattern? This is the overlap of EFT and context and is central to EFT's first step in therapy.

112 *Theoretical Application*

Anticipated Solution

As stated earlier, EFT places great emphasis on creating a safe physical and emotional environment for honesty and vulnerability. This is typically achieved in connection with someone else who can respond attentively and respectfully. Even individually, this can include the practice of self-kindness and non-judgmental language with ourselves.

Treatment may focus on improving trust between three important people in this system. First, therapy may address trust between Tawney and her mother through reflecting on the past breaches in trust and experiencing acceptance and expression of those needs. This will potentially be a challenge as, depending on the mental well-being of Tawney's mother, she may not be readily able to participate in this process. The second relationship to potentially address is building trust between Tawney and Jimiyu. Due to the child's age, this will not be traditional talk therapy. Instead, Tawney would practice playing and interacting with Jimiyu in a way that communicates love and trust. It is likely his behavioral outbursts are a response to the uncertainty of the present moment and homesickness. With validation and love, Tawney can impact these behaviors by approaching them with consistency and compassion in her response. The last relationship Tawney will not to focus on is the relationship with herself.

It is likely that Tawney would present to therapy and be in the first stage of EFT treatment. The therapist will assist her to identify her interaction patterns with others, identifying her emotions within those, and validate those contexts as part of her personal history. Tawney may reflect on feelings of weakness or loneliness, which would contribute to her continued work ethic, both professionally and as a caretaker to her family. This will be a time of de-escalation through increased awareness and affirmation. The therapist can then lead into potentially validating other perspectives, as was explored in this chapter as part of understanding differing contexts.

Example Questions

1   "Tawney, pretend with me that your life yesterday was the focus of a movie. Your whole day was on film, from start to finish. Tell me what I would see when you get upset with your mother."
2   "Tawney, you describe Jimiyu offering you a toy to play with him, trying to reach out and interact with you. You say when you are stressed and busy, you notice that you tend to try and calmly tell him, "Not right now," which leads to him throwing the toy and crying loudly. What happens after that? What thoughts and feelings do you have? What action do you take next?"
3   "Tawney, what would it be like to call Atticus and tell him about these fears you have of feeling so weak or alone?"
4   "Tawney, I wonder if there was ever a time when you were a child and didn't get some reassurance or message of love from you parent that you needed. Tell me about that."

5   "Turn toward your mother. Tell her what you just told me about why words of affirmation are so important to you."

Reader Reflection

1   What preferences do you have about your context? Do you prefer to spend time ...
   - Indoors or outdoors?
   - In nature setting or manmade structures?
   - In private or public settings?
   - Alone, with a few people, or in groups or crowds?
2   To what extent do you think it is appropriate to integrate these biases into your workspace?
3   What is a bias you are aware that you have about other people? Remember, these can also be presented as stereotypes.
4   How can you intentionally minimize the influence of this bias when interacting with others?
5   What are ways we cannot control or influence our context?
6   How could your own context, such as the closeness of family with which you grew up, be a blinder to the contexts of your clients?
7   Look at the four modality examples. Which one matches your worldview best? How so?

7 FST Concept IV
Co-occurring Systems

Let's begin with a geographical simile.

Reflect back on our discussion of holism and the holon. Despite being parts of a whole, each individual has the capacity to be whole within itself. This can be like geographical states and territories. They are parts of a larger nation, but they also function independently within themselves. They have their own laws, budgets, and leadership. Even inside those, states have smaller pockets of populations, such as cities or towns. However, the smaller systems must adhere to the laws and norms of the larger systems. In the United States, states laws are secondary to federal laws, and local governments must follow state regulations, too. Altogether, each region, state, district, city, community, suburb, family, and individual contribute to the nation's identity and functionality. This is the nature of co-occurring systems.

Definition and Description

Family systems theory uses ecological systems theory in its understanding of co-occurring systems. *Co-occurring* means the systems take place simultaneously, one within another. Systems can be large or small. Larger systems are called suprasystems; smaller systems within those are called subsystems. They impact one another in both overt and covert ways.

Suprasystems and Subsystems

To start, let me repeat the definition of a system, as introduced in the preface. A system is a group of interconnected units, often with a relationship linking them together. A system can be a family, a classroom of students and educators, a small group of religious fellows, collaborative coworkers, and bosses at a job, just to name a few. We will focus on the family system, but several of these concepts can be applied to other relationships. The family system, like other systems I just named, occur in context of communities.

Suprasystems are the external environments and communities surrounding the system, particularly the family system. Often, these contribute to a family's

DOI: 10.4324/9781003088196-10

identity, values, and beliefs. The family may identify themselves based on the suprasystems to which they belong:

- Extended families, the family name
- Racial and ethnic subcultures
- Religious affiliations
- Geographic regions
- National identity

In identifying as a member of a certain suprasystem, people may believe they are identifying attributes of themselves that align with the values of that suprasystem.

For example, years ago I was confiding to my father about a frustration I had in my job at the time. I described my annoyance and steadfast desire to maintain my way of handling the situation, even though I was not getting the desired results. I remember him saying, "Yes, we Suppes' can be a stubborn bunch." At first, I had a disappointed reaction to the word stubbornness, which had negative associations for me. However, as I thought about it more, I realized he was right. In being steadfast, I was being stubborn. It was interesting to me that this personal quality was attributed to my extended family – a suprasystem. It was an attribute my family as a whole seemed to share, even people with whom I had never interacted! But my father did not mean it as an insult; we both chuckled and moved on in the conversation.

The relationship between my father and I would be an example of a *subsystem*. Within the context of my immediate family – a system including my biological parents, my sister, and myself – he and I were a subsection. Subsystems can be in pairs, triads, or small groups. It most often consists of a pair, or dyad. These can appear in three versions in families:

- Parental dyad (can include parent and stepparents)
- Sibling dyad (includes biological, step-, or fostered and adoptive siblings)
- Parent/child dyad (biological or otherwise)

The dyads can continue to appear when the child or siblings are adults; it is not exclusive to youth or adolescence.

Sometimes subsystems bond in opposition to another individual or subsystem in the system. These subsystems may divide into alignments, coalitions, and triangulations. *Alignments* are individuals joined by mutual benefits, interests, or value. *Coalitions* are a team-up against a common "other," such as against a specific caretaker or extended family member. Unfortunately, subsystems can result in people getting "clumped" together or identified with the problems of one person in the same subsystem, such as troublesome sibling pairs. Therefore, sometimes coalitions can come together against a specific subsystem, not just one person. Lastly, when there is disturbance within a dyad in the system, a third person may be brought into the fold. This introduces a family systems theory concept of triangles.

116 *Theoretical Application*

Triangles

Triangles are a form of subsystem in a family system. Where there are close relationships between three or more people – where the interaction of persons *A* and *B* influence person *C* and all their relationships – there is a family system. This example would also meet the definition of a *triangle*. Triangles have been described as a two-against-one situation. In a triangle, a third person will be brought into a dyad to provide stability, destabilize, or to make up for excessive emotional closeness or distance in the dyad. Per Murray Bowen, a triangle is the smallest stable relationship unit. Think of it as a three-legged stool; when there are only two legs, it will topple over. It is by having that third leg that the stool is able to stabilize and be functional.

That being said, not all triangles will result in stabilization. Sometimes triangulation can be unhealthy or destabilizing:

- Gossip
- Taking a morbid interest in others' problems
- Focusing on a third party rather than problems in one's relationship or oneself
- Affairs

All of these are verbal and behavioral triangles. Triangulation can be achieved through spoken and nonverbal communication: It could be multiple extensive conversations between friends about one's romantic relationships. It could be a conversation between coworkers griping about a new boss' job performance. It could be a glance between a store cashier and the wife of a man who makes a passive-aggressive sexist remark. The triangulated individual is not necessarily someone in the system. In fact, it frequently is not, such as the store clerk mentioned earlier. It could be in-laws, a coworker, a friend, even a therapist.

It is important to note that triangles are not innately bad. People can benefit from an outside perspective or having "new eyes" on the situation. A third person can bring some much-needed objectivity and compassion (Heath, 2001). It can deepen and broaden one's understanding of a topic or problem. However, triangles do have risky implications. The third person may not be objective; they may have their own agenda in the situation. Their feedback may be highly subjective and unhelpful. They may not offer empathy. Sometimes they can do more harm than good. Paradoxically, the goal of triangulation is detriangulation: Temporarily including a third party who can be emotionally supportive but separate enough to remain empathetic but objective.

Roles in Triangles

Like family roles mentioned in Chapter 6, members of a triangle tend to fall into one of three roles. There is the generator, who is often the identified

FST Concept IV   117

patient or symptom-bearer. Second, the amplifier is often emotionally reactive to the generator and contributes to the symptoms' perpetuation. Lastly, the dampener typically acts to reduce symptoms, not necessarily in a healthy way, and in doing so, reinforces the process of triangulation.

Interlocking Triangles

To further complicate triangulation as a concept, triangles can influence other triangles. This is called interlocking triangles. Sometimes the third person of a triangle fails to dampen the problem. They fail to decrease or eliminate the stress of the relationship between the other two members of the triangle. They may go to someone else to discuss the problem or seek advice. This creates an additional triangle. The more people there are in a system, the more opportunity there can be for interlocking triangles. Triangles can become increasingly polarized as each side can be entrenched in their perspective, pulling in others to vouch for their point of view as the correct one.

Overall, the triangle subsystem can be helpful or unhelpful. It can stabilize or destabilize a relationship based on the addition or removal of that third voice:

- An unstable dyad can be stabilized by the addition of a third person.
- An unstable dyad can be stabilized by the removal of a third person.
- A stable dyad can be destabilized by the addition of a third person.
- A stable dyad can be destabilized by the removal of a third person.

Frequently, these subsystems are self-built and self-maintained. Triangles perpetuating triangles. This aligns with the cybernetic concept of autopoiesis.

Autopoiesis

Autopoiesis is the belief that systems are self-creating and self-perpetuating. They are self-built rather than externally built. This pattern appears in nature, life, and social structures; the family structure is a perfect example. Biological families self-perpetuate: Parents create and raise children in a family system. Even when parents separate, they continue to have emotional and physical influence over the child genetically and possibly through interaction. If a child is given to adoption, they can connect with a family and be indoctrinated into that system. Blended families come to have their own identities, unique from the families-of-origin of any parent or child. The family identity is self-defined, self-organized, and self-maintained. Their beliefs, values, and thought processes can meld with a specific system with whom they interact. The way parts of a system interact creates a pattern. This pattern can become an identifier of who is in the system and who is not. It distinguishes them from other systems within a suprasystem.

A small example of this concept is inside jokes. Inside jokes are communications that are exclusively humorous or have distinct meaning to

118 *Theoretical Application*

members of a specific system or subsystem. Only members of that system understand the joke to its full extent. Inside jokes are often born from a specific experience that bonded the system. Only those who were present for that experience have the full context of the joke. From then on, the inside joke is a means of remembering and reiterating that bond. Friends make inside jokes; inside jokes help maintain friendships. They contribute to the self-perpetuation of the friendship.

Autopoiesis is important to consider when we look at how people distinguish membership of a system. This can be true of all sizes of systems, which can go beyond supra- and subsystem delineations. There can actually be several sizes of systems even within those distinctions, as described by ecological systems theory.

Ecological Systems Theory

Ecological systems theory originated with Urie Bronfenbrenner (1979), a Russian-born American psychologist in the mid-twentieth century. His work looked specifically at the role of the environment on child development. He observed that, when growing up, children's identities are intertwined fully with their social environments. It is only as people get older and attain cognitive developments that increase self-awareness that a person develops an identity beyond their social contexts. However, when we are younger, we identify ourselves based on our social interactions. These can be from family ("I'm Rachel's sister") to school ("I go to Littlebrook High School") to religious and ethnic affiliations ("I am Jewish"). These environments are various sizes; there are four people in my family, 2000 students at my high school, and millions with whom I may share a faith and ethnic background. However, each system has the capacity to influence one another. They are interrelated. This becomes more and more evident as we grow older. Though Bronfenbrenner's research focused on child development, we see the influence of co-occurring systems across all stages of life.

Bronfenbrenner also observed that people in the same system can experience an environment differently. Despite being raised in the same home, attending the same school, and being members of the same faith, my sibling can have a very different memory of our childhood. This is due to our unique genetic characteristics, such as our individual temperaments and preferences, overlapping with our environments and specific events or interactions that may have occurred within those environments. All of these will influence our impression of past events and the perception (and choice) of systems in which we currently are members.

As mentioned earlier, co-occurring systems are the result of being members of multiple systems at the same time. These can be small, specific systems to larger, more abstract systems. Ecological systems theory describes six such level of external influence: Chronosystem, macrosystem, exosystem, mesosystem, microsystem, and the immediate self.

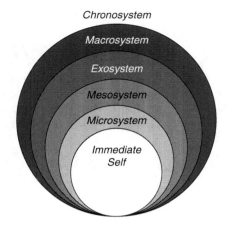

Immediate Self

This smallest system may be rather self-explanatory. It is the individual. It's you! Bronfenbrenner called this smallest circle the child, but I am editing the language somewhat to apply it across age groups. The self could be considered the ultimate subsystem. The *immediate self* will be a member of multiple systems. Within those many systems, a person may have varying roles and hierarchy placement from system to system (Markus & Cross, 1990).

When a therapist works with an individual, family systems theory would have us remember the individual is a member of these systems. They are influenced by the systems. Their membership in one system influences their experience in another system. Even when a client presents with a problem in a specific setting or relationship, we cannot discount the impact of other settings and relationships on the identified problematic one. The specific setting or relationship would likely be an example of a microsystem.

Microsystem

The *microsystem* is one's immediate environment. Typically, these are one's personal relationships: Close family, classmates, a teacher or supervisor at work, a caregiver. Close family includes those with whom one has regular contact; it is not necessarily just immediate family. It could be a grandparent who frequently babysits, mother's lifelong friend whom you grew up calling your aunt, or cousins who are close in age and attend the same school. It can also be a mother, father, step-parent, or foster/adoptive sibling. Even at this level, influence is multidirectional. I have the ability to influence other people, and they have the ability to influence me. This influence can stem into my other microsystems, called mesosystems.

120 *Theoretical Application*

Mesosystems

Mesosystems are known for the connection or overlap between microsystems. This could be parental involvement at school events, friends visiting your home, inviting church friends to a school or community event, or other such social circle intersections. This colliding of worlds can be exciting to some people if it does not happen often, or made mundane in its frequency for others. However, problems can arise when there is disconnect between environments. For example, it can be distressing when a caregiver dislikes their child's friend group. As a result, the child may feel torn in loyalties between the two systems. They may experience conflicting emotions and uncertainty, and this imbalance can negatively impact their development.

Exosystems

Up until now, there has still interaction between the immediate self and the micro- and mesosystems. Shifting outward, this direct contact becomes minimal. Unlike the circles of influence that came before, the *exosystem* is the indirect environment. These are the linked environments with which the immediate self may not interact. However, they can still impact the immediate self. Examples include settings such as a parents' workplace, school administration, extended families, or homeowner's associations (HOAs). For a family specifically, these can include my family members' other microsystemic relationships: A sister's peer group, mother's small group from the synagogue, or father's coworkers.

Even without direct interaction, these exosystems can influence me. They impact the moods of my family members, family reputation, time management of family members balancing different expectations and roles, and family attitudes about money. Exosystems also influence family attitudes. In the example earlier, my father's family-of-origin, including people I have never met, taught him the importance of responsibility and independence. He passes these on to me to impact my value system. This is seen to a greater extent at the macrosystemic level.

Macrosystem

The *macrosystem* is the largest social circle. They are the social and cultural patterns, values, and beliefs. More than the smaller systems, macrosystems connect people via concept rather than physical or tangible connection. Examples include regional, political, religious, and economic systems. People can be connected by the concept of their mutual faith, even when their physical spiritual meeting spaces are across the globe from one another. People can be connected by a common political party, even when their specific policy passions under that umbrella may vary. People may bond over their reciprocated struggles of a certain socioeconomic status and the restrictions and challenges that accompany it. People may connect with someone for being raised or currently living in a shared geographic location or climate.

Macrosystems do not exist in exclusivity. A person that grows up in the religiously and politically conservative part of a first-world country will experience cognitive, emotional, social, and physical development differently from someone raised in a war-torn country where access to basic necessities (food, clean water, shelter, clothes) are inconsistent at best. The macrosystems in which one is involved teaches you about social norms and acceptable behaviors and thought patterns, whether they mean to or not (Laveman, 1997). For example, I regularly interacted with multiracial families throughout my childhood. As a child, it seemed odd to learn there were people and places that did not accept this as normal or healthy. However, that same environment also taught me certain biases that were not challenged until I went outside my exosystem to meet new people and new ideas. Hopefully, with greater awareness of how my systems influence me, I can minimize those biases and develop into a better person over time.

Chronosystem

The *chronosystem* is measurement over time, both changes and consistencies. Examples of change could be shifts in parental employment location or employment status, changes in living arrangements, and larger macrosystem changes. These changes can occur at all system sizes. At the microlevel, family norms and rules change over time based on the ages and maturity of the family members; a child's curfew may change as they get older. On the other hand, the economic and technological development of the cellphone changed communication practices on a macro level. This included the shift in popularity of texting over phone calls, changes in social media usage, and even the cultural assumption that people have cell phones instead of home phones. Chronosystemic changes can be quick or slow and belabored. Regardless of the system size, change can be challenging. This is as true for a family as for a culture as a whole.

Ecological Systems Theory and Family Systems Theory

Ecological systems theory concurs with family systems theory's recognition of how people are influenced. Both look at how those influences are layered on one another. Individuals and families are influenced by our cultures as much as we are influenced by one another. This is central to family systems theory. As a suprasystem grows larger, it does not negate the intricacies of the subsystems; it incorporates them. However, it cannot give equal attention to all parts. There is an assumption that people will inevitably choose which system to prioritize their time, energy, and identity. This is the nature of social hierarchy.

Where There Are Systems, There Is Hierarchy

We all belong to multiple systems across multiple levels of systems. At any given time, we must choose which to focus on and prioritize. We typically choose based on context: In this moment, in this physical and social setting, which is most significant? Which demands my immediate attention? To what must I be most mindful? Based on these types of questions, one system will take import over the others at that time. Let's say that you both have a job and are in school. When you are at your job, you probably do not work on school material (homework, readings, etc.) unless there is a lull in your workplace responsibilities and you have permission to do so. While in the context of your workplace, the tasks, relationships, responsibilities, and roles of your employment are prioritized.

The challenge for many people comes when the context calls for one priority but another system is demanding it. For example, have you ever been at home but found yourself thinking of assignments for school that still need to be completed? Or been at work at the sacrifice of a social or personal event that was at the same time? These are ways systems co-occur. The challenge of the work-life balance is based in the hierarchy prioritization of one over the other.

The prioritized system will have its rules and roles prioritized, as well. Subsystems follow the rules of the system. Systems adhere to the rules of the suprasystem. This is how there can be cultural norms that transcend gender, race, socioeconomic status, religion, or other attributes. It is also how norms in a family can be carried into its subsystems such as sibling dynamics. Rules can also extend from system to system. If a family has a rule that discourages interruption or that a father figure has a last word, this can influence how a student may not interrupt peers who speak over them in class or accept a male teacher's grade on an assignment they feel is unfair. Though a child in one system and a student in another, both hold a similar subservient position in a hierarchy. Additional challenges come when a person is subservient in one setting but expected to be a leader in another.

In different systems, people will take on different roles. Unlike the example mentioned earlier, a person does not necessarily fall into the same role across all systems. Earlier, we identified common roles in a family system: Scapegoat, hero, rescuer, mediator, lost child, mascot, and cheerleader. A person may be a mascot in their professional settings but a lost child in their family-of-origin. They may be more outgoing in one system compared to another. How they enact these roles depends on their relationships in the system. If they are forced into a submissive role in their workplace, an adult may be authoritative at home. If a child bullies at school, they may also be a victim of bullying at home or in another peer setting.

That being said, general systems theory has a concept called *progressive centralization*. According to von Bertalanffy (1968), this is when a specific subsystem becomes more and more important and one's behaviors centralize around it. This means a subsystem, despite its size, becomes more prioritized and dominant, even in the presence of other systems. This subsystem becomes increasingly central to the identity of the individuals in it and its members become more unified. They increasingly take on the roles and rules of that subsystem and apply it to other systems of which they are a member. Von Bertalanffy asserts that the selection and emphasis on a specific subsystem as one's defining attribute is a form of progressive individualization, too. Specific identification of one's roles and rules in various systems can be an important step in therapy to provide clarity of systemic hierarchies and individual responsibilities.

Applicable Therapeutic Models

Structural Family Therapy

Structural therapy considers the influence of systems on and within one another. Additionally, how those microsystems and subsystems interact will influence larger systems. A person or system does not have to be physically present to be influential. Therefore, this model emphasizes the ability to do systems-based therapy even when the client is a lone individual. Seeing a person individually does not remove them from the context of their systems, and treatment will consider the client's membership various systems. It would be unrealistic to minimize the influence and significance of those relationships. This includes how those systems are structured that influence the individual's life.

Structural therapy highlights the role of social support, including family, in creating lasting change. Charles Fishman says, "Family therapy can decrease symptomology by addressing the patterns and transforming the system, the ways people interact around symptoms" (Guzzardo & Pina-Narvaez, 2019, p. 221). While family involvement in therapy is important, it is not essential. Structural therapy relies heavily on what is observed in session, but meaningful change can happen even at that smallest system – the immediate self – and move outward. Structural family therapy wants to know who is in the system, who is out, and about the hierarchy that is present versus the desired hierarchy, including division of power and role within the family system.

Common interventions in structural family therapy include tracking, joining, and particularly enactments. In enactments, a subsystem practices a typical interaction in session, and the therapist interrupts when the system's dysfunctional behavior comes out. They then redirect the interaction to be more functional and to assist in reaching the desired outcome.

Bowen Multigenerational Family Therapy

Bowenian therapy looks at multiple systems influencing one another over time – the chronosystemic influence across generations. Bowen also looks at how systems interact and are in relationship with one another. Each system includes three components:

- *Emotional system*: Instinctual, biological functioning
- *Intellectual system*: Human ability to think, reflect, and reason

124 *Theoretical Application*

- *Feeling system*: Bridge between emotional and intellectual systems, attaching meaning to emotional reaction

These can be observed at all sizes of systems. The emotional system, specifically, drives process within systems and the resulting relationship and interactions between systems. This relates to the Bowenian language of anxiety to describe the distress between system members and between systems; they are good intentions "run amuck," as Kerr would say (Popovic, 2019, p. 60).

A central Bowenian concept is societal emotional process, or the idea that societies shape families. That is to say, participation in suprasystems influences how we emotionally experience our microsystems. According to Kerr, a partner of Bowen, "The emotional system drives functioning at all levels – families, society, work, social organizations, and other nonfamily groups – reflecting the systemic consistency of Bowen theory" (Popovic, 2019, p. 52). In different systems, even outside the family, we see the same patterns of emotional tension; subsystem division and triangulation; emotional reactiveness, defensiveness, and counterattacks feeding systemic anxiety; and the pattern to spend emotional energy to calm the system. As with family systems, Bowen views societies as constantly having fluxes of progression, or prominent differentiation, and regression, marked by absence of differentiation. These are fed by environmental issues such as increase in population and exhaustion of natural resources, and restricted access to alternatives. Therefore, a person's level of differentiation can be impacted by their macrosystems' levels of differentiation and vice versa.

Client microsystemic family history is often learned through building a genogram in Bowenian therapy. Specifically, Bowenian therapists tend to seek information in three family generations or more. This simultaneous assessment and intervention look at how one generation influences the next – how the family-of-origin influencing nuclear family including family roles and rules. The genogram also draws to light the role of power of subsystems, particularly sibling positioning, more than other models might. Theoretically, increased family insight can lead to behavioral change. As the family is able to identify patterns of reciprocal functioning, they noticed when one person functions effectively at the cost of someone else in the system. Impressively, this is across systems of all sizes, including macrosystems. Common examples include over- and under-functionality, decisive and indecisive, and dominant and submissive. These "occurred with such precision that the presence of one train in one family member predicted the presence of its partner in another family" or system (Popovic, 2019, p. 44).

Lastly, as noted in Chapter 6 about the role of the therapist, it is important to be mindful of the therapist's systemic history and how it could influence treatment. It is possible to connect with and help a client system without emotionally pouring ourselves into it. Differentiation is what makes this possible through maintaining a sense of self in the system – a sense of one's immediate self, or *solid self* in Bowen's language. It is the ability to distinguish oneself from others in your microsystems, subsystems, and larger systems. Your solid self is what makes you unique and potentially what allows the therapist to uniquely balance between membership in the client system and separation from it.

Solution-Focused Therapy

Solution-focused therapy (SFT) looks at systemic interaction of all sizes as potentially part of the solution to any problem. As mentioned earlier, this is largely due to the role of communication and language in SFT. This is due to SFT's connection with social constructionism: Knowledge and meaning are built between people and their sharing of those. This is true both between people and between larger systemic perceptions shifting over time. For example, shifts in political power can impact a person's perception of that group and what it means to be affiliated with a certain political party.

Experiences that people have at different systemic levels impact their emotional, cognitive, and behaviors attitudes toward that system. This can be true in microsystems, such as getting in an argument with a friend. It can be true of a mesosystem, such as when one's friend group encourages misbehavior that would affect one's family, leaving the person in a moral dilemma and feeling pressured to respond a certain way. Experiences even occur between exosystems, such as the fear and uncertainty a person may have when they find out a loved one was fired from their job. In a macrosystem, hearing that a loved one is leaving their lifelong faith in pursuit of another can be jarring. The shift-over-time mentioned earlier of what it means to align with a specific political party or faith can be a very emotional chronosystemic change. Any of these examples, at all levels of systems, can be distressing.

All this to say, SFT depends on collaborative development of meaning and definitions of progress. Therapists, individuals, and families can create change in language to change perception of a problem in order to bring about lasting change. Additionally, change in one system can elicit change in another, for better or for worse. Hopefully, in therapy, it would be for the better. The same types of questions – miracle, scaling, exception-seeking, and presuppositional questions – can all be used to highlight meaningful change. For example, a therapist can ask a client about a time they have already produced the desired outcome in another setting, even just a little bit or for a little while. This would provide evidence that the client is capable of the desired outcome rather than it seeming an outright impossibility. That change can occur in an external system or the immediate self, which is most prominent in the next model.

Internal Family Systems Therapy

Internal family systems (IFS) therapy is known for its application of family systems theory even within an individual. The model takes the immediate self, the smallest unit in ecological systems theory, and explores it as multifaceted, too. IFS calls this internal multiplicity. With internal multiplicity, therapy can pay attention to the relationship one has with oneself. Specifically, it looks at

126 *Theoretical Application*

the multitude of relationships within a person with all their different parts. This is not to say all people have diagnosable multiple personalities. Instead, it normalizing that a single person can have multiple perspectives at the same time. The complication, of course, is when those perspectives contradict one another. Just like multiple members of a family, the parts within a person can disagree, even harshly.

Richard Schwartz, the founder of IFS, theorizes three types of parts in addition to the core Self. The latter is an unchanging internal entity who offers consistent fairness and patient insight, like an internal therapist of one's own. The other parts are managers, firefighters, and exiles. These parts are not divided by emotion; instead, they are divided by function, or role.

In life, sometimes things happen to us that lead to feelings of self-doubt. These expand into feelings of unworthiness, fear, shame, or other self-deprecating self-perceptions. These parts are called *exiles*, and they can be the source of many unpleasant emotions and choices. To avoid feeling these things, people have managing parts. *Managers* strive to prove those harsh self-perceptions wrong, such as overachieving to make up for feelings of inadequacy. They often do this through efforts to control oneself and one's surroundings, including relationships. However, sometimes these parts take things too far, reaching perfectionistic tendencies. As much as we don't want to admit it, that's not a sustainable state of being. In those moments of exhaustion, the exile can feel more raw and be more sensitive to external influence. When that happens, the *firefighter* parts of a person also leap to action.

Firefighters and managers are both protective parts; managers are proactive to avoid an exile's hurt, and firefighters are reactive. Firefighters act to stifle the unpleasant thoughts and feelings of the exile. They will do almost anything to prove those feelings wrong in the moment. This can be healthy coping, or it could include addiction, risky impulsivity, or other problematic behavior. Once these parts silence the exile, the manager typically finds it necessary to be stricter and more controlling in effort to avoid the situation repeating.

It is important to note that no parts of a person are innately bad. Like in external systems, people have both good and bad inside them; they become their ideal selves through insight, constructive self-reflection, and pursuit of meaningful change. While IFS is designed with individuals in mind, it works with systems, too. Microsystems can demonstrate similar role patterns as IFS parts. The exile is the identified patient or problem, compared to managers who try to maintain order, and firefighters who distract from the identified problem – be that a person or relationship. However, the parts of one person will inevitably interact with the parts of others. They are part of one another's context, after all.

The model uses the same interventions for individuals and relational clients, but their implementation can vary somewhat. There is increased emphasis on understanding and empathizing with one another's parts, along with the usual interventions of unburdening parts and increase of self-leadership. This will be demonstrated below.

Case Study – Billy's Night Job

Billy, 21, has come to therapy at the "request" of his mother. He put air quotes around "request" because she reportedly threatened to kick him out of the house if he did not go to therapy and get sober.

When asked to identify the problem for his perspective, Billy identified his living arrangement and his relationship with his mother, Tara. He lives with his mother and her boyfriend, Samuel, who have been together for ten years. Billy reports never having been close to Samuel and states he does not consider him a father figure. Billy's mother split from his father, Marcus, when he was six due to Marcus' alcohol addiction and resulting legal problems. According to Billy, Tara refuses to talk about Marcus except to say he "was a mean drunk and an asshole." Billy has had minimal contact with Marcus' side of the family. He briefly befriended a cousin, but says, "We didn't have nothing in common." Billy reports having no siblings and says Samuel has a son who "never lived with them, is much older, and lives across the country."

Billy works at a department store part-time and has an online videogame streaming channel that he hosts for several hours five days a week. Billy describes that he greatly enjoys streaming and hopes to eventually do this full-time. He reports he feels confident, funny, and talented during his gaming streams: "It's like I finally found something I'm good at." While streaming, he describes drinking "two or three beers or mixed drinks, maybe 4–5 when there's no work the next day." He occasionally smokes marijuana when he drinks. When asked if that seems like a lot, Billy waves his hand dismissively. When asked why his mother is worried about it, he replies, "She says I yell a lot when I drink and game, but that's just gaming. You talk some trash and get pumped up to play." He acknowledges he has yelled at her when she asks him to be quieter but also minimizes this: "That's just the adrenaline talking. I know she doesn't like that I play into the night, but that's when I have the energy, the time, and the privacy."

In therapy, Billy says he could work on his anger. He also wants to "convince Ma that the drinking's not a problem. It's just a thing I do." He reports he wants to live independently but is not financially prepared to do so. Billy reports having friends through both of his jobs but is not close with them. He denies involvement in community or religious organizations, though his mother raised him in both so he does, "Believe in God and being a good person and stuff."

When asked how he would feel about his mother joining them for therapy at some point, Billy stated, "I mean, sure, but she's always working, too. She works at a few retail stores full-time, like 70–80 hours a week. That's how it's always been with us." He says he respects his mother for her hard work raising him but that, as an adult, "It's time to let me do my own thing."

128　*Theoretical Application*

Treating with Structural Family Therapy

Before we look specifically at this model, let's do some assessment:

- Who are some of the subsystems in this case?
- What are some microsystems influencing Billy?
- How can previous membership within macrosystems have prolonged influence?

Remember, structural therapy pays special attention to the role of hierarchy in systems and how these are asserted and maintained.

Interpretation of the Problem

Based on the client's description, one of the most prominent subsystems to consider will likely be between Billy and Tara. Currently, Tara appears to be the top of the familial hierarchy, demonstrated by her enforcing Billy's attendance and making family rules, such as requiring behavioral obedience to continue living with her. Additionally, she has a history of being the enforcer of what the client knows about and how he has contact with his father. This further asserts her dominance in the family system. In many systems, the chief financial provider will be the top of the hierarchy; the same appears true in this family. Therefore, her perception of Billy's alcohol consumption may seem very important.

The presenting problem could be his perceived lack of individual power and diminished role in the family hierarchy. The client expresses dislike of current living situation but is there to maintain it due to perceived lack of option. It appears that streaming is the only place the client is the top of a hierarchy. His role there is very different compared to interactions with his mother or at his other job. Billy also appears to lack meaningful social support, noting that his friendships are not close and a lack of community associations. His mother reportedly offers support but appears to be frequently physically absent due to her work schedule. The stream is also likely where Billy receives the most social support and interaction.

Treatment will likely focus on exploring the family system and subsystems as related to hierarchy. Remember, it is possible to do systems therapy even without other system members present. For example, does Billy consider Marcus part of the family system? How might Marcus still be influential, even in his absence? Additionally, alcohol can be viewed as a member of the family system/subsystem, triangulated between Billy and his mother in a similar dynamic that it may have been between Tara and Marcus. There may be a pattern; Tara seems to cope with alcohol consumption is by removing the person from the physical system. Billy copes by minimizing. Lastly, when discussing hierarchy, we are innately also talking about power. Treatment will include conversations about how power is perceived to be dispersed among the family, among other topics.

FST Concept IV 129

Anticipated Solution

Tracking and reflecting will be particularly important with the client to empower him in the therapeutic setting. Theoretically, he could apply this empowerment in other settings and with other systems. There will be several areas to consider for this treatment process, but they influence one another easily:

1. *Broadening Billy's social support:* What social support does he currently receive? How does he respond when he receives it? What might be getting in the way of healthy social interactions?
2. *Explore age-appropriate roles in the current hierarchy:* Age-appropriate responsibilities differ between a young adult and an adolescent. What independence has been permitted so far? How can those be broadened? How can Billy show he can handle those reliably?
3. *Exploration of past systemic relationships:* This includes micro-, exo-, and macrosystems. Billy's inconsistent microsystemic relationship with his father may impact him more than he realizes. This goes beyond their shared alcohol consumption, though that can be a factor. It also can be what Marcus inadvertently taught Billy about being a man and father. Exosystemically, therapy can also look at what Billy learned about the paternal side of his family in his earlier interactions with them and to what extent he can identify to what is learned. Lastly, therapy can learn how Billy applies concepts and beliefs around the community and religious macrosystems with which he has previously been involved. Did he learn a sense of right and wrong, role of responsibility, etc.? These can seem like big-picture questions, but they tell us about Billy's value system and how he came to form it. This will be important when exploring what it will look like for him to achieve greater independence and improving his relationship with Tara.

Earlier I mentioned enactments are a common intervention in structural therapy. How do enactments work with individuals? Experientially, it can be combined with Gestalt's empty-chair technique. Even without that, Billy can practice what he would like to say to his system members, finding the most effective and accurate statements to reflect how Billy feels and thinks. This can be important whether or not the later conversation actually occurs. For example, Billy may have things he would like to say to his father even if he may not get the chance to do so. However, practicing what he would like to express to his mother could come fully to fruition. Those are conversations that realistically could occur over the course of treatment. Ideally, these conversations could include Tara coming to therapy with Billy, but it is not essential to do so. A few of the example questions include those that could be asked to Tara if she did get to accompany Billy to some sessions.

130   *Theoretical Application*

Example Questions

1   "Who do you think holds the most power in your family?"
2   "How do you think alcohol impacts your mom?"
3   "It seems like right now Tara and Samuel have really teamed-up while you are figuring out your streaming schedule and getting that business off the ground. What do you think?"
4   "What do you imagine Marcus would say about your situation?"
5   "Who do you feel supports you? What are some ways different people support you?"

Treating with Bowen's Multigenerational Family Therapy

Interpretation of the Problem

This model would have us consider 3+ generations of Billy's family, seeking patterns in behaviors, such as addictions, and emotional interactions. These may be drawn into a family genogram to help both the therapist and Billy better understand family dynamics. It may be pertinent to see if alcoholism runs in either family, which could contextualize Tara's response to it in both her former partner and son. The genogram can also include insight about the societal emotional process, or how societies shape families. An example of this is Tara's religious affiliation, Billy's rejection of it, and how that rejection impacted their relationship. Another example would be the family's socio-economic status. Having multiple family members working multiple jobs will no doubt influence their interactions, such as Billy's assumption that his mother is too busy working to be involved in the therapy she initiated for him.

This intersects with the emotional, intellectual, and feelings systemic components in the family microsystem. First the emotional system indicates biological functioning and what drives processes within and between systems. Billy is the son of Tara and Marcus, who was an alcoholic. Avoiding alcohol dependence is a goal for Tara of her son; this aligns with her role as his parental protector. Similarly, she may strive to make sure the alcohol is not impacting his ability to function, hence her intervention on his behalf. Tara is also a partner to Samuel, though this case study does not describe that dynamic in depth. Billy is a stepson to Samuel, though he does not attach to this role. Samuel may have been triangulated between Tara and Billy at different times in their ten years together, though no specific example is provided here.

The second component is the intellectual system, or the human capacity to think, reflect, and reason. Here the therapist can find out how Billy learned what is logical and reasonable versus what is not. The therapist can gage his ability to see from other perspectives, such as that of his mother, who is acting to protect him from the dangers and challenges of addiction. It also invites Billy to clarify why he keeps his emotional distance from Samuel. These questions echo Billy's relationship with his family-of-origin and how those have gone on to influence his other systems, both professionally and personally.

Finally, the feeling system bridges the emotional and intellectual systems, attaching meaning to emotional reaction. Any of the topics in the other components can be addressed here because the components overlap so prominently. Specific feelings-based questions can be considered indirectly or asked outright:

- *What is it like for Billy for his mother to place the expectation of sobriety on him?*
- *What might it be like for Tara to see her son go through similar consumption patterns with alcohol as his father, who got in legal trouble for it?*

With these questions, the therapist can listen for Billy's empathetic capacity to see Tara's sense of reason overlapped with her sense of compassion and potential fear for his well-being.

Additionally, this model reflects on symptomology as forms of anxiety in the system. In Billy, the anxiety will be around living situation, disagreements with mother, estranged from father he barely knows, starting own business. His anxiety may manifest in anger and alcohol consumption. For Tara, this could be financial responsibility for her adult son and concern that Billy is following his father's footsteps with alcohol consumption. Her anxiety appears in the use of ultimatums to try and manage her son's behaviors.

Anticipated Solution

As stated earlier, the genogram can be both an assessment and intervention tool in Bowenian multigenerational therapy. The information-gathering process can require family members to reach out and build connection to one another. In this family, Billy might be asked to reengage with his paternal cousin to learn about his father's side of the family more. The genogram will look at how one generation influences the next – how the family-of-origin influencing nuclear family, including family roles and rules. Learning more about Marcus' life growing up could provide insight to his adult behaviors. Learning more about Tara's upbringing could offer the same from her experience. How these two came together can provide insight and context for Billy's decision-making.

For example, building the genogram may reveal more about Tara's tendency to overfunction for Billy. As a young adult, she appears to still treat him like an adolescent. He works part-time at two jobs while she works full-time at two; how much of each of their incomes goes toward family expenses? This imbalance could be indicative of their current roles, where one party is allowing the other to remain in a juvenile role. Theoretically, this increased family insight can lead to behavioral change. Therefore, therapy can also further explore alternative behaviors and how those could impact others differently than the current course of action. This can include Billy's substance consumption

132   *Theoretical Application*

but is not restricted to it; it can also include exploration balancing freedoms and responsibilities between Billy, Tara, and Samuel. Additionally, increased awareness of others' perspectives and contexts can increase empathy. This can create a prominent difference because change in one system potentially changing another. This is the chief overlay between multigenerational therapy and co-occurring systems.

Example Questions

1   "Billy, how did adding Samuel to the family impact your relationship with your mom?"
2   "Billy, what would motivate your mother to tell your father to keep his distance from you?"
3   "Billy, what do you believe would change about your streaming channel if you got along better with your mom?"
4   "It seems like alcohol really serves a purpose between you and your mom. It's almost like a sibling, or another member of the family that we pull into our issues to help us deal with them. How has alcohol been there for you at different times and places in your life?"
5   "Billy, what would it be like to reach out to your cousin and find out more about your dad's side of the family? What do you think you would learn about them?"

Treating with Solution-Focused Therapy

Interpretation of the Problem

As the name of the model entails, this model focuses on solutions rather than problems; however, it is only fair to recognize current conditions that may be interfering with reaching the family's goals. First is a differing perception of alcohol between Billy and Tara and different ideas on what "better" looks like. For Tara, abstinence is the only identified version of "better," while Billy is more flexible in possible versions. Remember, our thoughts, emotions, and behaviors are interrelated. Billy's attitude toward alcohol and other substances when interacting with his mother could impact other areas of his life, such as other places where he is told what to do, like at his "day job."

Billy verbalizes an additional problem without specifying it overtly. He appears to lack confidence in settings other than his streaming service. If nothing else, he describes a difference in self-perception between systems and over time. We see the example of chronosystemic change; he changes in his macrosystemic involvement and identity due to not feeling it has been a good fit for him. It would be interesting to learn how he believes his mother perceives him and how this might impact him. Does he feel pressured to be a certain version of himself in different settings with different people? Overall, we must recognize systemic changes can be distressing. SFT will explore how Billy has persevered those.

FST Concept IV 133

Anticipated Solution

In SFT, the first step is to get the family system to agree on a shared goal for treatment. Billy is presenting seeking increased independence, including eventual independent living, and improving his relationship with his mother, specifically related to decreased anger. Tara is presenting seeking her son's substance abstinence, which she believes would also address his anger. With this in mind, we see some common ground: They both want to improve their interactions and improved anger management (Franklin et al., 2019). The role of substances in those goals can be explored in greater depth (CSAT, 1999).

Another early step in treatment will be to clarify more about the preferred future. They can agree they want improved interactions and anger management; what does that actually look like? What will be different when that has been achieved? How could living separately contribute to that? How could changing his alcohol consumption help him achieve this, versus how does his current alcohol consumption might be holding him back from it. Treatment will also further deepen understanding the meaning Billy gives alcohol versus what his mother seems to attribute to it.

As with other models, SFT will also explore how creating change in one system – including within himself – can influence other systems. For example, increasing awareness of his self-confidence while streaming, what helps him feel confident, and finding out if there is an equivalent to that in his other job. The goal, overall, is that increased self-awareness of capacity to create meaningful change.

Example Questions

1 "Billy, I hear you describing that you feel confident and competent when you do your streaming job. Tell me about a time you felt that same confidence or competence when interacting with your mom or at your other job."

2 "Billy, help me understand more about your relationship with your mom. Let's put it on a scale of one to ten, where one is the worst relationship imaginable and you never want to see or talk to her again, and ten is the ideal version of the relationship. What number would you say you are at with her right now? Tell me about that number. What does it look like? What would the next highest number look like? How would it be different?"

3 "It sounds like you don't view alcohol as much of a problem right now. Tell me, how would you know when it was a problem? What would be different then?"

4 "I hear you say you think your relationship with your mom will be better when you don't live together anymore. How do you imagine moving away and having that separate space will help the relationship? When that relationship is better, how do you think your time at work would be different?"

134　*Theoretical Application*

Treating with Internal Family Systems Therapy

Interpretation of the Problem

IFS focuses on the relationship one has with oneself and how it impacts relationships with others. For example, when a part of ourselves has an ulterior motive within ourselves, we may assume others also have self-serving motivations. Self-doubt leads to doubt in others; self-dislike can result in disbelieving others can like you. Billy appears to be coping with all of these in the form of an exile. He describes not feeling good at most things in life, possibly fearing being a disappointment. Keep in mind, the presenting problem is not always the exile; often it can be a firefighter, or the behavioral outpouring of exile denial. Billy's substance use could be considered a firefighter because it functions to numb or silence possible insecurity. What does that mean Billy may lack? A strong sense of self.

In Billy – the immediate self system – there appears to be a plethora of parts. He appears to have a manager that is aware of the need for anger management and a part that demonstrates a strong work ethic. He desires independence and demonstrates maturity to recognize he is not financially prepared to live independently but wants to find ways to be independent in the meantime. He does work two jobs, but only part-time each; he does not appear to be experiencing an extremist, overburdened version of that part at this time. Billy's firefighter, as mentioned earlier, includes turning to substance use to cope with uncertainty and possible fear. Further details are not provided in the case study, but it appears his self-perception and method of coping with this is impacting his external systems. Moving forward in treatment will include further assessing for and increasing Self-leadership.

Anticipated Solution

Increasing Billy's self-leadership will mean working with parts that may not trust him to make good choices on behalf of the internal system. The process of unburdening parts will overlap with this intervention. Two parts Billy may need to unburden are a manager who seeks to appease Tara and the firefighter substance user who presents too quickly to soothe an exile of ineptitude or worthlessness. To do this, the therapist coaches Billy to offer gratitude to his parts' efforts to protect and take care of him. He can acknowledge their hard work and potentially how exhausted they are. Next, he can ask his parts what would help the parts entrust Billy's core Self to take back a few responsibilities they have claimed as their own – things maybe he couldn't handle when younger but can handle now. As these parts witness Billy being able to handle stress and responsibility, this will both unburden parts and increase Self-leadership.

So how it would be different if the client came independently versus systemically, such as with Tara accompanying Billy? The therapist will now balance the microsystem in addition to the internal systems of each immediate self present. That means being attentive to how each person's parts are interacting not just within themselves but with each other. The therapist will still spend a lot of time validating different parts, particularly managers. In this case, the therapist can acknowledge both Billy's and Tara's work ethics, hard-working parts with possible overactivity due to interaction with caretaking parts.

The intervention process can allow one another to witness each other's parts. This increases awareness of how people speak from parts rather than their core selves. Remembering that Billy's anger comes from a part rather than his core Self, and learning the unmet needs and insecurities of that part instead could help Tara depersonalize the anger. It could also help Billy be increasingly mindful of his anger when he sees his mother react to that part from one of her own, perhaps her own firefighter. It is possible a firefighter seeking safety is the reason she gave him the ultimatum coming to therapy in the first place.

Example Questions

1 "Billy, tell me more about the part of you that feels streaming is the only thing you're good at."
2 "Tara, I can tell working hard is something you take a lot of pride in. There's a part of you that has worked long and hard for that to be the case, but I wonder if that part ever gets tired but is afraid to rest. What do you think about that?"
3 "Billy, it sounds like a part of you doesn't trust Tara's judgment about your drinking and smoking. What does that part of you want her to know about you?"
4 "Tara, what happens inside you when Billy yells at you when gaming? What do your different parts feel and say inside you?"
5 "Billy, how old is the part of you that tells you drinking and smoking is a no-big-deal aid to help you calm down and do your stream?"

Reader Reflection

1 Reflect on your family-of-origin. What subsystems do you remember being present in your childhood? How did those dynamics shift as you got older and became an adult?
2 Can it be healthy for the therapist to be the "third leg" of a triad sub-system? How so? How could it be unhealthy?
3 What can a therapist do to avoid being unhealthily triangulated into a client subsystem?
4 Identify three microsystems you're in. How do you behave differently in each of them?
5 Identify three macrosystems you're a part of. How do those big-picture qualities contribute to how you view yourself and how you might interact with others?

136 *Theoretical Application*

6   Reflect on how you prioritize your time and energy. Are there certain microsystems that tend to take that priority? Reflect on how you came to decide that microsystem is the priority.

7   Reflect on the challenge of adding a new role to an existing identity, such as becoming a student or parent. Have you had this happen before? What was it like? How could reflecting on this be helpful to empathize with a client in the future?

8 FST Concept V
Boundaries

Picture a fence around a home. Chances are, you just imagined a specific type of fence, but there are many different types of fences. They can be short or tall. They can be porous, like a chain-link fence, or impermeable and fully filled in like a concrete wall. They can be flexible and thin or rigidly thick and immovable. They might include an opening or gate; even so, the gate might be locked. A person's ability to pass from one side of the fence to the other depends on many qualities of it. Fences like these are physical boundaries, and emotional boundaries can be similarly varied.

Boundaries are an essential part of life. This includes physical boundaries like the walls and fences and emotional boundaries. The latter is strongly associated with family systems theory. People communicate their boundaries in a plethora of ways: How we behave, what we say, and the rules and roles we use. Boundaries deeply overlap with other family systems theory concepts: Context, communication, co-occurring systems…all of it!

All systems have boundaries. However, not all boundaries are healthy. Sometimes the boundaries are super strict; sometimes they are excessively lenient. There is a time and place for either, but for the most part, we want a balance in the middle. When the family's typical boundaries are at either of those extremes, it can be necessary to change those to achieve a healthier inter-action pattern. Setting new boundaries within families – or specific members of the family – can be challenging. That's what this chapter will explore.

Defining Boundaries

Salvador Minuchin, a prominent contributor at the Mental Research Institute, was highly influential to how family systems theory approaches boundaries. He defined boundaries as the rules that organize family transactions. Family transactions include the rules around system interactions, behaviors, and roles (Minuchin & Fishman, 2004). That is to say, boundaries determine how we interact and what is expected of those with whom we share a system. They surreptitiously communicate responsibility and authority in a family system. These rules can be overt and clear but are often unspoken or assumed.

The purpose of boundaries is the balance one's individuality and con-nectedness, or togetherness, with others. This could also be called managing

DOI: 10.4324/9781003088196-11

138 *Theoretical Application*

proximity, the balance of closeness and distance either between systems or between members of a system. Boundaries can be a tool to identify who is in or out of a system. Often, those outside of a system are held to different boundary regulations than those in a system – that is to say, we have different expectations of those with whom we share a systemic connection compared to those we do not.

Another purpose of boundaries can be to manage hierarchies in relationships. This addresses three questions:

1 Who holds power in the relationship?
2 How is power divided or distributed in the relationship?
3 How is that division decided?

Hierarchy also greatly relates to rules and roles of the family. This could also be called the structure of the family. Here we see more questions:

4 Who makes the rules?
5 Who enforces the rules, and how?

Take the example of privacy. A teenager may want to keep the door to their bedroom closed in order to have privacy from others with whom they live. However, their parent or guardian may be uncomfortable with this and assert the rule that if the teenager has the door shut, they cannot refuse the parent when they request to enter. The parent may agree to respect the teenager's request for privacy by agreeing to not enter without permission (such as when the teenager is away at school during the day), but asserts they have the right to search the room if there is something suspicious or concerning in the teenager's behavior. When the teen resists this – noting that the parent could use that excuse at any point to do whatever they want – the adult may reiterate that the room does not belong to the teenager but is a room in the adult's home.

Reflect on this example and answer the questions 1–5 given earlier. The parent or guardian holds the power, because they are the one making the rules and asserting them. However, they acknowledge and respect the teenager's desire for privacy; they do not outright reject it and therefore hope to create a rule that balances both the teenager's growing independence and the adult's continued responsibility for the teenager's well-being.

Boundaries in Subsystems

As mentioned earlier, boundaries can indicate who is in or out of a system. They do the same thing for subsystems. The mere presence of a subsystem indicates the presence of boundaries away from or with others in the system. To be a member of a subsystem can require certain criteria of commonality or connection: A romantic partnership, siblings, parent and child dyad, etc. These boundaries can also be established by the same tools and methods as larger systems: Rules and roles. To be a member of a subsystem may require something as simple as understanding an inside joke or as expansive as familiarity with the biopsychosocial of one or more members of the subsystem.

Those boundaries may be tested by other subsystems. For example, a marital dyad can be pushed by children, in-laws, and even those outside the system or who have been triangulated in. The partner/parenting dyad is among the most important to maintaining or creating family structure. Even when this structure changes, such as through divorce, it is up to that parenting team to establish what the new boundaries are or what boundaries stay the same. In this way, boundaries will look different depending on the power dynamic of the subsystem. As with larger systems, boundaries within and between subsystems may shift over time as people grow toward greater independence, personal authority, and responsibility. In this way, the dynamic between members of a subsystem can change. As a result, the way boundaries are asserted may also change.

How Boundaries Are Asserted

Boundaries are asserted through the flow – or lack of flow – of information between systems or members of a system. Sometimes withholding information is an act of setting a boundary, too. The information is typically passed via verbal or nonverbal communication. As given in the fences example earlier, boundaries can be physical or emotional. Physical boundaries are not just physical objects like barbed wire, though. They can also be expressed physically through gestures and body position.

What Are Unhealthy Boundaries?

Unhealthy boundaries are indicated by how unstable they are. These boundaries are difficult to maintain because they are not conducive to longevity. Unhealthy and unstable boundaries tend to show a lack of respect and a prominence of uncertainty. This overlaps significantly with lack of autonomy – not being able to make your own decisions or feeling unsafe to do so (Cohler, 1983). There can be a perceived need or dependence for others to make decisions for you, or, conversely, for you to make decisions for others. That depends on if you are in the role of power in the relationship. If you are in the position of power, you will make decisions for others, even when it is not appropriate to do so.

In the end, unhealthy boundaries can be experienced as emptiness – it's the question, "Who am I if not tied to the other person?" Unhealthy boundaries can be exemplified in two of Minuchin's types of boundaries, where family systems theory first explored boundaries.

Minuchin's Types of Boundaries

Minuchin identified three types of boundaries: disengaged, enmeshed, or clear.

1 **Rigid boundaries**

Rigid boundaries are like the concrete wall compared to the picket fence; they are fixed, strict, and unbending. However, this boundary type tends to be poorly communicated or explained. This may be a result of poor access to the authority figure, such as a parent or boss. The authority figure may not make themselves accessible to clarify a rule or may not give permission for others in the system to question or understand the boundary. Communication or expression in the system may be covertly or overtly discouraged or stifled. This may be associated with blind loyalty to a rule or a phrase like, "Because I said so!" Disengaged boundaries do not foster emotional closeness. On the other extreme, promoting excessive emotional overlap, is enmeshed boundaries.

2 **Diffused boundaries**

Diffused boundaries tend to be unclear and uncertain. At an extreme, these boundaries can be like a line of traffic cones, easily moved to meet the immediate needs but lacking in long-term enforcement. This can occur when the rules and roles in a system seem to constantly change. Responsibility and authority roles are inconsistent. As a result, a system's hierarchy may be imbalanced. For example, ideally, adults have more power in a family than children. However, sometimes children hold more power and influence than the adults in the system. They might control the adults' schedule based on their needs, their financial demands may be more highly prioritized, and they might skirt the rules routinely without consequence. The adults may strive to appease the child, giving them the power rather than holding it themselves. In these cases, the adult may be so flexible in their rules that they end up being meaningless or, as stated earlier, inconsequential. These types of highly fluid boundaries are not made to last and can actually be quite detrimental to the relationship and individuals in it.

3 **Clear boundaries**

These are the desired type of boundaries. These are explicitly communicated, and mutually understood between the members of the system. These healthy boundaries are a balance of flexibility and firmness in established rules of interaction. It is an awareness of when it is appropriate to alter the rules and when it is appropriate to hold steadfast. This is the healthiest type of boundaries, and the one people should strive to achieve. Having clear, healthy boundaries is beneficial to improving both relationship and individual functioning and well-being.

These foundational concepts were expanded upon by the circumplex model, which assessed these attributes as points on a spectrum of a single variable in boundaries.

The Circumplex Model

The circumplex model was designed in the 1990s by Candace Smyth Russell, David Olson, and Douglas Sprenkle. It takes Minuchin's boundary classifications and expands on it. Minuchin's measure of rigid and diffused boundaries can be simplified as a measure of family cohesion. Cohesion is defined as coming together as a whole, or a sense of togetherness. According to the circumplex model, cohesion is one of three assessment measures of relational connection. The model was designed as a relational assessment in the 1980s. At the time, it specifically focused on couples, but it is applicable in families, too. The three measures are cohesion, adaptability, and communication.

Cohesion

Cohesion means togetherness. Family cohesion is the emotional connection family members share with one another. This includes shared space, time, decision-making, interests, and identities. It is a balance of individuality and togetherness. These range from disengaged to enmeshed; both of these are considered unbalanced extremes. Between those two extremes are states of separation and connection, which are balanced mediums of the two extremes.

Disengaged boundaries can be compared to Minuchin's rigid boundaries. These families are minimally involved in one another's lives; everyone does "their own thing...with limited attachment or commitment" among family members (Olson, 2000, p. 149). There can be minimal sense of loyalty, support, or unity to one another or/and negligible interest in spending time together. As a result, disengaged or disconnected families tend to not know very much about each other. On the other end of the spectrum, enmeshment is intense and extreme emotional closeness and loyalty.

Enmeshed families tend to be very overlapped in one another's lives. They are highly dependent on one another and may have a difficult time making decisions independently because they are so sensitive to how the decision might influence others. Similarly, enmeshed individuals tend to be highly reactive to one another and have disproportionate emotional reaction to others in the system. This can result in easily raised tempers and emotional volatility. Additionally, enmeshed families allow minimal privacy or personal separateness. Family members know (or want to know) intimate details of one another's lives and spend an extensive amount of time together. As a result, the system may be judgmental or resentful when members want to go outside the system, such as to friendships, to meet a need. The family system consistently prioritizes what is in the interest of the family, not the individual. As a result, individual development can be stunted as exploration of it will likely be discouraged in enmeshed systems.

In between those are separate and connected relationships. *Separated* relationship includes a high focus on individual development and identity but not to the detriment of extreme disconnection. Individuals in the system will predominantly have their own interests, but there is commitment to hear one

142　*Theoretical Application*

another talk about those. There is still time spent together and emotional engagement with one another in the system. Many decisions are made individually, but those that highly influence the relationship will be made mutually and with support.

Connected families, on the other hand, are still focused on the emotional connectedness of the relationship but allow space for individual development. Families may be highly intentional and prioritize time spent together, but this time may be more limited to allow for some time alone. Members of the system may have friends and other support systems; however, those additional systems may be shared. For example, a couple may have friends who are also couples, and when they spend time together, it is as a couple unit. In connected relationships, there may be greater emphasis on having common interests and activities rather than individual interests and activities.

Both separated and connected levels of cohesion are considered balanced and healthy. Families in these medium options tend to experience optimal functioning both individually and systemically. Attempting to function in the extremes long-term tends to cause problems in the relationship and the individuals in it.

Adaptability

Adaptability can also be called flexibility, or the extent of change tolerable in the system. Over time and due to various circumstances, the rules and roles in a system will change. The will! It's inevitable. These can include leadership/hierarchical shifts, as pertaining to control and discipline, and negotiation skills. Successful adaptation is indicated by a movement toward balance and stability even amid or shortly after change. While early family systems theory work focused just on cohesion, it similarly focused on systemic means of stability rather than how the system functions in times of change. Both change and the status quo are inevitable experiences in a family system; there will potentially be times of both in the duration of the relationship. Therefore, an indicator of functionality individually and as a system can be recognizing when to initiate change, accept change happening around you, or when to strive to hold the status quo. We'll talk more about this in Chapter 9.

As with cohesion, there are unhealthy extremes of adaptability and healthier balanced levels. The extremes are rigidity and chaotic. More balanced versions of those are structured and flexible. *Rigid* adaptability is indicated by restrictive and strictly enforced rules and roles. These rarely change – if ever. The only person able to change them is the individual with the most power, the person at the top of the system hierarchy. This person tends to offer minimal rule and role negotiation and does not invite input from other system members. They can be very controlling within the system, offering an authoritarian style of leadership.

Chaotic system adaptability, also called diffused adaptability, is indicated by a laissez-faire leadership style. In chaotically adaptive structures, there may be a person who is titled the leader, but the hierarchy is almost non-existent. Leadership and organization are unreliable and unpredictable in chaotic systems. The family rules and roles in a chaotic system are inconsistent and unclear. They lack guidance from leadership. Decisions made by the leader tend to be impulsive and poorly delivered. The leader may not even be the one making the choice, but have allowed anyone else in the system to make it instead. Understandably, this type of leadership can result in either dependence and enmeshment (refusal to make one's own choices) or inversely hyperindividualistic.

Between these two extremes are flexibility and structured. One step in from rigid boundaries that lack adaptability is that of structured boundaries. *Structured* boundaries are a version of democratic decision-making between the higher and lower people in the hierarchy. In structured dynamics, the leader may receive input form others parts of the hierarchy, but there still tends to be a designated person to make a final decision on the matter. Roles seek to be stable but can be shared as needed. Rules will not be changed beyond necessity and still will be strongly enforced. Connections to individuals outside the system are permitted or encouraged, but the family dynamic may be treated as the dominant prioritized system. As structured systems increase in fluidity, they could shift to being classified as a flexible system instead.

Flexible systems are marked by egalitarian democratic leadership styles. Negotiations are open across levels of the hierarchy, including children. Like with structured families, a specific person may make the final decision, but it will be with careful consideration and significant compromise. Roles are shared and change when convenient but with ability to revert when needed. The same could be said of rules; they exist, but they are easily influenced by the system members over time. When rules and roles do change, they are to an appropriate extent. As with structured dynamics, the changes do not topple the hierarchy but may broaden it. For example, they would not include a child taking over a parental role, but it could be a parent stepping into their partner's role at home when the latter is having increased demands at their job.

Communication in Boundaries

In the circumplex model, communication is a facilitating dimension that helps dictate the other two dimensions. It focuses on "listening skills, speaking skills, self-disclosure, clarity, continuity tracking, and respect and regard" (Olson, 2000, p. 149). Generally speaking, more balanced systems will have better, more clear communication and problem-solving skills. This, of course, is also a stand-alone concept for family systems theory. It is integral to the expression and setting of boundaries. Those boundaries range in their cohesion and adaptability.

These concepts were designed as a four-by-four grid called the Couple and Family Map (Olson, 2000). This grid can look like a graph with one axis

144 *Theoretical Application*

indicating degree of cohesion and the other, flexibility. While communication is an important variable, it is woven into the other two. Here is a visual representation of this grid:

Circumplex Model: Couple and Family Map

		Low ------ Cohesion ------ High			
		Disengaged	Separated	Connected	Enmeshed
High	Chaotic	Chaotically disengaged	Chaotically separated	Chaotically connected	Chaotically enmeshed
	Flexible	Flexibly disengaged	Flexibly separated	Flexibly connected	Flexibly enmeshed
	Structured	Structurally disengaged	Structurally separated	Structurally connected	Structurally enmeshed
Low	Rigid	Rigidly disengaged	Rigidly separated	Rigidly connected	Rigidly enmeshed

(left axis label: -----Adaptability-----)

The three shades of color indicate the healthiest, moderate, and highest risk versions of cohesive and flexible boundaries. The goal is for balanced levels of cohesion and adaptability. You want to steer clear of the extremes. In the center are the four healthiest boundary dynamics. Here, there are not rigid, chaotic, disengagement, or enmeshment extremes. Instead, there is flexibility, structure, separation, and connectedness. It is important to note that even within this healthy dynamic, there is a range, not a single ideal structure. This allows for families to determine for themselves what their unique ideal structure can look like and how it functions.

The outermost corners indicate extremism in both adaptability and cohesion. These are indicative of combined rigidity or chaos and disconnection and enmeshment. Working with these systems can be very difficult, as they may not be aware of the harm their dynamic can cause to the individuals in the system. The more moderate parts of the grid border – those in the medium color – have one extreme measure but one that is healthier and more reasonable. In these cases, change can still be intimidating but may call for less modification than those corners.

To help couples and families identify their positioning on the grid, Olson created the aptly named Family Adaptability and Cohesion Evaluation Scales (FACES-IV). This is an assessment that has been updated over the years and is currently on its fourth variation (Olson, 2010). It asks about the family's adaptability, communication, and degree of cohesion along with the reader's perceived satisfaction with their familial dynamics. It uses a Likert-style numeric system, meaning each item (62 in total) is a statement with which the reader states they strongly agree (5), agree (4), neither agree nor disagree (3), disagree (2), or strongly disagree (1). The satisfaction section modifies this somewhat to measure from being extremely satisfied (5) all the way to very dissatisfied (1). In includes six subscales; two balanced – balanced cohesion and flexibility – and four unbalanced – rigidity, chaos, disengaged, and enmeshed. The assessment has been deemed appropriate for ages 12 and up.

It can be used in therapy to start conversations around desired boundaries and as a quantitative measure of progress and change as the family moves toward those desired boundaries.

Examples of Practiced Boundaries

Below are various examples of physical and emotional boundaries. Reflect on these; consider whether you view them as healthy, unhealthy, physical, emotional, etc. Additionally, reflect on how they may be somewhat healthy if approached in a balanced way:

- Child refusing to hug a relative they don't know
- Restraining order
- Parent telling their adult child personal health details
- Feeling unable to say no to someone
- Feeling the need to address others' needs before your own; being a people-pleaser
- Feeling unable to state own opinion even when asked
- Irreverence for others' feelings/perspectives

Further consider, also, how power plays a role in any of these scenarios: Who holds the power? How can these situations be handled in a way that is healthier? These are the types of situations that you may work with in a therapist role. Consider how changing boundaries to be healthier can be a therapeutic goal and how those changes could be achieved.

Goals of Boundaries

As a general rule, the clearer the boundary, the higher the functioning of the individuals in that system or subsystem. That means covertly communicated rules would work better to become more overt. Doing this will allow people to function independently better. Healthy boundaries also serve to balance systems, establishing the healthiest hierarchies and structure. To do this, there must be a balance of cohesion, flexibility, and communication. None of these should be extremely rigid or elastic, enmeshed or estranged. Overall, boundaries should be clear enough to establish a person's separateness and autonomy but also permeable enough to ensure systemic support and affection. Of course, this is the healthy ideal of boundaries. That is not always what happens. A common discussion that occurs in therapy can be how to have better boundaries, which can require some uncomfortable change.

How to Have Better Boundaries

Squeezing this into a small section of a book seems improbable and impractical; volumes of whole texts have been dedicated to this effort! Therefore, this will be an overall summary of the idea of how to set and create better, healthier

146   *Theoretical Application*

boundaries. This process could be called assertive acceptance (Bennett, 2014). It is a balance of recognizing what capacity you have to change and influence and what you do not. Overall, there are four steps: Define the desired boundary, protect those boundaries, respond to offenders, and propose an alternative course of action.

Define the Desired Boundary

When expressing desired boundaries, it is important to be firm but flexible. There is probably a reason a new boundary is being set, either the previous boundary was ineffective or not present at all. The firmness of the boundary emphasizes the importance of having one, but the flexibility acknowledges that the person setting the boundary is not the only one contributing to it. If I am setting a boundary of how often I talk to my parents, I want to be mindful to their schedule and availability, too. It is also important to be consistent once the boundary is set. A person on the receiving end of the boundary is likely to push them out of their own discomfort. In the example of talking to my parents, one parent may attempt to call sooner than the scheduled time. It would then be up to me to choose whether or not to answer that phone call, which will either hold the boundary or allow it to be overstepped. This is part of protecting the boundary.

Protect Those Boundaries

Protecting boundaries includes both identifying and reinforcing the boundary with others. Once the boundary has been established and decided, it will be the boundary-setter's responsibility to let others know about it. This coincides with the earlier mentioned need for consistency. Protecting the boundary is part of nurturing yourself and giving yourself value. When talking to others about this boundary, you are not asking permission for respect, you are establishing respect as the expected norm. As stated earlier, others will inevitably push the boundary for a multitude of reasons. There will be times when the boundary is pushed for extenuating circumstances, such as a family emergency. Part of setting the boundary can include space for emergencies, but this may require a conversation with the other system members about the definition of emergency. How you respond to boundary-pushers and -offenders is just as much a part of the boundary as the newly established rule.

Respond to the Offenders

More than the previous two sections, this truly demonstrates assertive acceptance. Boundary offenders are unavoidable; however, this is not to say it is acceptable for them to continue doing so. People may not realize they are breaching a boundary. Bennett (2014) called this ignorant disregard: People may not realize they are offending a person or a boundary because they do not know what matters to boundary-setter. They neglect the boundary due to ignorance or habit. As a result, they may take it personally when we enforce a new boundary. The offender may not realize that setting the boundary is an act of healing necessary to improve personal and systemic well-being. Hopefully, when kindly confronted with this new boundary, the offender will be receptive to this and recognize the change comes from a desire for that improvement. However, there can still be resistance, uncertainty, or confusion, such as asking, "Why now?" or saying, "I thought things were fine. Why didn't you say something earlier?" Even when challenging, treating these statements as curiosities rather than accusations can make a significant difference in both how the boundary-setter respond to the offender's statement and how the offender receives the newly clarified boundary.

Keep in mind, ignorant disregard is different from inconsiderate disregard. For the latter, "reminding others of our personal boundaries doesn't have much effect. These are the people who just don't care" (Bennett, 2014, p.126). Those with inconsiderate regard tend to be disrespectful and perceive their perspective as more important or more accurate than that of others. Even after asserting the boundary and non-defensively clarifying why it is necessary, the inconsiderate offender may be uncaring to their impact.

For example, if a nonbinary or transgender individual identifies their correct pronoun, people may respond in one of three ways: (a) receive this without question and promptly shift out of respect to the boundary-setter, (b) express confusion, request additional information that the boundary-setter may choose whether or not to provide, and hopefully ultimately will respect this change and make efforts to use the correct pronoun, or (c) express their sadness, disappointment, or overt rejection of the change, making statements such as, "You'll always be [biological gender or birth name] to me," or some version of, "There's only man or woman and that depends on what's between your legs." In these situations, more direct and judicious measures will likely be necessary when creating a boundary.

Propose an Alternative Course of Action

Regardless if the offender (or potential offender) is ignorant or inconsiderate, sometimes reinforcement of the boundary can be helpful. In this context, reinforcement can also mean consequence. Therefore, offenders would need to experience a consequence for their continued lack of respect. This consequence does not have to be extreme or excessively harsh. Breaches in the boundary do not have to result in the end of a relationship. The purpose of a consequence in this context is the same as child discipline: To emphasize that decisions have logical outcomes. Therefore, the selected consequence should also be logical. When we restate the boundary, we can include a follow-up statement of what would happen if it continues to be breached. Throughout this conversation, it may be important to clearly state the importance of the relationship with the person, validate their frustration, and reiterate the boundary is not a personal attack as much as an act of protection.

148 *Theoretical Application*

Applicable Therapy Models

Some models of therapy more openly address boundaries than others. However, they remain an important attribute in all models of therapy because boundaries are the embodiment of balancing individual identity and connection to those around us. It also considers the role of power and influence. Therefore, this concept appears, in some form, in all systemic therapy models, including the four below.

Structural Family Therapy

Structural family therapy is the first model to consider boundaries, specifically the cohesion aspect. Minuchin did not focus as much on the adaptivity or communication facets. Instead, the model focuses on the part of roles and rules in systemic cohesion. These include asking questions like:

- Who is the parent? Who are the dependents?
- Is the parent at the top of the hierarchy, or has a dependent taken over that role inappropriately?
- What responsibilities are expected of the different roles?
- What's allowed or not allowed compared to other roles?

Part of structural therapy is often to rearrange roles and boundaries to adhere to healthy family dynamics. As you can see from the above questions, hierarchy and boundaries are deeply tied to role clarity. Structural family therapy assumes the desire is for balance and to maintain the status quo in the system. According to this model of therapy, a challenge to family hierarchy includes risk of boundary ambiguity. Boundary ambiguity is a state of uncertainty, particularly relating to hierarchy and role confusion.

Remember, boundaries can be experienced and expressed physically and emotionally. In therapy, "boundaries can be communicated and challenged through seating arrangements in the therapy room" (Minuchin & Fishman, 2004, p. 6). This is a form of therapeutic intervention. Other structural interventions include:

1 **Making a family map**
   Like a Bowenian family genogram, this is a family-tree-like tool that identifies family members and their relationship. It is a visual representation of the family's degree of cohesion and identification of subsystems. The structural family map places great emphasis on boundaries of who is in the family versus outside of it. It is a strong assessment tool to help the therapist better understand the hierarchical dynamics and to make those overt to the client, too.

2 **Tracking**
   This is a verbal tool of the therapist, directly using the client's words back to them in how they describe other people and their relationships. This

creates room for the client to be faced with their perception, potentially correct themselves, or recognize the limits of their insight. Repeating back client terminology and beliefs around boundaries can help them realize what is unhealthy or problematic.

3 *Reframing*

Similar to tracking, reframing takes the information the client presents and shifts the perspective on it. It provides an alternative explanation for behaviors and beliefs. This could include viewing a boundary in a new light or the need for a boundary in a new way.

4 *Physical rearrangement*

As mentioned earlier, boundaries can be demonstrated and communicated in the seating arrangement in the therapy space. Therefore, intentionally rearranging the family physically can challenge their unhealthy status quo and allow them to explore the emotional impact of doing so.

Structural therapy's boundary work is central to how it creates change. Therefore, when the client's presenting problem specifically includes imbalanced hierarchy and power distribution, structural family therapy can be a strong approach to address this.

Contextual Family Therapy

Key concepts of contextual family therapy pertaining to boundaries include trust, give-and-take, and entitlement. When setting boundaries, a level of trust is necessary for both the setter and receiver of the boundary. The setter has hope that setting the boundary will improve the relationship; the receiver needs to know that the setter still values their relationship together. Additionally, there needs to be trust that a boundary will be appropriately flexible. This relates to the necessary give-and-take in relationships.

There is a balance of influence between members of a system, even across hierarchies. This is connected to the pursuit of more egalitarian boundaries. That egalitarian, mutual respect and sense of value, is part of entitlement. Entitlement in boundaries can include what is owed multidirectionally across generations. Parents owe kids safe well-being; children are entitled to safety, acknowledgement, and praise. Kids owe parents appreciation and reason- able obedience. These are called constructive entitlements because they use appropriate boundaries to allow a balance of responsibility to family and self- ownership. This differs from destructive entitlement, when old hurts lead to perceived right to free action without consequence. These can look like rigid, uncompromising boundaries, which are understandably undesirable.

These concepts overlap with some Bowenian multigenerational concepts. This includes attentiveness to generational influence and family history. Often, older generations have the power to make the rules in the family, even when they do not live together. This can be a form of enmeshment, including emo- tional influence. Boundaries are deeply associated with emotional reactivity; enmeshed relationships tend to have high emotional reactivity. Decreased

150   *Theoretical Application*

enmeshment helps decrease emotional reactivity, and vice versa. Lastly, both models highlight responsibility to make one's own decisions and have a unique identity, or differentiation of self. These could be called identity boundaries and can be addressed with contextual family therapy.

Contextual family therapy emphasizes the importance of seeing as much of the system as possible, not just a certain subsystem. With as much of the family present as possible, the therapist is able to witness boundary dynamics that otherwise only could be described through a limited perspective. Having more of the family present also allows for multidirectional partiality: Empathy for all, give credit where and how you can, acknowledge efforts and contributions (for better or worse), and highlight individual client accountability. All of these can be part of setting boundaries and discussion in session of what holding that boundary might look like. A prominent boundary- and balance-central contextual therapy intervention is rejunction, which explores the client's capacity to create balance, including through boundaries. Therapy will include conversations of how family members help and care for one another, and how they use and rely on one another. These questions reveal the cohesion and flexibility in the family along with identifying preferred boundaries and confronting potential discomfort making that change.

Symbolic Experiential Therapy

Experiential therapy intentionally uses here-and-now in-session experiences, playfulness and activity, and emphasizes the role of spontaneity, intuition, and personal growth in systemic connections. It places a sense of importance on person identity and sense of self. While people can be influenced by our family-of-origin's values, beliefs, and cultural identity without being consumed by or limited to those. In this model, the therapist takes on a parental role in session, climbing to the top of the hierarchy and becoming a decided influence on family boundaries. A responsibility of the therapist is to listen for the client's current boundaries: Are they a closed, troubled system, or an open, nurturing system? This language differs from other models' understanding of boundaries, but it describes the same concept; it remains an assessment of cohesion and adaptability.

As with other models, to assess for boundaries, experiential therapy reflects on three generations of family influence. Satir referred to this as the three-generational family reconstruction process. This transformational process hopes to bring a shift in family members that allows for them to make independent choices unhindered by history and based in realistic hope. The therapist works with the client to acknowledge family history, particularly reflecting on how a client came to have certain beliefs and values. It recognizes the role of emotions and the cognitive and emotional responses to those emotions. This will be present in the model's interventions.

There are four interventions that experiential therapists can use with families to explore their current boundaries and identify their preferred ones. These are parts parties, family sculpting, family reconstruction, and the use of metaphors.

1 **Parts party**

According to Satir et al. (1991), the parts party intervention serves to help clients "identify, recognize, use, and transform their inner resources into a new and integrated self-worth" (Robinson, 2019, p. 171). In this intervention, a client identifies external roles they play and how those interact with the world around them and the client's internal being. Each of these parts are imaginatively "seated" in the room, and the client moves around between those seats, speaking to the perspective and experience of each one as if the parts were different people have a conversation. The different parts can seek to with one another in their roles and stresses, and the therapist may help to reframe these as strengths. This intervention is comparable to the concepts of IFS therapy, described in the next section.

2 **Family sculpting**

This is a second activity-based intervention, but unlike the parts party, it is used almost exclusively with systemic clients such as a couple or family. Clients will physically position themselves and family members to be a living portrait of family dynamics. People can be positioned around the room physically close to represent emotional closeness, stand on a chair to represent being high in power, etc. Along with the physical positioning, the person arranging will explain their reasoning and emotional process of the placements. This can be used both to portray how the boundaries are or how the individual would like them to be.

3 **Family reconstruction**

This intervention is similar to sculpting but requires a bit more. People or objects are placed to represent broader system members, resources, and emotions in addition to the nuclear family. Similar to sculpting, the family member can arrange the people and objects to reflect the family's level of cohesion and what roles they tend to fill. The purpose is to have family members identify one another as unique people, not stereotypical roles.

4 **Metaphors**

Metaphors are a linguistic tool to create a parallel between a personal situation and a similar fictional situation. This tool engages the client's creativity. It provides ongoing language that can cushion wording around emotionally intense situations. This method tends to give clients a way to open up and explore their problem without looking at it personally or head-on, which could be emotionally intimidating. The goal is to make the topic more approachable, but it necessitates follow-up of practical application.

Internal Family Systems Therapy

In previous chapters, we introduced internal multiplicity as defined by IFS therapy. Types of parts include managers, firefighters, and exiles, along with the aspect of Core Self. In this model of therapy, the client is confronted with boundaries not just with other people but between their internal parts. Parts, just like relationships with other people, desire to have balance in resources, responsibilities, influence, and boundaries. Those resources include material, leisure time, nurturance, attention, and guidance in relationships. Responsibilities include addressing physical health of self and others, generating income, developing and maintaining relationships and interests including with those outside the family system, and organizing and maintaining a home. Additionally, influence and boundaries are multidirectional between parts and between people.

Internal parts awareness can help challenges to boundaries be validated and moved forward. Internal parts can help enforce boundaries with others. It is common to have a defensive firefighter part who advocates for healthy boundaries. However, setting boundaries with others can trigger other parts within ourselves, parts of self-doubt, shame, or feeling undeserving. To address this, the client system will need to increase self-leadership.

"A family functions best when each member is a part of the subsystems they need in order to develop, and the boundaries around each subsystem are balanced between access and privacy" (Schwartz & Sweezy, 2020, p. 193). All people want to feel important and like they are contributing to a system's functionality. At the same time, people need to be given space to have their own unique identity. This is the balance of cohesion, and it is equally applicable between internal parts. The Self has the responsibility to be a leader over the parts, but the parts also need to give the Self the chance to do that. To increase self-leadership, the Self will need to demonstrate boundary-setting with external system members and, when having internal dialogue with parts, not allowing others to interrupt. Self-leadership includes setting those boundaries; this is the aspect of oneself that should be setting boundaries with other parts because it is the top of the hierarchy. The more the Self demonstrates the capacity to lead, the more the parts will trust the Self to act in the interest of the person's whole being. Similarly, when people function from their core Self, they exude confidence, calmness, and compassion that allows them to interact in a healthier way with others, too.

Case Study – Lola's Limits

Lola initiated couple's therapy for herself and her partner, expressing frustration and fear for her romantic relationship's future. Lola is in her late thirties; she is divorced and has two teenage children, Tomas (age 13) and Isabella (age 15). Lola divorced their father, Anthony, three years ago due to irreconcilable differences, but Lola also describes him as verbally abusive. Lola describes their divorce process and current relationship as "tense, like he'll do something to discredit me and take custody in a moment's notice." Lola says she believes Anthony it still angry at her for initiating the divorce, which she did after they fought when she came out to him as bisexual. Lola has been dating Valerie for about a year and a half. The couple live together and have shared custody of Lola's children. Valerie has no children of her own.

Valerie does not get along with Anthony, and her relationship with the children is impartial at best. Tomas largely ignores Valerie and says he does not view her as an authority figure. Over the past year, he has started treating Lola with similar harsh indifference. Lola says she has gone out of her way to rebuild this relationship, purchasing expensive computer and video gaming equipment to "connect" with him, though they do not play together. He also has increasingly been spending time isolated in his bedroom with the computer, playing games throughout the night despite his mother's passive objections.

Isabella has also been increasingly keeping to herself. Valerie describes Isabella's behavior as "secretive," and "like she thinks she's older than she is." The latter is in reference to Isabella's recent tendency to stay out past curfew and not disclose her whereabouts when asked. Valerie has occasionally attempted to reinforce parenting rules with Lola's children, and when they reject her efforts, she becomes frustrated and may let this out on Lola, calling her an ineffective parent and threatening to break up.

When asked what she wants out of therapy, Lola identifies several goals including, "getting Anthony to chill out and let me be a mom," "get the kids to respect Valerie," and, "Make sure Valerie knows how much I appreciate her and want this to work." She is tearful as she describes these goals, adding that her parents have "barely spoken to" her since coming out.

Treating with Structural Family Therapy

Interpretation of the Problem

According to this model, the problem rests in lack of hierarchy unity and hierarchy imbalance, both of which impact familial cohesion. All three individuals in parental roles, or those closer to the top of the hierarchy, that brief case summary describes all three contributing to disfunction. Lola is fearful of Anthony undermining her and hyperfocuses on this, potentially letting it interfere with her parenting. In Valerie's verbal barrages, she is disrespecting and belittling Lola's parenting efforts. This could decrease her parental confidence, impacting how she interacts with the children. Anthony is not shy that he does not respect Valerie or Lola, possibly based on their sexuality; this is inevitably going to influence how he interacts with them and how he talks about them with the children. If he insults and discredits them to the children, this contributes to toppling the appropriate hierarchy.

At this time, the hierarchy is imbalanced as the children hold an inappropriate amount of power in the family. Lola is attempting to appease Tomas and improve their relationship by purchasing him desired items. However, this is without sustained follow-through on the expectation that he would use the

154 *Theoretical Application*

item to connect with her. Similarly, both Tomas and Isabella are disobeying rules, such as staying up or out late into the night, without consequence. In doing this, the children are essentially making the rules and upsetting that parental hierarchy. This inversion impacts their expectations of others and the ability to cope with disappointment when those do not go well. It also impacts familial cohesion.

The shift in hierarchy is impacting both the adults and the children. Anthony, it seems, wants to remain at the top of the hierarchy rather than share it with Lola and/or Valerie mutually. This interrupts his connection both to them – not as a friend or lover, but as a co-parent – and the children. We also see the hierarchy change impacting cohesion with the children. Both appear increasingly disengaged; they are spending more time alone or away from home with peers. They also appear to be disregarding the stepparent figure because they are unattached emotionally. While it was not specified, the case does not describe a close relationship between the siblings, either.

Additionally, while there is no specific mention of adaptability problems, we see increased family disengagement. The divorce occurred three years ago and Lola entered a new relationship two years ago; these are both drastic life changes! The family is not adjusting to these changes together; they are isolated and turning to outside systems (peers) to cope. This is not innately unhealthy, but at this extent, the family does not appear appropriately connected or even separated. It is worth noting that this seems to upset Lola, which could be indicative of mom wanting a more enmeshed connection, reaching for the other extreme to make up the difference. This is the right idea to help rebuild connection but done in an unsuccessful effort.

Anticipated Solution

Structural family therapy would have two important steps and goals for this family. First is to bring hierarchy back to balance, giving the power back to the parents. This will include practicing creating boundaries, defining them to the children with love, and following through on consequences. The children will inevitably push against this shift initially, but eventually can understand it as a new norm. To do this requires consistency and support between parents, which is the second goal – to increase co-parenting cohesion. Parents do not have to like each other to not actively undermine one another. That person is still a leadership figure in the child's life, and attempts to take away that power will potentially harm the child and your relationship with them long-term. Simply put, it's not about you, the parent.

All three adults in this system have a responsibility to improve co-parenting dynamics. This is interesting because the three parents are a subsystem, but there are dyads within that triad, too. According to Minuchin and Fishman (2004), "one of the spouse subsystem's most vital tasks is the development of boundaries that protect the spouses, giving them an area for the satisfaction of

FST Concept V 155

their own psychological needs without the intrusion of in-laws, children, and others" (p. 17). Others include a co-parent. The Lola and Valerie dyad needs to be strengthened in the interest of the overall system. That relationship needs to be secure so that they can turn to each other when other subsystems are difficult.

However, it is also important to strengthen the dyad of Anthony and Lola. They can be united in the goal of raising upstanding adults who can think independently, act responsibly, and maintain family and cultural values. They can share this goal even if they do not like each other. To address this, the parenting team will need to agree to have similar rules from one home to another, maintain consequences from parent to parent, and encourage communication and relationship between the child and other parent. It will also be important not to insult one another in front of the children, even when they disagree with personal life practices. Disagreements need to be addressed, but not necessarily in front of the children. They do not need to be triangulated because that would pull the child back into a parental hierarchy role. Remember, though, that the child can be part of the conversations around boundaries and consequences. The family can practice these in sessions.

All of the interventions identified earlier can be applicable with this system. Building a family map can easily take a whole session as the therapist asks adults and children may draw it differently. The therapist can also begin to ask how the adults feel about surrendering their control and leadership to teenagers. Throughout conversations, therapists can offer tracking and reframing, examples of which are below. Lastly, the therapist can rearrange the room as needed, depending on who comes in and where they sit. In this system, likely Lola and Valerie will sit together; that is not innately problematic. Teens will likely require prompting to attend, but this can be an introductory boundary issue to practice enforcing. The therapist and parents could all possibly draw them to attend with emphasis of wanting to hear their perspective.

Example Questions

1   "Lola, who do you think holds the power in the family right now? How can you tell?"
2   "Valerie, what do you think is your role with the kids? What are your responsibilities to them? How is that different from their biological parents?"
3   "Tomas, how did house rules change between your mom and dad after the divorce?"
4   "Isabella, tell me about how you act older than you are."
5   "Lola, it sounds like you bought Tomas his computer so that the two of you could spend time together, but it's having the opposite effect. Tomas, what are your thoughts on playing games with your mom?"

156   *Theoretical Application*

Treating with Contextual Family Therapy

Interpretation of the Problem

Contextual family therapy places great emphasis on trust pertaining to boundaries in a system. It is appropriate to ask, where is the trust and where is it absent? In this system, trust appears to be lacking overall. Lola, Anthony, and Valerie do not seem to trust one another as parents or even as people, which the children can see and replicate. They do not seem to trust one another to take care of the children or lead by example. The family also demonstrates lack of loyalty evidenced in poor boundaries and imbalanced ledgers. The children may perceive that Lola and/or Anthony were disloyal to the family by electing to get divorced and therefore do not feel it is important for them to be loyal, either.

Similarly, the children may feel owed certain things due to the emotional distress of the divorce, including lack of consequences for their actions. For example, Isabella goes out without getting punished for breaking curfew and Tomas stays up late, both of which are currently without consequence. This destructive entitlement will need to be addressed in the therapy process. Additionally, therapy will need to address parental undermining, similar to the lack of unity in structural family therapy.

Anticipated Solution

First, contextual family therapy will strive to see the whole system: Lola, Valerie, Anthony, Tomas, and Isabella. Once there, session will focus on learning to set boundaries with explicit consequence. This includes stating the boundary, the potential consequence, and a possible explanation or emphasis on importance of the relationship. Additionally, the family can practice figuring out how can it be flexible and receive input from the kids. Using the computer time as an example, parents can choose to have an established permitted length of time by time of day (4 pm–6 pm) or maximum seat time (2 hours). Alternatively, they could discuss whether or not game time with family counts as an incentive. A second example would be between Valerie and Lola, who will need to talk about how it is unhelpful to put down her parenting efforts in front of the children.

The second intervention will focus on noticing where both destructive and constructive entitlement is currently happening. The therapist can have the adults and minors make lists of what the children and parents offer and owe each other. It would be important for both levels of the hierarchy – adults and children – to hear the other's perspective. This awareness overlaps with the practice of rejunction and identify cross-generational expectations.

Rejunction will be an appropriate intervention for this family. It connects balance and boundaries, focusing on how each family member contributes to the presence or absence of balance in the system. Therapy will include conversations of how family members help and care for one another, and how they use and rely on one another.

Lola contributes to the imbalance by giving without expectation of return to her children; she has a desire for return, but minimal hope or effort for it to occur. Lola also does not support Valerie as a parental figure when allowing the children to disrespect her without consequence. The children knowingly participate in these dynamics, too. Tomas uses Lola's guilt to use his computer more. Isabella demonstrates destructive entitlement to come and go as she pleases, likely reinforced by Valerie's verbalizations about doing so being an act of maturity. Valerie is also undermining Lola by putting her down in front of the children. This contributes to the imbalance in the system because it discredits her efforts to bring balance, too. Drawing attention to these concepts – balance and entitlement – is essential to contextual family therapy. However, beyond insight to these ideas, the family and therapist will explore what comes next and what changes can be made.

Example Questions

1 "Lola, what's it like when Isabella and Tomas ignore the rules you set at home?"
2 "Isabella, how do you rely on your mother? Your brother?"
3 "Anthony, what are you teaching the kids when they see the way you treat their mother?"
4 "Valerie, how do you show the kids that you care about them?"
5 "Tomas, why do you think your mom wants to set new rules around how you use the computer?"

Treating with Symbolic Experiential Therapy

Interpretation of the Problem

To begin building a connection and establishing a hierarchy with the family, the therapist will acknowledge they are currently in a closed, troubled system. This is observable in the family's tendency to reach for extremes of cohesion and adaptability rather than balance. The children lean out toward detachment, Valerie excludes herself from system decisions, and Lola leans in toward enmeshment, seeking connection that way but also appears fearful of seeming controlling. This could be associated with her fear Anthony will attempt to decrease her parental rights, too. This speaks to Lola's value of compassionate, nonauthoritative parenting style.

This sort of information will be very important to understand why clients do what they do, including what boundaries they do or don't set or reinforce. The therapist will want to learn Lola, Valerie, and Anthony's family-of-origin's values and beliefs, including how those might be contributing to current decision-making processes. Additionally, the therapist should consider how the clients' cultural identities may be contributing to the problem?

158 *Theoretical Application*

For example, Lola's Hispanic heritage and her parents no longer speaking to her, likely related to her nonheteronormative sexuality, are probably impacting how she parents now. It may reinforce her desire for compassionate connection with her children because it is something she craves but does not seem to have now.

Anticipated Solution

Part of the solution is going to be recognizing the influence of family-of-origin. In addition to learning about the adults' family-of-origin beliefs and values, the therapist will want to hear about these from the children, too. Additionally, the family's present and desired emotional connection can be a pathway to discussions around boundaries that may seem less harsh. In a way, these are goal-oriented conversations of boundaries – what is the desired outcome, and how can each person in the family act toward that? This overlaps with the therapeutic intervention exploring each person's responsibilities in and contributions to the problematic relationship and interactions. This includes contributions to create the desired outcome, too. Emotional connection will also be explored at a meta-level, such as exploring present emotions when talking about past events and emotions. These conversations can be woven into the intervention of sculpting.

In this family, sculpting will provide valuable insight to perceived boundaries and hierarchy. It will be important to allow all members to voice their perception in sculpting; this is not a breach of hierarchy, it is permission to express and an important example in appropriate flexibility. In therapy, over multiple sessions, the therapist can have the family members organize and arrange one another into postures communicating perceived and desired boundaries. Family members seeing one another's perception and hopes can be deeply influential to help one another see and validate each other.

Metaphors or similes can serve a similar purpose. The creation of an analogy can help depersonalize the situation and decrease the emotional intensity of the topic. Therapist can say,

> When we're born into a family, it's like the start of our stories. Have you ever read a book thinking it would go one way, and then some big plot twist happens and the book shifts in a total new direction? When that happens to me, sometimes I get irritated that this isn't the book I wanted to read. It's not what I signed-up for! But that doesn't mean it's a bad book. Just different than I expected. And before I can enjoy the book, I have to work through those feelings of irritation or disappointment that this isn't what I expected. Right now, Tomas and Isabella, you might feel like that big plot twist happened when your parents got divorced. And you might have a lot of feelings about it, maybe even some feelings you don't quite have words for. That's ok. You don't have to have it all figured out. What's different about this story is that you get to help write it. All of you, together.

Example Questions

1 "Lola, as we talk about your family history, there seems to be a lot to unpack. What feelings come up as we discuss your family history?"

2 "Tomas, when we did the sculpting exercise, I noticed you had Valerie stand on the chair over everyone else. How did you decide to place her there?"

3 "Isabella, I noticed a tear in your eye that you wiped away when your mother talked about coming out as bisexual. What thoughts and feelings were you having as she described that?"

4 Related to the earlier metaphor: "Isabella, what's something you'd like to see happen in your family in Chapter 9 that would let you know this book is going to be ok?"

Treating with Internal Family Systems Therapy

Interpretation of the Problem

From the IFS therapy perspective, the primary problem with this family is everyone's lack of self-leadership. Instead, the family is functioning primarily from manager and firefighter parts, both of which are protectors – proactive or reactive, respectfully – of damaged exiled parts that are based in hurt or shame. Lola seems to be acting from a manager that is fearful of losing relationship with her children, partner, and parents. Tomas is withdrawing due to possible exile and firefighter activity around fear of abandonment. Isabella is functioning from a manager that is seeking validation and acceptance outside the family, instead seeking it among peers. Valerie appears to lash out from a firefighter too, speaking for an exile fearing rejection as a partner and potential parental figure. It is unclear how Anthony is functioning, but his active blame and rejection of Lola as a person, not just a past partner, speaks to his own possible feelings of insecurity. However, it is important to note that while each individual contributes to the dysfunction, even one person shifting to self-leadership can impact the whole family. Self-leadership will include improved boundaries both between people and between a person's parts.

Anticipated Solution

Since the problem is the absence of self-leadership, it makes sense that the anticipated solution will be to increase everyone's self-leadership, especially Lola as the presenting leader of the familial external system. While IFS can be completed in a family unit, it tends to involve a lot of individual deep-dive work. Lola can work with a therapist to practice turning "inside," a beginning meditative practice, to contact and converse with her internal parts, including those that are upset with her family.

It is likely this process will include specific work on boundaries. Right now, a manager part is attempting to function as the internal system leader not

160 *Theoretical Application*

because the Self can't lead but because it is not being given the opportunity to. Lola's internal parts need to see that the Self is capable of asserting and holding boundaries to entrust it with internal system leadership. This will be a process of increasing internal trust. She can do this either individually or with Valerie present, if safe to do so. Valerie can support Lola's Self, but like the other parts, she cannot be the leader for Lola's Self. She may review what she realizes with her partner or children later, when the internal system feels safe to share with others. Other family members can do a similar process, particularly with Lola leading by example. She will be able to demonstrate the qualities of the Self – compassion, calmness, creativity, confidence, clarity, curiosity, courage, and connectedness – to set and hold boundaries in a balanced way rather than leaning into rigidity or enmeshment. The presence of these eight Cs will indicate presence of Self and increased potential for Self-leadership.

Example Questions

1 "Lola, it sounds like there's a part of you who doesn't want to upset your children by enforcing rules. What does that part believe would happen if it held firm about a rule or consequence?"
2 "Lola, I hear you describing a manager part who is working really hard – working overtime! – trying to do a job that it isn't made to have. What would it need to see from the Self to trust it to enforce a boundary with Tomas' computer use?"
3 "Valerie, you described having anger toward Lola for not enforcing rules. Where do you feel that anger in your body? What would that part like to be called?"
4 "Isabella, tell me about the part of you that decides when to come home and when to stay away. How does it make that choice? How did it get that job?"
5 "Lola, how do you feel about the part of Isabella that reaches out to others, instead of family, for support?" (This question is to gauge for Lola's current presence of Self; does she respond with any of the eight Cs, or something else?)

These types of questions would not happen sequentially; these would occur progressively working with each person as the therapist seeks to understand the clients' parts and increase their Self-leadership one by one.

Reader Reflection

1 Reflect on your family-of-origin. Who made the rules in the family and how were they reinforced? Who was responsible to reinforce them?
2 What's an example in your life of different subsystems having different boundaries?
3 Reflect on the extremes of cohesion – disengagement and enmeshment. Do you personally believe one is worse than the other? How so?

4 Which do you think is harder to change, emotional boundaries or physical boundaries? Why?

5 What step in boundary-setting do you think would be the hardest for people, or for you? How could each step be a challenge?

6 How might boundaries look different in a therapist relationship than a familial relationship?

7 This family systems theory concept differs from others in there being a predetermined range of healthy versus unhealthy boundaries. Do you believe there is an ideal boundary type? Or that it should be entirely left up to the client what healthy boundaries look like?

9 FST Concept VI
Circular Causality

To start, grab a writing utensil. On a piece of paper, draw a circle as best you can. Theoretically, after completing the loop, a later observer would not be able to tell where you started and closed the ring. One of the defining features of a circle is its lack of definite beginning or end. People can assign a starting point, such as the top of the clock indicating the beginning of an hour. However, the circle existed prior to that point. This is different from a straight line, which has definite beginning and end points. Comparatively, even if a single conversation has a start and end, the communication and relationship go beyond this interaction in both depth and width. Circularity is a family systems theory concept of recurring influence; there is more than the immediately apparent.

Defining Circularity

Go back to the drawing from last paragraph. A skilled artist could use it to draw another circle and create a bicycle. On a bicycle, the two circles individually spin in sync to create forward motion. *Circularity* entails cycles, spinning around to move forward. The wheels impact one another and other parts of the bike. A rider can kick the pedals to make the wheel move, and moving the wheels can push the pedals in their circular motion, as well. One impacts the other; their interaction is dynamic. It is reciprocal. The same can be said of relationships: They are reciprocal. A person's behaviors and words impact another person. In turn, the second person's behaviors and words impact the first person. This is called circular causality, which differs drastically from linear thinking/linear causality.

Circular Causality

Circular causality considers all the variables that contribute to a pattern of interaction. According to family systems theory, there are always multiple contributing factors. Even a single person is involved in multiple systems, which multiply exponentially the more people and relationships

DOI: 10.4324/9781003088196-12

you involve. Unfortunately, the more complex and multifaceted a system is, the more opportunity there is for problems. If a problem sticks around, it is not the fault of a single person; all parties and systems involved contribute to keep it going, even unintentionally. Once a cycle is established, finding the beginning becomes inconsequential. Often, an interaction pattern is deeply rooted between people. It is the norm between them! Regardless of where it began, its perpetuation is the responsibility of all parties who contribute to it.

This multiple causality perspective can feel disheartening. Knowing there are so many contributing factors can make it challenging to figure out where and how to initiate change. Fortunately, the more steps there are in the cycle, the more potential points of intervention and cycle interruption. Remember what we said earlier about equifinality: Multiple paths can lead to the same end. Interrupting a pattern of interaction at any point can help you leave the cycle. This differs from the perspective of linear causality.

Different from Linear Thinking

Earlier I mentioned how circles differ from a straight line. Circular causality is similarly different from linear causality. Linear causality could be summarized as a one-directional cause-and-effect relationship. If one thing happens, the next will logically follow. For example, if you leave milk out on the counter for a long time, it will go bad.

$$A \longrightarrow B$$

In family systems theory, linear thinking looks like a client coming in and saying, "If he hadn't yelled at me, I wouldn't have left." In this case, the graphic would appear:

$$\textit{He yelled} \longrightarrow \textit{She left}$$

By itself, this is linear thinking. However, something came before the yelling. The male partner may have a different version of events: "I wouldn't yell if you didn't talk down to me!" Now the image would be:

$$\textit{She talks down to him} \longrightarrow \textit{He yelled} \longrightarrow \textit{She left}$$

The conversation continues back and forth. It seems like there is always something that came before, leading into the next action, thought, or feeling. Eventually, a cycle emerges:

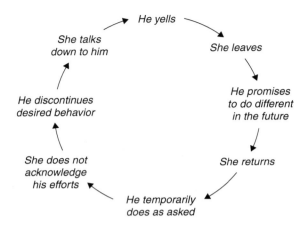

There are now repetitions in steps. Actions, thoughts, and feelings occur in the context of the previous actions, thoughts, and feelings. A cycle occurs in those interactions.

These cycles do not always have so many steps. Sometimes it only has a few: "You treat me like a child, so I might as well act like one"; "You act like a child, so I might as well treat you like one."

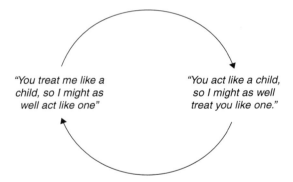

In this second example, the attitudes of each person perpetuate the behaviors of both parties. If an adult is assumed to be irresponsible, rude, or childlike, no matter what, they might not be motivated to be responsible, polite, or adultlike. They may say, "Might as well be irresponsible if it's what people expect, anyway!" The other person, seeing this attitude, may view the childlike behavior as evidence of why the person should be treated as a child rather than given more mature responsibilities. And thus, a cycle of interaction is developed. Both parties contribute to it continuing, even when they do not like the outcome. These cycles of interaction are perpetuated by feedback from the other person.

Perpetuated Cycles of Interaction: Positive Feedback and Negative Feedback

Let me reiterate from Chapter 5: We are constantly communicating. Similarly, we are constantly influencing one another. Sometimes the way we influence someone is intentional, sometimes it is not. Sometimes it does not go as planned, and the outcome is different than expected. Not only this, but sometimes we do not even realize how we are influencing that outcome. We may not realize the cycles we help perpetuate or recognize how we contribute to them.

Generally speaking, circles tend to be indicative of cycles. This can be true of behavioral cycles. These are called feedback loops. There are two types of feedback loops: Positive and negative:

- Positive feedback encourages behavior or a specific response.
- Negative feedback discourages behavior or a specific response.

In this sense, positive and negative are not indicative of good or bad. In psychology, B.F. Skinner introduced positive and negative reinforcement and punishment. In his terminology, positive meant adding stimuli and negative meant removing one. Whether or not the behavior was encouraged or discouraged used the language of reinforcement or punishment. In family systems theory, positive feedback means reinforced, and negative feedback means punished or discouraged. However, sometimes we unintentionally discourage good cycles with negative feedback or encourage problematic cycles with positive feedback. Either form of feedback can create or maintain problematic or good, constructive ones. We can inadvertently encourage problematic behavior or discourage good behavior.

In this way, circular causality can actually be a good thing. Circular responses, where certain behaviors are encouraged or discouraged, are how we teach social etiquette to children. Children learn to follow social rules based on how their peers and mentors respond to their behaviors that break or follow the social norm. Consider how preschool and early education focuses on establishing social norms. It is where children learn to take turns, stand in line, and use verbal manners such as saying please or thank you. Pleasant behaviors are rewarded with pleasant responses, which encourages the pleasant behavior. This can teach healthy and helpful behavior patterns through feedback loops.

Recursion

All communication is a series of feedback loops. This is called recursion. *Recursion* is that constant dynamic interaction and influence between people. It is the shared responsibility of those people to maintain the feedback loop or potentially end the loop to create a new sequence of interaction.

166 *Theoretical Application*

This is not just true between people. Recursive (ongoing) feedback can be between people, events, settings, or any level of system influencing another. To reiterate, in recursion, identifying the beginning point – which person or system influenced the other first – is both impossible and unnecessary. What matters is how the feedback loop currently is perpetuated, even when it is vicious and problematic.

Vicious Cycles

The term vicious cycles became increasingly common in the first half of the twentieth century, a time when cycles of global war were destroying economies, communities, and lives. Vicious cycles occur when two or more systems (including individuals) interact in a way that exasperates and intensifies one another, progressively worsening a situation or relationship. These cycles emphasize the problematic patterns of interaction, such as meeting aggression with aggression. This also can be phrased as meeting aggression with firmly negative feedback. It discourages the previous response but, unwittingly, is contributing to the behavior sticking around. In this sense, no one wins. All parties can be left feeling they have lost the battle for good relationships. When we fight with loved ones, or even strangers, we do not leave the situation victors. The very act of vicious cycles can be detrimental to the relationship and often to the greater goals of the system.

The assumption is that the aggressive or rebellious person behaves this way due to feeling misunderstood or unaccepted. When their self-expression is insulted or rejected by others, this belief persists, or "proves" they are correct. This includes when a therapist may unknowingly seem to side with the other family members, apparently against the agitator. The way to end vicious cycles is to mindfully respond to the aggressive person. Intentionally respond with something other than harsh negative feedback. Minimize behavioral resistance in your response. When you stop resisting aggressive behaviors, the other will not have to resist yours. Keep in mind this is not the same as permitting unhealthy or dangerous behavior. It is more like acknowledging the other person's actions as their own and your actions are your contributions. It is also a reminder there is more to that person than their problematic behaviors. Circular causality invites us to think of blame and responsibility in relationship dynamics differently.

Fault and Responsibility in Circular Causality

In family systems theory, knowing the origin in the argument – "Who started it?" – is inconsequential. Generally, it is hard, maybe even impossible, to find the starting point. The beginning of one difficult conversation is a follow-up to previous conversations, previous interactions, even previous relationships. Finding the first catalyst for a behavior response could require a lifetime of backtracking. Arguably, this insight is not essential to figuring out how to move forward from the present problem.

FST Concept VI   167

In a current problematic interaction, all participants contribute to the problem continuing. Placing fault in circular causality can be a sticky topic. First and foremost, let me iterate that all participants contributing to the problem is not to say there is equal contribution. Responsibility is shared but not necessarily evenly. We want to avoid language of victim-blaming. That being said, remember that blame and responsibility are not the same thing. Responsibility takes personal accountability for the role you play in a situation. Fault and blame seek to displace one's responsibility away from oneself.

Let me give an example. If I go through a difficult break-up with a partner, my first inclination may be to blame them for the relationship not staying together: They avoided difficult conversations, and maybe they were disloyal. However, with introspection, I can recognize how I also contributed to the break-up: Perhaps I also avoided those difficult conversations because I assumed how my partner would respond. Maybe I was emotionally withdrawn and harsh to the partner, and they elected to spend time with someone else who was more attentive to their emotional needs. That's not to say I am to blame for the ex's choice to cheat; it's to say I played a role. I have shared responsibility. I did not make their choices for them; that is still the former partner's responsibility.

Sometimes, people learn the difference between blame and responsibility based on how they see those concepts played out in their families of origin. Changing those perceptions can be difficult, just like the difficulty in changing communication patterns we might have learned early in life. Bowen's whole multigenerational therapy theory is based on this idea that we repeat what is demonstrated to us behaviorally, cognitively, and emotionally from our families-of-origin. However, just as all parties contribute to a problem, all parties have the capacity to contribute to new, better possibilities.

Circular Causality and Change in the Family System

Change has come up before in other section of this text. In Part I of this book, I talked about first- and second order-change when exploring different modalities of therapy. Remember, change can be strictly behavioral (first-order change) or can alter the meaning-making cognitive and emotional process (second-order change). Earlier in Part II, I identified the relationship between holism and change. One person doing something different can change the whole system. Similarly, change in relationship changes the people in it. This includes perception of the relationship. In either case, it can be difficult for someone to initiate or maintain that change.

Generally speaking, people do not like change. We can tolerate a certain amount, depending on a multitude of factors including adaptability levels and ambiguity endurance, but rarely does someone enjoy drastic change. Change often challenges a system's sense of normalcy, or the status quo. The status quo can also be called *homeostasis*. And people tend to cling to normalcy, enjoying its predictability and familiarity. Unfortunately, sometimes people will cling to that normalcy even when it is more than uncomfortable; sometimes it

168 Theoretical Application

is downright unhealthy. As a result, efforts to create change are frequently resisted or thwarted. However, change is inevitable! It occurs in three ways:

1 Organically, through normal development such as stage of life transitions. Puberty or moving away from one's family-of-origin may be two examples of this type of change. This includes *non-purposeful drift*, or the slight changes that happen in a system's structure throughout life without a specific goal in mind.
2 Incidentally, through atypical life experiences such as natural disasters, societal unrest, or disruptions to stage of life development.
3 Intentionally, through challenges to the current, potentially unhealthy, norm. In therapy this is called a *perturbance.*

In any of these three situations, people may attempt to hold onto their homeostasis. Homeostasis is sustained using negative feedback, which rejects change. Positive feedback, as said earlier, allows for or encourages change. When change does happen, systems can do one of two things. For one, the system can resist change and stabilize the system using old patterns, sometimes to a greater extreme. This would be called *morphostasis*; the back half of the word stems from the same linguistic root as *static*, or unchanging. Alternatively, the system can adapt to the change, evolving as needed to grow; this would be called *morphogenesis*. The latter, obviously, is more indicative of positive feedback.

Interestingly, there is also overlap between family systems theory's perception on change and chaos theory. There are four overlapping concepts between these theories: Systems function out of equilibrium, nonlinear causality, self-organization, and patterns in apparent chaos (Ward, 1995). According to chaos theory, when left unattended, systems will fall into a state of disorder. This is called *entropy*, the tendency to fall into chaos, or unpredictability. The more chaotic a system is, the more *entropic* it is. A small-scale example is a child's bedroom getting messier and messier without parental intervention. This would imply a sequence of negative feedback interactions that unwittingly allow or encourage the pandemonium. Alternatively, negative entropy, or *negentropy*, is the tendency to fall into an orderly state. For example, when something bad happens, a family might come together and experience increased structure and cohesion to achieve peaceful interactions within the system during a time when a macrosystem might be more disordered. This demonstrates the bridge between circular causality, boundaries, and change.

Another aspect of chaos theory that family systems theory adopts relates to chaos theory and entropy's state function. Chaos theory concludes the entropic unpredictability is not dependent on randomization of events between the start and finish. We can anticipate an ending but it may be unpredictable how we get there. Family systems theory has two subconcepts around this idea. *Equifinality* states there are multiple means to reach the same ends. A therapy example of this is that different models of therapy can achieve the same desired outcome for the client. Inversely, *equipotentiality* asserts there can be multiple ends to the same efforts. A therapeutic example here is an intervention that is well-received by one client may be ineffective or detrimental to another. Unfortunately, this has been a criticism of systems theory; there is no "how to create the desired change." As mentioned in Part I of this book, this can be as freeing as it is exasperating. There is not one right way to create change in a system; instead, it can be achieved in a plethora of means.

Applicable Therapeutic Models

In therapy, we use circular causality to understand our clients' contexts even further. Learning the events, thoughts, and emotions that lead up to actions helps us make sense of their situation. Not only can we understand the situation better, we better understand their decision-making process based on that situation. In the following four models of therapy, circular causality takes a different role both in understanding the client and creating space for change.

Strategic Family Therapy

As one of the very first models of family therapy, strategic family therapy was the first to notice that sometimes our solution attempts end up contributing to a problem. As a result, the problem sticks around or worsens. Typically, people will reach for the opposite of the problem with the assumption that it will create a solution. If a room is cold, we add heat. Theoretically, this will bring back a balanced norm. If the room keeps getting colder, we keep doing more of that same thing – turning up the thermostat, making a fire in the fireplace, putting on layers of clothes and blankets to warm up. However, this linear solution does not always work.

When a child misbehaves, it is typical that their parent or guardian will inflict some punishment or negative consequence that discourages that behavior. If the child does it again, the parent may repeat the punishment, perhaps increasing it in severity or duration. The child, possibly in a display of steadfast stubbornness or desire for selective independence, has determined this behavior to be their battleground to assert themselves. The more the child is punished, the more the child feels the need for freedom. Suddenly we are in the midst of a small but definitive cycle: The negative feedback is not deterring the original problem. Sometimes we need to look beyond doing more of the same. Namely, when more of the same is not working.

Strategic family therapy poses that we do something drastically different instead of more of the same. Back in Chapter 5, we talked about paradoxes as barriers to effective communication. Interestingly, paradoxes can also be effective interventions in therapy – do what is unexpected to yield a different result. These are called *counter-paradoxes*, or a contrasting paradox from the original conundrum. This option would have us do the opposite of what might be expected. For the child in the paragraph above, instead of applying a punishment, this child might be permitted to do the misbehavior (assuming it is not harming someone) without reaction from the adult, or even actively

170 *Theoretical Application*

encouraged until the child is bored with it. They may even be assigned to do the misbehavior regularly, even after it has lost its interest. The theory is that the purpose of the behavior – to assert independence – is taken away and no longer effective. In this way, the cycle of interaction is interrupted.

I recognize that this is not viewed as a traditional or typical response. That is, in a way, its exact appeal. We need to do something different, something unexpected, in order to break the current cycle of interaction. In this case, that is achieved in an unorthodox, yet frequently effective, method of shifted interaction.

Bowen Multigenerational Family Therapy

Bowen's multigenerational approach to therapy carefully considers patterns that are passed down from generation to generation, often viewing these as cycles. This can include learned behaviors like how to talk to other people, but it can also include multigenerational pass-downs such as career choices, mental health problems, addiction, and geographic location. It can be relational patterns like divorces and multiple marriages, adoptions, children born to young parents or out of wedlock, and relationship cut-offs. This is one of the main concepts in Bowen's theory: *Multigenerational transmission process.* Families are breeding grounds for patterns because that is where we learn so much about what it means to be a person and a contributing member of our social systems. There is circularity between generations.

According to Bowen's theory, all people have a balance of individuality and interdependence with others. This is called their level of differentiation. According to multigenerational transmission process, families project their level of differentiation from one generation on to the next using positive and negative feedback to reinforce or reject certain behaviors that deviate from their normal functioning. As a result, it can be very hard to become more differentiated than your family because it can be very anxiety-inducing to introduce change to those deep-rooted ways of functioning. That is to say, families learn to function in a certain cycle, and introducing change to that can be very difficult because it is so uncomfortable for everyone involved.

An additional version of this same concept of differentiation can be seen in contextual family therapy. While they use different terminology, this model of therapy draws attention to the balance of entitlement and indebtedness among a family. Neither entitlement nor indebtedness are innately bad. For example, my parents put a lot of time, energy, and money into raising me; therefore, when they are older and less physically healthy, I owe it to them to take care of them in return. Similarly, they raised me to believe I am entitled to being well cared for by a partner and treated like an equal rather than subservient. This was a value my family taught me related to my differentiation. I learned this by experiencing it with my parents, receiving positive feedback when I took initiative toward individuality without sacrificing the togetherness of my family bond. Multigenerational patterns taught me about these social norms with the expectation that I will pass the cycle forward to future generations, as well.

FST Concept VI 171

Acceptance-Commitment Therapy

Acceptance-commitment therapy (ACT) is frequently used to treat various types of anxiety including situational and social anxieties, paranoia, and obsessive-compulsive disorders (OCD), along with depression and substance abuse. Its core belief is that it is unnecessary or counterproductive to believe you have the capacity to control several aspects of one's life. However, instead of using interventions aimed to stop those behavioral efforts for control (first-order change!), ACT focuses on embracing one's thoughts or feelings rather than avoiding them or feeling guilty for them. That is how it interrupts problematic or negative cycles: Through self-acceptance.

This mindfulness-oriented therapy model seeks to break negative feedback loops of criticism and judgment both internally and in relationships with others. It achieves this by having people assess their psychological flexibility through six key factors. This is called the *hexaflex*. The six key factors were identified in Chapter 6, with particular emphasis on one:

- **Present moment**
  This is a behavior- and body-based awareness of being in the present. It uses your sense to ground yourself in the present when our minds so easily get distracted by the past and future.
- **Values**
  This factor asks, "What is most important to you in your life?" What gives your life purpose? What matters most to you? Once we are able to answer these questions, we are able to identify actions we take that lead us closer to living out those values. Living out our values provides us with greater internal peace. Identifying our values also helps us strive to spend time with people and be in places that match those as well as can be expected.
- **Committed action**
  Expanding on what was stated about values, committed action looks at the practical steps to align with our values when our thoughts, feelings, and actions deviate away from those values. Additionally, this factor considers the action itself, not just the outcome, for how it relates to our values. It believes there is meaning in the process and the experience that counts for something. Instead of the misnomer *the end justifies the means*, this factor would say *the means explicate the value*. Even the cycles we get stuck in having meaning. We just want to look at how that meaning parallels our greater values.
- **Self as context**
  As I described in Chapter 6, the self as context allows a person to objectively reflect on themselves. It is a heightened level of self-awareness. They can reflect on past and present behaviors, thoughts, and feelings without judgment. Instead, a person can use mindfulness to say to themselves, "Oh, that makes sense why I made that decision." This is not to justify all our choices – we can still make some bad ones – but we can better understand how a part of us came to choose that course of action. Logically,

172 Theoretical Application

this also helps us learn ourselves better to spot the problems earlier in our internal cycle, too.

- **Cognitive defusion**
  Like self in context, this process looks to defuse ourselves from an experience. In this, we essentially pull the emotion out of a thought and treat them as two separate things rather than one fused together. As internal family systems therapy would say, you are speaking for a part of you, not from it. This also has the goal of increased objectivity in self-reflection, along with improved ability to offer empathy to the parts of us that may carry heavy or harsh self-beliefs.

- **Experiential acceptance**
  This is the part I mentioned earlier about accepting what we cannot change. We can do this by having increased awareness of activities as separate from ourselves. Things can happen in the world that are separate from ourselves; we do not need to immediately personalize them, but sometimes we do it anyway. This part would have us focus instead on what is within our control, laying down responsibility for what is not within our control, and, in the wise words of the Serenity Prayer, the wisdom to know the difference.

Any of these six can influence one another and contribute to the perpetuation of unhelpful mental cycles and cycles of interaction with others. Understanding how these interact with one another and impact a person's decision-making process helps us be better clinicians and provide more effective, individualized treatment. When we understand someone's cycle practically, not just abstractly, we have an improved ability to nonjudgmentally challenge specific assumptions that are occurring between those factors. This can increase awareness of the hexaflex and mindfully shift cognitive perceptions toward a healthier alternative.

Emotion-Focused Therapy

Working with couples, cycles play out repeatedly both in session and outside of it. In the Gottman approach with couples, they highlight the presence of bids for acceptance and connection that can be either rejected or accepted though negative and positive feedback loops. Emotion-focused therapy (EFT) includes an intervention of identifying a couple's "dance," which is the step-by-step drawing out of their cyclical interaction. From there the couple strives to create emotional security together, trusting one another with vulnerability from one past that inadvertently taught a person about how to connect with others. Emotion-focused family therapy (EFFT) utilizes a foundation of attachment theory. It believes previous attachments to loved ones, such as to parents, impacts how we give and receive love as we age and mature. We can be taught healthy dynamics, called a secure attachment, or less healthy dynamics that result in disorganized, anxious, and ambivalent styles of attachment.

FST Concept VI 173

Circular causality is another way of looking at the couple's interactions with the context of their attachment style. This may include divulging specific hurtful memories of past loved ones and how interactions with the current partner inadvertently replicated those. According to EFFT, change happens in a system when a person feels emotionally and physically nurtured in their relationship. To achieve this, EFFT describes nine steps that occur over three stages.

Stage 1: Assessment and Cycle De-escalation

In this stage, there are four steps. The therapist works with the client to build rapport (Step 1) and understand the interaction dance, or cycle (Step 2). We also strive to help each individual learn the deep emotional source of distress associated with the interactions (Step 3). This is overlapped with the perspective shift of viewing the interaction as the problem, not placing blame on one person or the other (Step 4). Instead, both parties are responsible for contributing to the problematic cycle of interaction and can mutually come together with the common goal of overcoming the negative cycle rather than overcoming one another.

Stage 2: Changing Interaction Positions

This stage holds the next three steps. Here, couples learn to engage with one another without withdrawing or by softening their approach to be more invitational than demanding. Then, the pair can hear out one another's attachment history and current needs without blame (Step 5). Members of the relational dyad now have a better understanding of one another's internal process and how it contributes to the negative feedback loop. This promotes acceptance and creates opportunity to have a new positive feedback cycle replace the previous negative one by shifting interaction responses (Step 6). This new cycle allows the pair to express their needs and wants safely, hopefully experiencing positive feedback interactions that encourage engagement with one another (Step 7).

Stage 3: Consolidation and Integration

This final stage holds the last two steps. Now that a new cycle of interaction is emerging, the couple may address old problems from this new perspective with the potential for new solutions (Step 8). We have diverted from their old cycle of blame, embraced responsibility, and found a new cycle that is more positive. The therapist is also able to solidify the changes in their interaction cycle – creation of a new dance – and address any final concerns about applying this new cycle into different situations (Step 9).

As you can see, EFT greatly utilizes cycle recognition and shifts in interaction loops to create change in a system. Though this example uses a couple, it can also be applied to families creating those initial attachment bonds among

174 *Theoretical Application*

children. This aims to increase the family adults' awareness of the attachment styles they are giving as examples to the children.

Case Study – Erik's Dilemma

Erik presents to therapy reporting feeling overwhelmed with numerous problems in his life. He tearfully says, "It all started when my girlfriend, Melissa, left me." He describes two years ago Melissa cheated on him with a coworker and subsequently left him to marry the other man. Since then, Erik says he has suffered from substantial depressive episodes. Those episodes have included and resulted in fluctuating weight, losing his job due to lack of attendance or attentiveness, and difficulty maintaining or making new friendships (many of which were already strained since the break-up). He has said, "I just wish life could be as easy as it was before Melissa left. It was so much less stress." However, specific stories he tells about his life at that time are not consistent with that claim.

Erik uses conflicting language in session. He alternates between statements such as, "I don't deserve this," and, "It's my fault all this is happening." He also demonstrates inconsistent dedication to therapy, some days expressing optimism that things will get better and other days wallowing in self-doubt and hopelessness. In therapy, he has learned behavioral coping skills related to anxiety and depression but struggles to implement them at the time of distress. Erik has started a new job in the same industry, working for a family member. He makes less than his previous job but has potential to return to a similar leadership position and income. Erik frequently expresses uncertainty about this job choice and whether it is "the right move" for him.

In the months initially following the break-up, Erik reports having experienced prominent anger and sadness. He stopped talking to Melissa because she no longer responded to his calls or texts. He remembers sleeping excessively and eating very little at first, but then shifting to working out regularly, then excessively, and hyperfocusing on his calorie intake. He recalls the workout was helpful to distract himself, but he discontinued when he lost his job. A friend at that time had suggested he attend therapy, but Erik denied the need for this. Instead, he continued turning to that friend until they withdrew, claiming the need to "set boundaries." Overall, Erik describes few other attempts to move past the break-up, stating that just getting through each day should be good enough: "Time heals all wounds, right?"

The thing that pushed Erik to come to therapy was Melissa recently reaching out to him via text, triggering a panic attack. He describes "mixed feelings" of excitement and anxiety when talking to her. He sees on his ex-girlfriend's social media that she is separated from her husband and seems open to seeing him again. At this time the pair is texting daily, but when she goes several hours without responding, Erik notices feeling increased anxiety symptoms including chest and stomach pains. Erik recently said, "Even with everything we've been through, I still love her and want to be with her. But I know people will judge me if I go back." Shortly after stating this, Erik acknowledges he is not totally certain though, because he still resents her choice to leave him two years ago.

Treating with Strategic Family Therapy

Interpretation of the Problem

Erik appears to be in the exact dynamic strategic therapy seeks to address. His solution attempts seem to contribute to a problem sticking around or worsening instead of getting better. That being said, the case example does not describe many of his solution attempts after the break-up. These include attempts to cope with depression then or anxiety now. Based on what is described, he has not been consistent with his efforts to cope with the break-up. He is stuck in a negative feedback loop that paradoxically views Melissa both as the source and solution to his problems. Because of this, he lacks true motivation to put the relationship behind him or the capacity to fully recommit to it again. His inconsistency, both behaviorally and cognitively, contributes to the lack of sustained change.

Anticipated Solution

According to strategic therapy, sometimes we need to look beyond doing more of the same. Namely, when more of the same is not working. It would seem whatever solution attempts Erik has attempted have not been followed through – the negative cycle persisted. His behaviors and thoughts were not properly deterring of his continued fixation on Melissa and their previous relationship. Treatment could focus on interrupting the cycle somewhere other than the perceived problem spot. Therefore, a paradoxical intervention could be appropriate.

The strategic therapist could challenge Erik to not attempt to distract himself from the previous relationship and instead encourage the focus on their relationship (as long as it does not reach a dangerously obsessive extent). The therapist could have Erik intentionally set aside time to reflect on their past relationship, both the good and bad qualities, and write these down. He can do this every day for a set length of time. He must dedicate the whole duration and only that duration of time to this topic. If he thinks of things about the relationship outside that time frame, he can write those down briefly and come back to them at the designated time. The intent with this approach is that his solution attempt – to avoid thinking about the relationship – was not working and, in a way, contributed to his fixation and blame cycle. Therefore,

176 Theoretical Application

instead of avoiding the topic, we are intentionally focusing on it. We can look at the relationship for what it was instead of idealizing or villainizing it or the individuals in it.

Example Questions

1 "Erik, tell me what you liked and disliked about the relationship when you were in it."
2 "I hear you describing efforts you made just after the break-up to move past the relationship, but that those didn't seem to stick. Why do you think that is?"
3 "Erik, it seems like your friend encouraged you to try therapy before, but the timing wasn't right. What do you feel is different this time?"
4 In the session after the paradoxical intervention is introduced: "How was it helpful to set aside that time every day to think about the relationship and Melissa? How do you feel about the prospect of continuing to do that?"
5 "Erik, I hear you saying that you're not sure your job is the right move for you. Talk to me about how you know when something is or isn't the right move for you."

Treating with Bowenian Multigenerational Therapy

Interpretation of the Problem

Two attributes of Bowenian therapy appear in Erik's situation. First is consideration of intergenerational patterns and cycles. What did Erik's family-of-origin teach him about romantic relationships? What was healthy? What was normal? Remember, those two things are not one and the same. He likely learned that the best way to cope with distress, including a break-up, was to distract himself. While it may seem initially off-topic, we know Erik has continued interaction with his family since they were able to help employ him after losing his previous job. Therefore, including them in the conversation does not have to seem disconnected or random. They are relevant to how Erik learned to be in a relationship, be single, and cope with uncertainty.

The second aspect to consider per this modality is the role of differentiation. Erik's attentiveness to this relationship may be due to a lack of self-differentiation. He appears to overidentify with the relationship and now feeling a lack of identity since its dissolution. That is to say, he doesn't know who he is without Melissa or their relationship. This could have been furthered when he also lost his job – another identifier – after the break-up. Erik's difficulty moving past the relationship, and even his willingness to return to it when doing so may be an unhealthy choice, indicate a lack of differentiation. This will likely be a focal point in treatment with Bowenian therapy.

FST Concept VI 177

Anticipated Solution

Bowenian therapists are attentive to how one's past influences one's present. This can include family-of-origin, but also previous significant and/or romantic relationships. An early part of the therapeutic process for Erik could be learning more about his past to provide insight to how he learned about healthy and normal relationship interactions. What did he observe was normal in his family? In previous romantic relationships? What felt abnormal? How has he learned to deal with stress and disappointment? Learning these may help the therapist better understand why Erik has responded so poorly so far and offer validation to Erik that this is learned behavior that can also be unlearned and taught differently.

Much of therapy will likely focus on increasing Erik's sense of self-differentiation. It is important that he have an identity separate from this romantic relationship considering the future of the relationship is unclear. This includes exploring how he might want the relationship with Melissa to be different from their previous attempt should they decide to get back together. To do this, therapy will ask questions with four purposes: (1) To increase his self-awareness through "I" statements ("I feel _____ when you/they _____ because my context is _____"), (2) To practice personal ownership without projecting onto others, (3) To identify where there is a realistic absence of control, and (4) to set necessary boundaries with others to establish appropriate independence. This process is called increasing *self-focus*, and doing so is not a selfish act but an essential tool in identity development.

Example Questions

1 "Tell me more about who you are outside this relationship or this break-up. How did you identify yourself before that relationship?"
2 "Have you seen anyone else in your family experience a break-up? How did they handle that?"
3 "If you thought about it, how do you feel both you and Melissa contributed to that relationship ending?"
4 "Give me an example of something you feel when you think about your relationship with Melissa, using an 'I' statement."
5 "How do you believe your family views you differently as a single man compared to when you were in a relationship?"

Treating with Acceptance-Commitment Therapy

Interpretation of the Problem

According to ACT, the source of the problem is in Erik's difficulty separating what is within his control and beyond his control related to this relationship. He also appears to assume that avoiding the unpleasant emotions through distracting behaviors is the best way to move forward. Whether this be the

178   *Theoretical Application*

workout regimen or his current day-to-day activities, he appears to believe that time will ultimately separate him from his pain. Similar to Bowenian therapy, he also appears to not have a strong identity outside the relationship, which helps it make sense that the break-up would be so challenging. Treatment will likely focus on these three as they apply to the sectors of the hexaflex.

Anticipated Solution

Erik's presenting problem and potential solution tie to all six areas of the hexaflex in ACT. He can interrupt his negative cycles that result in lack of lasting change through radical self-acceptance.

1   Erik will need to practice being in the present moment. Therapy can teach him to notice when he is excessively focusing cognitively and emotionally on the past or pondering excessively on the "what might be" of the future. Once he can notice these tendencies as they occur, he can learn to bring himself back to the present. The therapist can teach Erik to use mindfulness practices to accomplish this.
2   Values and committed action – The therapist will be able to assist Erik to identify what is important to him, besides this relationship? What about being in a relationship, especially this relationship, is so important? What do those say about his values, and how do we live out those values instead of feeling stuck waiting to live them in the next relationship?
3   Self as context – This is Erik's call for objective self-reflection. The therapist can help Erik honestly reflect on his past and present behaviors, thoughts, and feelings nonjudgmentally. This can be connected to how Erik feels these beliefs do or do not reflect his values or sense of identity.
4   Defusion – As a reminder to Erik, we are more than our emotions and thoughts. This includes those regarding this relationship and the meaning-making he ascribes to either not being in it or potentially returning to it.
5   Experiential acceptance – At this hexaflex phase, Erik can learn to depersonalize events in his lives. Pain is a common human experience; even when we all experience it uniquely, we are not failures for experiencing it at all. Erik must recognize what is in or out of his control. Melissa's choices were her own at that time; he gets to make his own choice about what moving forward in a romantic relationship looks like, regardless of with whom he moves forward.

Overall, Erik must embrace his behaviors, thoughts, and emotions associated with his anger and sadness rather than avoid or berate himself for them.

Example Questions

1   "What do you notice your mind is doing as we talk about Melissa?"
2   "Erik, how do you tell the difference between your thoughts and feelings and fact?"

FST Concept VI   179

3   "What do you believe it says about you that you still want to be with Melissa? What are the advantages and disadvantages to those beliefs?"

4   "If I were to ask someone who doesn't know you, someone who doesn't have any investment in taking sides between you and Melissa, what do you think they would say about your continued interest in a relationship with her?"

5   "From what you've said, I can tell this relationship has been really important to you and how you see yourself. Tell me about how important it is to you to be in a relationship, particularly this one?"

Treating with Emotion-Focused Therapy

It may seem odd to think of using EFT with an individual, but as we know from previous chapters, the individual self is the smallest system. Erik is still a mess of perspectives within himself interacting with the external world, including Melissa. EFT is designed to be usable with individuals by decreasing defensiveness and self-judgement. A treatment goal for Erik will be to increase trust in himself including accepting his perspective/experience as valid. We want him to feel like a worthwhile person and be willing to feel his emotions, including unpleasant ones. Moving toward this state of self-acceptance (noticing that theme?) will enable him to have healthier external relationships moving forward.

Interpretation of the Problem

EFT utilizes language of the "dance" to describe the step-by-step cycle of interaction that results in and leads to cyclical thoughts, emotions, and behaviors. This pattern can appear with such consistency, people start to anticipate the acts of others based on previous performances of the dance. For Erik, this could include anticipating Melissa's thoughts and actions based on their past experiences together. However, he may not be as aware of his internal interactions with himself, such as judgmental language "dancing" with language of self-blame.

We know EFT utilizes attachment theory. Erik's attachment style seems to be anxious and preoccupied. He craves emotional intimacy even when other parties are not as invested. He can be approval-seeking and often need reassurance from others. He is easily made to feel anxious and has difficulty making decisions independently. He may rely on others for decision-making. For example, Erik offers inconsistent perception on the past relationship or his current life situation. He seems to seek input from others to tell him the "right" way to feel or behave. His anxiousness could be why he is so triggered by Melissa not responding to him even now. This fear for the security of their relationship is based on his attachment style.

To move forward in treatment, the therapist may want to learn about specific attachment injuries – times when Erik was left feeling unsafe with his attachment figures – that impact his current attitude toward relationships.

180　*Theoretical Application*

Does he have any specific hurtful memories from childhood or previous significant relationships, including past romantic relationships, that could provide insight to why he attaches this way? And moving forward, how can he practice meeting his own needs to avoid attachment injuries with himself?

Anticipated Solution

In individual EFT, the therapist aims to create emotional security through entrusting oneself with vulnerable honesty. He will need to be able to access underlying, unaddressed emotions with self-kindness. The therapist must first build rapport and assist Erik to identify his patterned internal interactions. Eventually, we hope to identify and address the unmet internal emotions he briefly identifies as anger and sadness, taking personal responsibility for contributions to the cycle and its continuation. This would be Steps 1–4 in EFT's first stage.

To do this, we can learn a bit about Erik's attachment style history. What attachment styles did Erik observe in his family-of-origin? What has he previously experienced with Melissa when they were together? How securely is he attached to himself – does he view himself as untrustworthy or problematic? What would it look like to build up his trust in himself?

Example Questions

1　"Erik, what I hear you describing sounds a lot like a cycle. It sounds like sometimes something triggers inside you that makes you feel unimportant or incapable of being a good boyfriend. It sounds like that leads you to lash out at yourself and maybe reach out to someone else for comfort. Then, if they don't respond quickly or in a way you like, it feels like that fear is confirmed. It's like it makes you question how important you are all over again. That leads you to behave in a way you aren't proud of, which you now see causes that person to stay away instead of comfort you, which is what you really want. Does that sound right?" (This is an example of a cycle being summarized. Please note that sometimes there will be more steps in the cycle when there are multiple people because you are describing the behaviors, thoughts, and feelings of each person interacting with one another. This example also includes details that were not explicitly given in the case study. This was done for the sake of providing an example of how the therapist can summarize a client's "dance" and should not be said without evidence from the client.)

2　"Erik, tell me about a time you saw your parents interacting. What do you think that taught you about how love is given and received?"

3　"Erik, what similarities do you see between your relationship with Melissa and how you remember your mother seeming to talk down to you?"

4　"Imagine turning within yourself and stating, 'I know you've had a hard time thinking this relationship is really and truly over. That's ok. Relationships are difficult, and we don't know the future of them.' Tell

FST Concept VI   181

yourself that out loud now. Then tell me what it was like to receive that message." – This question is comparable to the couple-based intervention of an enactment.

Reader Reflection

1   Reflect on a time when you were taught something is unacceptable not because someone outright said so, but because of the response you got from other people. What was that like for you? What did you learn as an outcome of that interaction?

2   What role might peer feedback play in teaching/encouraging questionable social mores among adolescents?

3   In some situations, insinuating a victim has any role in their abuse can be very invalidating. How can we as therapists potentially handle that? Remember, shared responsibility is not equal responsibility.

4   How could viewing the family as a circle of influence, constantly influencing one another, make it harder or easier to initiate change?

5   How can a therapist encourage positive feedback loops without exposing their own biases?

6   When exposed to negative feedback loops, how do you typically respond? Does it cause you anxiety or immediately overwhelm you? Do you view it as a problem to be solved? Or something to be avoided? How could this potentially impact you as a therapist?

7   To what extent do you believe people are capable of change? How did you come to this belief?

Part III
Additional Considerations

10 Role of Individual Psychology in Family Systems Theory

Back in Part I, I described marriage and family therapists as having a *nondiagnosing stance*. That is to say, we have the training and capacity to assign a mental health diagnosis to a client, but due to our systemic lens, prefer not to. The systemic perspective asserts that problems are based primarily in interactions, not individuals. That being said, it would be ignorant to pretend individual psychology and mental health are not factors in systemic well-being. The Palo Alto Team noticed this in their research with individuals diagnosed with schizophrenia and their family interactions. However, what they considered causal distress, I will explore as correlating.

This chapter is dedicated to finding the balance and role of individual psychology in systemic approaches to therapy. I will define aspects of mental illness, including connections between physical and mental health; look at how different systemic models incorporate individual psychology and theorize its origins; and discuss how it is possible to treat individuals through systemic modalities of therapy. Because while family systems theory focuses on interaction patterns and dynamics, individual mental health is an ongoing influence, too.

Mental Health, Mental Wellness, and Mental Illness

Mental health is the spectrum of mental wellness and mental illness. A person is not either well or ill; most people fall somewhere in between. *Mental wellness* is typically associated with mental and emotional stability. This includes the ability to handle distress without feeling total loss of control or loss of identity. It also includes internal acknowledgement of one's humanity and capacity to be in the present without getting mentally swept away ruminating about the past or anxiously anticipating the future.

Unlike mental illness, mental wellness is viewed very broadly; there are many ways to be mentally healthy without specific qualities of life being present. On the other hand, *mental illness* tends to be tied to specific symptomology, categorized and classified depending on how it intrudes upon one's ability to function in day-to-day life. This includes one's ability to share some perceptions of reality and social norms alongside others within your culture and surroundings. Specific types of mental illness are characterized by

DOI: 10.4324/9781003088196-14

186   *Additional Considerations*

the means, frequency, duration, and intensity of interruption. These are the grounds for a mental illness diagnosis. Diagnoses tend to be given to individuals, not systems.

According to famed psychiatrist and founder of individual psychology, Alfred Adler (1973), mental illness stems from a mismatch between one's lifestyle and one's worldview. When your perceived reality does not match your life experience, you increase the risk of mental illness. Intuitively, mental wellness would therefore be experienced when one's perceived reality matches one's experiences. However, family systems theory notes this is not always the case. Mental health is dependent on so many facets including physical health, personal resilience, and systemic interactions.

Mental Health, Physical Health, and Systemic Health

It is undeniable that there is a tie between physical and mental health. When I feel anxious, I have a stomachache and tense muscles. When I am tired due to lack of sleep, I have a harder time concentrating, may be more likely to get stuck in my thought processes, and can be more easily overwhelmed by my feelings. When I finish a therapy session as a client, discussing my emotional processes can leave me physically feeling drained and exhausted. That is because my body and mind are not mutually exclusive; they are united by the brain. The brain is a perfect metaphor for holism – there is so much more to it than its physical parts.

In western cultures, it is not uncommon for mental health to be boiled down to neurological atypicality – the brain is not "quite right." However, this medical approach can be a bit shortsighted. It is true that brain chemistry is a significant factor in mental health. Brain chemistry and brain structure do impact mental health. Anxiety and distress tolerance are based in the limbic system. Depression is influenced by the presence, absence, and speed of neurotransmission of chemicals including serotonin, dopamine, and norepinephrine. There can be structural imperfections in the brain. Changes in white matter impact learning, memory, cognitive processes, and attention; gray matter impacts motor control, balance, precision, and coordination. The physical state of the brain and body is one part of mental health, but it is not the whole picture.

The same can be said for the genetic components of mental health. Genetics are personal attributes that are passed down from our biological parents – they are intergenerational patterns. These can be physical traits like eye color and height or emotional and cognitive predispositions. Autism has a genetic prevalence as high as 90%; schizophrenia can be as much as 79% genetic predicated. Research about the role of genetics in bipolar disorders varies from 60 to 80%. Depressive symptomology can be seen across families in about 40–50% of researched cases. Attention disorders, particularly attention-deficit hyperactivity disorder (ADHD) is only 20–25% genetically correlated. This goes to show that genetics can be an attribute of one's mental health, but it is not the only influencing factor.

Role of Individual Psychology 187

So are some people's brains just doomed to mental unwellness? Maybe in some ways, but we also know life circumstance is a prominent variable. The human brain continues to develop from before birth all the way to 25 years old. The mind is constantly developing and open to influence throughout life. Continuing to take care of your neuroplasticity throughout childhood, adolescence, and adulthood influences memory, critical thinking, and other cognitive processes right into elderhood. Neuroplasticity is impacted by both genetics and lifestyle – that is to say, both nature and nurture.

There is an unfortunate social science dichotomy that seeks to specify the roles of nature versus nurture in human development. Natural is genetic predisposition, and nurture is life development and interactions. People seek to identify how the two balance together but still view the pair as separate. However, that is far from reality. As said earlier, the human brain continues to grow and develop into adulthood. Its structure and composition at a biological level can change as we participate in life through interaction with our surroundings. Nature and nurture are enfolded together, working harmoniously and collaboratively toward a person's burgeoning identity. Therefore, mental illness cannot be labelled as one or the other. It can be biological shortcoming or short-term situational chemical responses to external stressors. The external stressors often relate to systemic health – the well-being and functionality of the family.

There is a cyclical relationship between mental and physical health; they impact one another. Similarly, the mental or physical health of an individual can influence family dynamics. Family dynamics can impact the physical and mental health of each individual within the system. Physical, mental, individual, and systemic wellness cannot be divided into unique categories, nor can they be treated that way therapeutically. Holistic treatment means acknowledging individual brain chemistry and systemic interactions are circular. Studies have shown the systemic treatment of a person with a mental disorder impacts the disorder's presentation more than the genetic component alone. We must remember, even as we treat individuals, systems continue to be influential. The brain is where the body and mind collaborate; there is more to the mind than the brain.

One response to the medical model of mental health – perceiving mental illness as a brain malfunction – can be a reliance on medication. This "quick fix" (though many people who have tried medication can attest that it is often not very quick) can feel more like a temporary relief than a cure. It is a first-order change. This change can diminish capacity or desire to deepen one's understanding of one's own emotions. The experience of painful emotions is not readily understood as due to chemical imbalance or brain malfunction, but this is exactly what mental illness includes. Ideally, it can be more beneficial to ask what problematic behaviors are expressing, what unmet needs may be present, and what we can do in our lives differently to address these behaviorally, cognitively, and emotionally.

188　*Additional Considerations*

Systemic Perspectives of Individual Psychology

Family systems therapy models do not ignore individual psychology and mental health. Remember, the individual is the smallest system according to the foundational ecological theory used in family systems theory's concept of co-occurring systems. In fact, several models specifically look to individual health as indicators of systemic health. Two examples of this are Bowenian multigeneration therapy's attention to *self-differentiation* and internal family systems (IFS) therapy's concept of the Core Self. Amid these is also the idea of the relational self, which is founded in identity theory. These are three ways the autonomous self can be central to treatment, even with family systems theory.

Bowenian Self-Differentiation

In Bowen's multigenerational therapy, one of the goals of therapy is to increase one's self-differentiation. Self-differentiation is the pursuit of an identity outside your roles to others. It allows individuals to assert boundaries that enable that identity to grow without influence or hinderance by others. Differentiation is measured as a spectrum; at one end is complete individuality, at the other is complete enmeshment and sense of togetherness. The greater one's sense of individuality, the more differentiated a person is. Differentiation also includes responsibility for self: "thinking through situations, making decisions, and accepting the consequences of those decisions" (Papero, 2011, 68). Strong critical thinking skills is essential to self-differentiation. This includes awareness of one's subjectivity and how systems influence it.

According to Bowen's theory of change, this is each person's therapeutic goal, even within a systemic client: To increase a sense of self separate from others. Bowen theorizes symptoms manifest in response to family distress. This level of emotional reactivity is due to a lack of self-differentiation. Bowen titles all versions of distress, all symptomology, as anxiety. This includes various mental illness diagnoses and individual psychology. This anxiety is experienced individually and is treated in therapy by looking at the individual's family history and having the individual practice moderate boundary-setting. This is how Bowenian family therapy considers and addressing individual psychology from a systemic perspective. It is not the only model to do so.

IFS Self-Leadership

IFS is known for its application of internal multiplicity to conceptualize individual mental health. The collection of internal parts has a natural leader – the Core Self. This aspect of oneself is not a part, but something more and different. Like a sun in the solar system, it is not a planet but is an essential piece of the whole. And like the sun, it is the central life force of the system. It demonstrates eight key qualities of a leader: Calmness, curiosity, clarity, compassion, confidence, courage, creativity, and connectedness. When the Self

Role of Individual Psychology 189

is in its proper position of being the leader of the internal system, a person functions optimally. This is called *Self-leadership*.

As the leader of the internal system, the Self is responsible to delegate responsibilities among the parts. It can encourage the parts to maximize the use of their natural abilities. When the parts do not function as they are designed to, these can result in mental illness. When the Self is allowed to lead effectively, each part functions as it is supposed to, using its strengths as needed and leaning on the Self for guidance and support. This can help decrease or eliminate problematic symptomology. When the Self and the internal system work as designed, it allows that person to interact with their external environment, including other people and systems, more effectively. In this way, as with other models of family therapy, individual psychology is essential to systemic functionality.

The Relational Self

The *relational self* could be considered the ideal balance of individuality and togetherness. Bowen's modality assumes more individuality is healthier, and IFS believes in the innate systemic existence of the individual. The conceptualization of the relational self finds balance between the two by focusing on microsystemic influence. However, it is not the same as codependence, which lacks personal identity overall. Relational self differs from the individual self, which neglects relationships or context, and the collectivist self, which considers more macro- and chronosystems.

Remember, microsystems are the direct relationships we have. This balance of individual and systemic identity emphasizes personality, personal attributes, and role-based identity traits. It considers the context of directly relevant meaningful relationships. These include familial relationships but are not exclusive to them. Reflect on the early psychological theory of symbolic interactionism. We create our reality through our experiences, including relationships, and how we perceive others to perceive us. The latter highlights the overlap of the intrapersonal and interpersonal. People can listen to the thoughts, feelings, and behaviors of others and personalize them, experiencing them vicariously to create one's own meaning-making. Additionally, people evaluate themselves in comparison of others and may change their thoughts, feelings, and behaviors accordingly. With this in mind, remember that the self can only exist in context with others. Personal identity, the Self, exists only in context of our history and present context. This demonstrates how the self is innately relational.

The relational self impacts several areas of life (Kağıtçıbaşı, 1996). This includes a person's affect and emotions, goals and motives, self-regulation, and interpersonal skills. It strives to contextualize one's psychological experiences and meaning-making that contribute to personality development. This again highlights how personality develops over life, often through experience. Experiences occur in all stages of life from infancy through elderhood. The relational Self constantly seeks to be its best Self, similar to IFS. Therefore, this personal assessment and reflection is essential for the relational Self. It is an

190 *Additional Considerations*

amalgamation of one's self-aspects built through self-perception and perception of others over time. This balance of past and present and individuality and sense of shared togetherness all play into the family systems theory concepts covered in this book; they are not removed from individual psychology, nor vice versa.

Family Systems Theory Concepts Overlapping Individual Psychology

It would be inaccurate to treat individual psychology as opposite or vastly different from family systems theory concepts. Alfred Adler, a foundational observer of individual psychology, noted several systemic concepts interwoven into individual identity. As the smallest ecological system, individual psychology is a pivotal variable to consider in systemic health. It is present and influential in all the family systems concepts addressed thus far: Wholeness, communication, context, co-occurring systems, boundaries, and circular causality.

Wholeness and Individual Psychology

From the very beginning, we talked about the holon – the whole within the whole. The same can be said in tandem with individual psychology. Each person is a complete and complex being. This remains true when people are also parts of a whole. While we are inevitably linked together as a system, we are also free to act as we please within the system. Parts of the whole are connected constantly through feedback loops – the individual is a function of the system and the system as a conceptualization of the individuals within it.

Cooley (1902) wrote, "the person and society are two sides of the same coin," and asserted "people perceive themselves through the eyes of others, particularly important others" (qtd. in Chen et al., 2006, p. 152). In being part of a significant system, we adopt those principles into our identity. Individual psychology is impacted by the sense of belonging one has within different systems of which we are members. How that belonging is communicated, to what extent one belongs, can be part of communication between the individuals in the system.

Communication and Individual Psychology

Individual psychology presents in communication through individual meaning-making. Earlier I identified the contributors to communication and similar places that communication fails. So often that is due to the meaning-making each individual has toward the conversation, the other person(s), and their relationship with the other person(s). When meaning is different from person to person, it can make communication challenging as people make different assumptions about the motivations, intentions, and ideas of the other person. We ascribe different meanings to different behaviors, thoughts,

Role of Individual Psychology   191

and emotions based on personal history. Meaning-making does not happen in seclusion; it is influenced by external systems, both big and small, past and present. But it occurs and manifests in the individual mind and psychology. Therefore, individual psychology is essential to address meaning-making in communication in systems.

Context and Individual Psychology

Symptoms of individual mental health serve a purpose in social context. That is to say, all things make sense in context, including individual decisions and reactions that may not immediately appear sensible. Context is everything because individuals are socially embedded. Therefore, individual beliefs and values – and the behaviors, thoughts, and emotions that accompany them – stem from their social context. Gestalt theorists call this *"figure and ground"*: Systemically, we observe individual choices (figure) as part of their context (ground). Adler also gives abundant attention to context. He asserts it would be unscientific – an incomplete picture – to study people without taking their context into consideration.

Context includes constructivism – the fluid experience of reality that is central to postmodernism. This perspective rejects the ability to perceive absolute, objective truth. Instead, all reality is subjective truth. It is, in the words of Rudolf Dreikurs (1972), an associate of Alfred Adler, an approximation. People construct their own reality. Adler observed that one's beliefs and attitudes are built on one's experience of reality. Additionally, individual context influences a person's ideas, thoughts, meanings, and creativity. Adlerians call this the *creative self* – the subjective perspective of oneself and others in a systemic context, full of interpretations and meaning-making within each interaction with the world around us. It relates to how individuals develop a unique worldview, including perspectives on mental health and its management.

Co-occurring Systems and Individual Psychology

Co-occurring systems overlap with both wholeness and context in how it utilizes individual psychology. Personal identities are formed by individual attributes and role-based self-conceptualization. The self is naturally interdependent; people are naturally relational. When we view ourselves, it is often through the roles we play in conjunction with others. Remember social interaction theory related to roles? A teacher requires a student; parents require a child; leaders require subordinates. One's sense of identity as an individual cannot be fully removed from one's identity within the different systems with which we belong.

However, it can be a source of individual distress when we are members of a system but do not identify with its espoused values and beliefs. This can cause psychological anguish as a person attempts to balance these two juxtaposing ideas. Such a personal process leans heavily into how individual psychology and the systemic concept of boundaries intersect.

192   *Additional Considerations*

Boundaries and Individual Psychology

It might be difficult to see the bridge between boundaries and individual psychology because boundaries automatically require the presence of someone else for whom we are setting that boundary. However, remember that the purpose of boundaries is to balance a sense of individuality and togetherness. Individuals, not systems, define for themselves their preferred levels of cohesion. Individuals, not systems, hold and change hierarchical boundaries to be appropriate for them. Every single person in the system can implement change in a system. This includes asserting their desired boundaries, whether those be separate or connected.

Individual psychology also relates closely with adaptability. The circumplex model's conceptualization of adaptability portrays a range from rigid to chaotic, balanced within structure and flexibility. As a system uses these to cope with change, system members cope through personal *resilience*. Resilience is part of individual psychology. It is the ability to "bounce back" to a state of normalcy after or during a stressor without psychological deterioration. It is, in a word, personal morphogenesis. Resilience is associated with personal hardiness, positive emotions and affect, positive self-esteem, extraversion, self-efficacy, and spirituality (Schwarz, 2018). Resilience is also affected by larger systemic factors such as socioeconomic status, financial and communal resources and perspectives, education level, and microsystemic support. Therefore, individual adaptability, like other forms of individual psychology, remains systemic.

Adler says humanity and society continuously adapt and transform toward a goal, seeking balance between stability in change. He calls this pursuit of equilibrium. This adaptability, shifting between accepting and rejecting influence, ties closely to circular causality.

Circular Causality and Individual Psychology

Circularity occurs in the direct interactions of individual people and wider systems. It is a sense of mutual influence in relationships – recursion. Adler was mindful of this interconnectedness. He asserted that circularity is not contrary to self-determinism, or individual meaning-making of experiences. If anything, the complex circular relationship between systems is proof of self-determinism because it demonstrates the influence relationships have on individual psychology. That being said, "We are not just links in a circular chain of events; we are people with names who experience ourselves as centers of initiative" (Nichols, 1984, p. 35).

Change – morphogenetic shifts – occurs in shifts of the individual's behavior, thoughts, and emotional reactivity. Systemic change begins with individual change. Systemic psychology begins and continues in individual psychology. Therefore, we as systemic thinkers must be respectful of the individuals in the system, treating them as the autonomous, whole beings they are, with all the potential for change held within them.

Role of Autonomy in a System

What is autonomy in the context of individual psychology and mental health? It is the self-determined balance of individuality and communal identity. Autonomy is not the antitheses to relationship or intimacy. While Bowen considers more individuality to be desirable, he also recognizes that a person cannot feasibly be fully individualized. Complete autonomy is impossible because, as context says, we are inevitably influenced by our systemic interactions from a very young age. This includes prior to hippocampal development, or before formal memory can occur. Even then, we are influenced by our environment and our relationships. Therefore, we cannot remove all contributions from our systems because it is more deeply engrained than we are consciously aware.

So what is the ideal balance of individuality and togetherness? According to research, the ideal balance will still be a range. There is not one perfect balance that fits all people. Each person must have the autonomy to determine what the ideal balance is for them based on their experience and their desired relationship dynamics. This necessitates a personal belief system, including a personal sense of morality and responsibility. Autonomy includes recognizing personal responsibility and contributions to both problems and solutions instead of displacing those onto others. Similarly, a sense of autonomy can create personal investment toward desired change or outcome both at micro- and macrosystemic levels – in families and in societies.

Individual Psychology in the Microsystem

Human behavior can be indicative of internal processes, including meaning-making and personality. How a person's personality develops and their meaning-making processes are influenced by our microsystemic interactions. In the microsystem, it is important to remember that the system and the self are two ways to describe people's lives; they cannot be separated as dichotomous. When you work with an individual, you influence the microsystem. That means problematic interactions contribute to the individual psychological symptoms being maintained.

The Palo Alto Team discovered this in their studies with families including individuals with schizophrenia. Family systems theory does not believe interactions cause mental illness, but interactions can perpetuate it. The symptomatic behaviors of the individual made sense in the context of pathological family communication. The individual's psychosis reflects the system's "crazy-making" environment and interactions. It no longer works to banish the problem person under the guise of doing so to improve family functioning. When the individual returns to the system, if the family continues to perceive them in their previous version – symptomatic and problematic – then the patient will not get better. They will return to that previous version because the familial homeostasis demands it. This is not personal failure; it is human nature. It is a reflection of microsystemic norms colliding with individual psychology.

194 *Additional Considerations*

Our thoughts and perspectives are inevitably influenced by others. This is particularly true in those with whom we directly interact – our microsystems. We cannot be entirely independent, but we decide to what extent others influence our decision-making. How individual autonomy is respected by system members is a part of circularity – respecting individual autonomy encourages the balance of individuality and togetherness; discouraging autonomy can result in the extremes of cohesion (disengagement and enmeshment). From the lens of attachment theory, secure attachment allows for autonomy because it recognizes emotional and physical distance is not a threat to the relationship.

Microsystemic relationships are how we initially learn values and belief systems. Even among a family, personal belief systems create a sense of individuality and autonomy. This belief system can be a means of resilience and adaptability; therefore, autonomy means relying less on others to cope. One's sense of togetherness with family can help build resilience and diminish role strain and overload along with coping during life stressors, both routine and irregular. Family ties can actually be strengthened by increased autonomy as we get older, shifting from adolescence to young adulthood and especially into middle adulthood. Autonomy can actually help families function better together.

Individual Psychology in the Macrosystem

Cultural pressures influence individuals, which influences the system. Pressures of the macrosystem – expectations based on one's sex, age, ethnicity, or career; economic distress; and technological developments – influence the individual. How people view us impacts us, whether we want that to be true or not. It potentially impacts how we view ourselves. Additionally, it can create an illusion of what Carl Jung would call a sense of otherness that separates one person from another:

> The us-against-them attitude is a consequence of deemphasizing the human side of human beings. Sometimes we must recognize collective entities – family systems, communities, nations – but we need not dehumanize them by forgetting that they are made up of individuals. When we are sympathetic to and respectful of the individuals who make up families, we make them our allies, not our enemies.
>
> (Nichols, 1984, p. 20)

Systems are made up of individuals. While the whole is greater than the sum of these parts, it is also essential to remember each of those individuals is a complex being with their own motivations, defenses, and sense of identity. David Shapiro, a renowned poet and literary critic from the United States, has said, "The functions of the organism – or the activity of the organism as a whole – are regulated by processes internal to it. These processes confer a certain degree of autonomy...and endow the organism with a range of adaptability" (qtd. in Nichols, 1984, p. 145). This adaptability is essential to

Role of Individual Psychology   195

personal and systemic development and may be the central focus of potential psychological treatment.

Treating Individuals with Family Systems Theory

Marriage and family therapists, who frequently utilize family systems theory, are able to see groups, romantic relationships, families, and individuals as clients. As evidenced by the content of this chapter, systemic perspectives are still applicable when working with individuals. This is because, phrased differently, we work with individuals when we work with relationships, too. And individuals are incredibly powerful.

Individual dynamics and family transactions are two sides of the same issue; we can potentially approach treatment from either angle and create space for meaningful change. However, this must be done wisely as there is such a complex relationship between the two: "Lasting change takes place through a spiraling process of altered [interpersonal] interactions and enriched [personal] understanding" (Nichols, 1984, p. 65). As we begin to discuss the balance of individuality and systemic inclusion in psychotherapy, consider the plethora of ways people have meaning-making around pursuing and receiving therapy as individuals or as a family system. Exploring this is also part of the therapeutic relationship that contextualizes treatment for the client.

An additional consideration is identifying the goal(s) for treatment. This can include the absence of a problem and/or the presence of a preferred future. Both individually and systemically, it is essential to differentiate symptom management (absence of a problem) and symptom alleviation (presence of preferred future). Symptom management focuses on decreasing symptoms but anticipates their inevitable return. Symptom alleviation, on the other hand, would have symptoms decrease with the hope the client will reach a place of no longer having them. Remember though, others' attitudes toward the client's ability to overcome their diagnosis and/or symptoms makes a difference in their perceived ability to do so. This is an example of circularity and feedback loops.

In my exploration of individual therapy without a systemic perspective, I learned about coping skills as a common psychotherapy tactic to deal with problems. Basic fully individualized psychology would have you believe coping skills are a collection of behavioral practices a client can pick from their cognitive tool box to manage their mental health symptom in the moment. However, I propose a different definition. Coping skills are indeed tools, but they are not just behaviors. They can be thoughts and emotions; they include external resources and internal, such as how a person talks to and about themselves. It also includes intentional practices of how they talk to and about their significant relationships. Coping is not emotional suppression. It is the ability to address the problematic thought, behavior, or feeling without being overwhelmed by it.

In addition to common individual-based interventions like emphasizing coping skills (which would likely only offer first-order change), there are

196 *Additional Considerations*

common assumed individual-based presenting problems. Examples include anger management, anxiety management, sexual dysfunction, addiction, grief, trauma processing, and personal growth. Many of these can be treated systemically but typically are not. In this section, I will explore how we will incorporate individual psychology in systemic psychotherapy.

Generally speaking, psychotherapy can be divided into three phases: Assessment, intervention, and termination or conclusion of treatment. The assessment process is not exclusive to the beginning phase of psychotherapy. Throughout the therapeutic relationship, the therapist will learn new information about the client that could impact the direction and duration of treatment. Similarly, the assessment phase can in-and-of itself be an intervention. Therefore, while the stages may appear linear, we must always be mindful of the inherently circular nature of all things, including the therapeutic process.

Systemic Considerations in the Assessment Phase

In the beginning phase of therapy, the therapist frequently collects background information of the client. This can include information about family-of-origin, current relationships, past treatment received, past and current problem conceptualization and overcoming, and other relevant information. During this time, the therapist is assessing for the problem outside a specific individual. Remember, per systems theory, a person is not the problem. This is part of the nonpathologizing stance; a person can have symptoms rather than overidentify with them. There will be ongoing reassessment of the source of distress. During assessment, the therapist is also listening for the balance of internal experience interacting with external relationships and fluctuating perceptions of reality. These are demonstrated through observable or described systemic communication and circularity. All three are understood as aspects of the client's context and provide insight for the therapist about how to approach the next phase of psychotherapy.

Systemic Application in Individual Intervention

As said earlier, when working with an individual, systemic influence remains present. Therefore, it may be appropriate to try and consider systemic influence wherever possible, particularly the family-of-origin and nuclear family systems. Adler acknowledges family interactions as highly influential to individual psychology. In treatment, he encouraged exploration of family constellations (the role or niche each person fills in the system), sibling dynamics and birth order position, parental relationships (what was observed, experienced, and possibly replicated), social roles (larger systemic considerations), and feedback loops. Overall, Adler would proport that if the family cannot or will not be present in session, they can still be included in session content and processing the individual's emotional experience of that content.

Throughout this interventive phase of psychotherapy, it is the therapist's ethical responsibility to treat clients with their context in mind, including their family and systems. To treat the client as if they lived in a vacuum of influence would be inauthentic and, frankly, unrealistic and unhelpful. When we work with individuals or systems, we balance attention to both individual psychology and interaction patterns. We must be mindful of these multiple levels of what it means to be alive, what it means to belong, and what it means to pursue happiness.

A Final Note on Therapist Responsibilities

In every phase of therapy, the therapist must remember they do not create change, they create space for it. Similarly, "systems don't change; people change" (Nichols, 1984, p. 38). Therapists can initiate change, systems can experience change, but the ones actually doing the change are the individuals within the system. Do not lose sight of individual personalities and influence in pursuit of systemic understanding. Be careful not to limit your eyes to only see interactions; this is as misleading as ignoring them. This could also result in missing a significant contributor to the externalized problem. To work with individuals from a systemic lens may require they "but in" to systems thinking. They must be willing to perceive the problem and potential solution(s) in a new way. As with change, this receptivity occurs on an individual basis.

Lastly, consider the therapy space and relationship as another system in which the individual(s) are members. Therapists do our best to create a space of safety and openness, but even this occurs in context. Turning toward therapy is no longer synonymous to turning away from stressors outside the walls of the therapist office. Like with work and home lives, "leave it at the door" is not as feasible as some may wish it to be. Be patient. Be tenacious. And through it all, be mindful of the balance of external and internal experience – of interpersonal relationship dynamics and intrapersonal meaning-making of both the client and yourself.

Another Resource to Consider

Michael Nichols wrote *The Self in the System: Expanding the Limits of Family Therapy* specifically about individual psychology addressed in the system. It is worth a read. It looks at the importance of individual psychology in second-order change. If we only aim to address dysfunctional behavior patterns, we risk making merely superficial changes – first-order changes. Instead, we must explore the depths of the dysfunctional behavior, including the meaning-making of the individuals involved in it. Meaningful change can only be achieved through individual psychology. Individual psychology is how we understand coping skills, resilience, and a sense of self within the system. We are not merely parts of the system, we are holons – wholes – within it.

11 Cultural Considerations of Family Systems Theory

Prior to writing this book, I read through several of the primary texts on family systems theory. This included works by Murray Bowen, Jay Haley, Don Jackson, Richard Fisch, Salvador Minuchin, Charles Fishman, Paul Watzlawick, and John Weakland. Between these men – predominantly Caucasian from the United States, New Zealand, Austria, and Argentina –consideration of the client's culture was conspicuously absent. It might have been acknowledged as part of the client's context, but exploration of its influence was minimal at most. This chapter is written with that in mind. First, I will explore in greater depth how we can mindfully acknowledge the theory's initial limitations without dismissing it as a whole. Second, I will reconsider how culture impacts each of the core concepts of family systems theory, even if not originally validated.

Defining Culture

Often when people think of cultural diversity, they specifically think of ethnic diversity. However, culture is more than this. The American Psychological Association (APA) defines *culture* as "the distinctive customs, values, beliefs, knowledge, art, and language of a society or a community." These are passed down across generations and can be separated within particular groups in society including professions, social class, age classifications, and even culturally divided perceptions of mental health and socially acceptable behaviors (popular culture, cancel culture). They inherently include the presence of subcultures designated by differing details of the culture such as sexual and gender identities, disabilities, and education. Larger cultural and social constructs can include religious culture, ethnicity, regional geography, and nationality.

There is more than one way to study and assess culture. Cultural psychology is the specific study of how one's culture influences the psychological well-being of its members. That is to say, how a macrosystem influences the microsystem and individual system. There is also cross-cultural psychology, which looks at themes of human behavior and cognitions that are not restricted to the members of one macrosystem or another. Instead, the traits might permeate throughout multiple cultures, though perhaps are labeled and treated differently. Let me next articulate the differences between cultural awareness, sensitivity, and competence (Hastings, 2002):

DOI: 10.4324/9781003088196-15

- ***Cultural awareness***: Intellectual mindfulness; knowledgeable cognizance of differences between cultures. Clinically this can include the cultures of both the client and clinician.
- ***Cultural sensitivity***: Affective mindfulness; intentional appreciation and respect toward various cultures.
- ***Cultural competence***: Combined knowledge of, empathy for, and experience with specific cultures. With this combination, a clinician may better be present and process with clients of various cultures and subcultures, even those with which the therapist is not themselves a member. Part of competence is constant learning and openness to increasing one's awareness and sensitivity and, as a result, one's competence.

With these distinctions in mind, let's review how those applying family systems theory concepts can move from awareness to sensitivity to competence. While there are many facets to culture, one of the most influential that is experienced globally is the difference between collectivistic and individualistic cultures.

Individualistic and Collectivistic Cultures

Collectivistic cultures/societies typically are distinguished by how their parts prioritize systemic well-being – or really, systemic peace or homeostasis – over that of the individual. It can also be experienced as prioritizing the well-being of others over oneself. Inversely, as the name implies, individualistic cultures focus on individual functionality with the assumption that individual well-being will result in systemic well-being. Both of these are versions of isomorphism; elements of one system replicate in others, such as microsystem to macrosystem, familial to cultural norms, and vice versa.

Another difference between individual and collective cultures could be distinguished as hierarchical collectivism and egalitarian individualism. In the hierarchical collectivism, a person's identity is rooted in their roles; there is prominent respect for harmony and order and emphasis on obedience to authority and self-restraint. Egalitarian individualism, on the other hand, fuels identity through personal qualities and achievements, and places greater importance on equality and democratic representation (Christman, 2004).

Collectivistic cultures often have very defined social hierarchies (Shen, 2020). This can result in greater perceived authoritarian leadership that does not allow for questioning of their rules and roles. Common examples of collectivistic cultures are east Asian cultures, the Middle East, and Greece. It is worth noting that compared to the white citizens of the United States, many moderate individualistic cultures such as Italian and Latinx cultures may appear collectivist. Collectivistic cultures identify positive traits of individuals to include generosity, selflessness, helpfulness, and dependability. On the other hand, western psychology emphasizes personal agency, independent thinking, and freedom of speech. It can go on to include idealized versions of self-perception, attachment, parenting styles, even romantic relationship expectations. Individualism tends to appear in western European cultures,

200   *Additional Considerations*

such as Germany and Ireland, and global locations previously colonized by the west, such as Australia and South Africa.

Concepts such as fairness also are dissimilar. Rather than language of equity, collectivistic fairness emphasizes the responsibility to respond to inequity with virtue. This demonstrates exactly why family systems theory ideas of balance can be so difficult to cross cultures – balance can have different meaning to different people. This culturally normalized imbalance can result in a culture-wide minimization of self:

> What is supposed to be a principled act, stemming from a firm interior consciousness of the self, often becomes an act that responds to external demands and other-oriented, being sensitive to others' opinions, standards, and criticisms, and trying hard to conform in order to give a good impression to others rather than intrinsically motivated.
>
> (Cheung & Chan, 2002, p. 215–216)

This perspective normalizes, even praises, suffering at the cost of self, perhaps indefinitely. This idea is not exclusive to collectivistic cultures and is becoming increasingly present in individualistic cultures, too.

The two are not as separate as some may perceive; instead, collectivism and individualism could be viewed as the two extremes on a spectrum with most cultures falling somewhere in between. In fact, there could be three points of extremes. Cultures must balance individual values, family values, and culture-wide values. Arguably, this balance is exactly where family systems theory has not properly considered collectivistic values in its design.

Using Family Systems Theory with Collectivism in Mind

As said earlier, family systems theory was designed in a western culture. Some models of therapy have demonstrated effectivity with white audiences – cognitive-behavioral therapy (CBT) and emotion-focused therapy (EFT), in particular, have heavily relied on Caucasian participants in their research sample. However, instead of throwing the models, or family systems theory, out all together as irrelevant, I propose an alternative. Knowledge is passed down through tradition and education from one generation to another. It is the responsibility of the listeners to be critical consumers of the messages it receives. Similarly, listeners must be mindful of what information may be left out by the speaker for various reasons. As systemic thinkers, we must consider the systemic features (rules, roles, etc.) that contribute to how cultural attributes are portrayed moving from one generation to another. We must *contextualize* the information we receive. This will determine how we use the information and potentially apply it in clinical settings.

Constructivism is an example of culture. What it means to have a gender, ethnicity, religious identity, and other identifiers vary depending on perception. That perception, however, is impacted by the societal norms that delineate one culture from another. We must remain respectful as we bring

Cultural Considerations 201

the western philosophy of family systems theory, such as interventions from Bowen and Satir, to collectivistic cultures.

Bowen's Self-Differentiation in Collectivistic Cultures

As mentioned earlier, family systems theory was designed in a western culture that praises individuality. This is evident in the continued dominating narrative in the Unites States that mental well-being is bound in individual psychology and the medical model. Bowen's multigenerational approach ironically bridges this gap. It both considers the wounds and strengths that generations pass down to one another and idealizes differentiation of self from that family as the means of healing. He goes so far as to say the more individuation, the better. He acknowledges that perfect, complete individuation is impossible to achieve but asserts this should be a therapeutic aim nonetheless.

The Bowenian concept of intergenerational transmission includes the idea that people typically remain in the same approximate range of differentiation as what is observed and experienced in the family-of-origin. That is to say, individuals who come from families with poor differentiation – those with high enmeshment or disengagement or prominent maladaptive behaviors – tend to also have low self-differentiation themselves. Low levels of differentiation are also associated with relational and personal dysfunctionality including daily stress, anxiety and depression, high emotional reactivity or cut-offs, somatic and obsessive-compulsive symptomology. People tend to be drawn to others, including potential romantic partners, with similar levels of differentiation. This could also be true across cultures; people may be drawn to those of similar cultural experiences – religiosity, socioeconomic status, education, career path, or ethnicity, for example – due to similar levels of differentiation those facets of identity experience and express. However, this is not consistently demonstrated or explored in research.

It could be considered shortsighted to assume increasing one's sense of individual identity away from other systems and its members is the solution to one's problems. At the very least, it is one-sided. For many people, this is true; emotional fusion with system members is a breach of boundaries that results in discomfort and even resentment. However, this is not always true, particularly in more collectivistic cultures.

Most studies on Bowenian concepts are predominantly Caucasian samples and almost all are based in the United States. However, a study out of South Korea found that familial enmeshment was not associated with individual dysfunction. Instead, high fusion and high levels of self-differentiation not only coexisted but actually improved family functioning (Kim et al., 2014). In another study, Korean adolescents also showed positive correlations between family fusion and higher self-esteem (Chun & McDermid, 1997). A study of Italian adolescents found more family fusion did not correlate with anxiety or depressive symptoms. In an additional study with Filipino families, fusion with family members was not related to psychological distress (Tuason & Friedlander, 2000). All of these examples disprove Bowen's original theory of

202 *Additional Considerations*

linear correlation between self-differentiation and emotional attunement with one's systems. Of course, these are also further complicated by the legitimacy of assessment measures across cultures and whether or not these studies used culturally valid and reliable tools with non-white participants. Research frequently runs into such concerns across many fields in social sciences, including marriage and family therapy.

This is just one example of how family systems theory's conceptual origins could be considered limited by its individualistic origins. However, with intentionality, the two are not so juxtaposed. There can be culturally defined self-differentiation, particularly related to fusion with others. The same could be said in Satir's therapeutic intervention tactics.

Satir's Experiential Systemic Work in Collectivistic Cultures

Virginia Satir was one of the members of the early Mental Research Institute (MRI) team that created and revolutionized systemic therapy. She focused on the power of experience and immediate interaction. However, she still did these from a western philosophical lens. Despite this, collectivistic cultures have adapted her work to be considerate of collective-cultural norms. This posed a few challenges. Satir's work is still rooted in the American dream: Egalitarianism; individual uniqueness; individual capacity for change and growth; the essential role of self-discovery and self-fulfillment in pursuit of self-esteem; and free expression.

Satir's method of exploring and creating self-fulfillment includes work toward personal congruence. She calls this congruence between self, other, and context. To achieve this, Satir breaks congruence down to three levels, all of which can relate to cultural mindfulness:

> *Level (I) Feelings. Focus on awareness, acknowledgement, ownership, management, and enjoyment.* Be aware of your own emotions, how others may experience your emotions, how others experience their emotions, and how you experience the emotions of others. Acknowledge and own your role in those (relates to circular causality); manage that which is within your control; and pursue understanding, peace, and enjoyment within yourself, with others, and appropriately in context.
>
> *Level (II) The self ("I am"). Focus on centeredness, wholeness, and harmony.* This level of increased mindfulness emphasizes self-awareness moving into sensitivity and consideration. It seeks to be centered, whole, and harmonious within oneself as one interacts with other people and other contexts, including other cultures. That is to say, this level focuses on congruence within oneself in order to interact authentically and congruently with others. Be authentic but aware how your self-perception will differ from how others perceive you based on their own balance of self, other, and context. Remember, in their mental space, you are the other and they are the self.

Cultural Considerations 203

***Level (III) Life-force.** Focus on a sense of universality and spirituality.* I refer to spirituality as a sense of *existential belonging.* This level aims to move beyond awareness and sensitivity and specifically aims to build bridges through a shared desire for safety and belonging among all peoples. This perspective can aim for congruence between self and others, finding common ground and building off that rather than focusing on differences. It is rooted in compassion as Satir's core quality in empathic communication.

Satir's emphasis on congruence between self, others, and context includes cultural context. Satir is mindful of cultural context, that is, sensitivity to the demands of culture. For example, she acknowledges how the family, particularly parents, teach children cultural values and family values. They teach children how to live and work with others, the importance of and means to fit and belong, and how to cope with demands of cultural expectations such as getting a job, being respectful, develop self-reliance, and the like. The family, uniquely, determines what all of these ideally look like and how to instill those values. Cultures will have different ideas of how to do this, such as parenting tactics of shame and praise, consequences through rewards and punishments, and how love is expressed or withheld.

Satir's model also addresses stress, a global phenomenon and perceived source of problems. However, her methods to address stress are quite individualistic. Directly confronting challenges and directly identifying assets of resilience are rooted in individualism. In one study out of Hong Kong, researchers noted in a culture that is rigid, some participants struggled to express themselves overtly because this contradicted their cultural norms. It felt unnatural to outright express appreciation and gratitude toward microsystem members. Discussions about and with family are viewed as intimate, private, and difficult to share. This difficultly could be due to cultural minimization of individual thought and emotional expression. It seemed to discourage choice-making without familial input; directly facing conflict was counterintuitive to the participants. Therefore, even as Satir's model works to identify strengths of self and others, it continues to be steeped in culturally meaningful assumptions that can be addressed sensitively.

In a purist version, Satir's growth model uses six individualistic assumptions. With flexibility, it allows collectivistic cultures to maintain their values while broadening them, too:

1   Permission for "both/and" language rather than "either/or," therefore allowing exploration of hierarchical rulings without necessarily attempting to challenge or overthrow them. Instead, the pursuit is understanding, which is a prerequisite for meaningful change.
2   People can appreciate their cultural and familial roles rather than feel pressured to change them. We can view them as conformity for the sake of survival and inclusion. They still allow for unique individual strengths and grant permission to offer self-validation and self-valuing.

204 *Additional Considerations*

3   In a relationship of equals, people will serve and instruct one another in different contexts. Therefore, even between perceived equals, people will alternate between serving and receiving roles. Similarly, we can explore with collective cultures how, even in a defined hierarchy, multiple parties can be both a servant and leader in different contexts.

4   People can respect sameness (thinking, feeling, and act like one another to meet external norms) and differences. The challenge is to discover within oneself when or where there are problems in those norms, where they are dysfunctional. This can allow people to make discoveries about oneself and others and their extent of influence in the system.

5   Rather than there only being one right way to live and exist, many options are present. There may be an expert – maybe! – but you are allowed to critically assess that. This can be understandably challenging in highly rigid settings and should be approached with respectful pacing for those who struggle with this idea.

6   Look beyond the face of an experience to understand its context and numerous contributing factors, not just accepting an authority's version of events. Like the previous note, this can be challenging when it contradicts lifelong, even multigenerational, messages.

Through these six assumptions, Satir's growth model strives to bridge collective thought with individual capacities.

Even the call to address these overtly is a very eurocentric approach that leans on being direct and openly discussing a potentially uncomfortable topic. As therapists, we must be cautious any time we bring western, individualistic ideas to other cultures. We must be mindful of the colonizer/colonized dynamic that already exists and asserts a lingering power imbalance. This can influence a person's receptivity to family systems theory as one that originated in a white, western culture. Adaptation and respectful consideration are key. As we now look at how each family systems theory concept, we must be mindful of how others may hear these messages as contradictory to their values and instead highlight their commonalities and practicalities, not just differences. Therefore, let us approach each family systems theory concept with this same mentality. Let's look at how different aspects of culture play a role in each of the six family systems theory core concepts.

Holism across Cultures

Culture, as one of the largest groupings in the world, "is the unwritten and time-tested norms of how to make meaning in order to succeed within the organization [or setting] and for the organization to succeed as a whole" (Stevenson, 2018a, p. 169). Remember, holistic success depends on the functionality of the holons within it. If we view a culture as the whole, each community, family, and individual within it are holons. These are independently functioning but still interdependent for optimal systemic functioning.

However, collaboration and dependence are not the same as codependence. The parts are able to function independently but acknowledge when and how relationship must be prioritized for independence to thrive. To say it another way, autonomy and relatedness can coexist; they are not just opposing ends of a spectrum.

Individual autonomy and accepting influence from others are not juxtaposing concepts. Bowen says, even in complete individuality, a person must be able to reflect on how others have and continue to influence them. This is particularly true with family-of-origin. Consider a late adolescent who is determined to be nothing like their estranged mother. The young adult speaks angrily of her mother's shortcomings and failures and with tones of bitter determination to do quite different when they become a parent. In this focused attempt to be different from their mother, the person is still responding to and being influenced by the parent. This is particularly evident in their emotional reactivity to the person. According to Bowen, decreased emotional reactivity is proof of strong self-differentiation. That being said, it is important to recognize how this young adult's parent influenced them as a whole. Despite what the late adolescent thinks, pretending the mother never existed is not the solution. Instead, the person could reflect on how the experience contributes to their autonomy now, for better or for worse.

In the ideal world, autonomy and relatedness more than coexist; they cooperate together. Rather than treating autonomy as a lack of interconnectedness with others, let's view it as a personal sense of agency (Benito-Gomez et al., 2020). This logically leads to the next question – What is the purpose of agency? In individualistic cultures, it is to achieve personal goals. In more collectivistic cultures, it aims to achieve interpersonal goals (Manzi et al., 2006). Systemic goals can vary based on cultural norms, too. In individualistic cultures, these can be to accomplish mutually beneficial achievements, possibly through compromise and collaboration. In collectivistic cultures, systemic goals lean into obedience, loyalty, and belonging. Therefore, a sense of wholeness within the system may require a balance of these – personal and interpersonal achievements, mutual and exchanging benefits. Success in each holon in addition to the whole.

Treating each holon functioning as an island – uninfluenced and uninfluential – is not realistic. It is important to allow different holons to explore their own sense of balance between individuality and togetherness – both in the family and culture. For example, in some families and cultures, the previous provided definitions of nuclear and extended families may be more blended than it seems. Some cultures value extended family, even those not related by blood, as immediate members of the family. This is often due to the pervasiveness of their presence and influence. For example, family-of-origin figures and family friends may live in the home; contribute to chores, finances, or childrearing; and provide a sense of extended family that is quite central to daily functioning. These extended family members greatly contribute to the nuclear family's sense of wholeness. Therefore, their contributions should not be discounted.

Culture Influencing Communication

Communication style invariably varies depending on the system. This is true in systems of every size, from the macrosystem, such as cultural groups, to the smallest system, the immediate self. Communication serves the purpose of expressing oneself, one's needs, and one's understanding of others and their needs. In western cultures, there is frequently emphasis on congruent communication – using compatible words, tone, and body language to convey a single message. Congruent communication would be juxtaposed by the double-bind, or mixed message that is convoluted by incongruence between verbal and nonverbal communication. In some cultures, incongruence is not viewed as problematic, perhaps because it is so common to set aside oneself in the interest of appeasing others. However, I propose a different perception of congruence that would allow it to be both individualized and communal.

Congruence considers all facets of communication, including oneself, one's relationship with whom they are speaking, and the context of the interaction. It does not prioritize self over other or context. Instead, it allows space to explore all three as contributing factors to communication patterns and relationships as they are and how the members would like it to be. It acknowledges the importance of the relationship and making that relationship function better. It does not get much more systemic than that! To love and value others best, we must also love and value ourselves. To love ourselves best, we must consider how we love and value others – including how we communicate that message.

Different cultures can have different perspectives on appropriate types and extent of communication. For example, per Satir, communication should strive to be clear, direct, specific, honest, respectful, and freely expressed. All of these are entrenched in western values of individual expression over systemic comfort. However, in some cultures, such as China, direct conflict is avoided because it is viewed as unhelpfully aggressive. Part of cultural sensitivity and competence includes being mindful of these cultural differences in the nuances of communication practices.

One of the most pointed examples of this is cultural implications of silence (Shearer, 2020). Remember from the principles of communication, not speaking still communicates something. You cannot not communicate. Different cultures ascribe different meaning to silence in conversation. Western individualistic cultures frequently struggle with accepting silence as part of conversive norms; they can become uncomfortable within a few seconds of silence between people. Conversely, social collectivistic cultures such as some Asian cultures can frequently tolerate a minute or two of silence before becoming uncomfortable. Familial collectivistic cultures such as Latinx and Italian cultures can have such a disdain for silence that their conversational contributions overlap one another – they talk over and interrupt each other – for a constant flow of sound with minimal to no silence between them.

Cultures, not just ethnicities, can be divided between listening and speaking cultures. These can often seem parallel with individualistic as speaking and

Cultural Considerations 207

collectivistic as listening, but this is not always the case. In more hierarchical cultures, age and sex can also be a prevalent division between listener and speaker. In many societies, communication from one's elders is treated as wise and contributions from more senior peoples are treated with greater reverence than those offered by younger system members. In patriarchal societies, messages from men are treated with greater respect. Even in some societies that identify as egalitarian; these underlying patterns can resist pure democratic representation and speech. This can be attributed to the role power plays in communication. Those in power carry the privilege to speak unencumbered. This power differential can present in numerous ways, but one of the most obvious is through speech and silence. This will be further explored in the section for boundaries below.

Context of Culture, Culture in Context

This entire chapter could probably be summarized as this section – take culture, all levels and types of culture, into consideration. From Chapter 6, we described context as the physical and emotional space in which communication takes place. Culture is part of both of those. Attitudes toward familial cohesiveness in collectivistic societies versus individualistic societies and how this context may influence treatment goals and how "ideal" relationships look. For example, ideal relationships with and discipline of children will vary in different cultures and contexts:

> In low-include and/or rural context, children have economic utility, as they contribute economically to the family when they are young…. Hence, in a family where children have an economic and instrumental value, high independence of children is discouraged, while loyalty, belonging, and interdependence are promoted.
>
> (Erdem & Safi, 2018, p. 474)

This is also an example of differentiating individualistic and collectivistic norms in context. One of the challenges of individualistic cultures understanding collectivistic cultures is recognizing the distinction between self in the family and self within a culture. Both of these are distinct contexts with different degrees of influence, depending on the system. We can be slightly different people when we are alone, with family, or in different physical and emotional contexts. As Satir covered earlier, incongruence between these can be detrimental. However, the three do not need to be far apart; believing so could be dangerously individualistic to assume. In the study out of China, congruence of self, other, and context is essential but can be discussed gently:

> "Taking other and context into consideration does not mean conforming to the other or to the demands of the context. One learns to be respectful to the other. This does not mean taking care of the feelings of the other,

208 *Additional Considerations*

but rather trusting that the other has the ability to take care of his or her own feelings."

(Cheung & Chan, 2002, p. 212–213)

This can understandably be challenged by hierarchies present, such as giving people in a submissive role permission to speak to those in dominant roles in egalitarian language. Some collectivist cultures normalize keeping to oneself, not drawing attention to oneself. However, Satir would notice that this individual anxiety will eventually impact the system. Therefore, we want to respect their silence while also ensure there is invitation for input.

So what does it mean to take the context of culture into consideration? More than anything, it means to intentionally include conversations about meaning-making. Meaning-making is highly prevalent in the United States culture right now, especially personalizing the opinions of others about broad concepts such as politics or religion. USA citizens can be quick to make assumptions about others based on their faith, political affiliations, geographic location, or even where a person chooses to grocery shop. These can be explored through exception-seeking language, such as deterring the misinformation that assumes one facet of a person's identity makes them a good or bad person. Additionally, therapists can explore microsystemic dysfunction as unclear role expectations often rooted in family-of-origin and cultural differences and possible presence of mismatched levels of acculturation.

It is also possible to use cultural meaning-making as a source of strength. Strategic family therapy uses culture as context for resources such as the theoretical availability of a close-knit family in Latinx cultures, or faith as a source of resilience and hope. Gottman's approach to couple's therapy assumes cultural discrepancies are part of every partnership's challenges, rituals, and both individual and relational goals (Kelly et al., 2014). These are also influenced by how each person expresses and makes meaning of emotions, both their own and their partner's. Therefore, the process of meaning-making is one of seeking clarification. It can include behavioral normalization and understanding, such as how common physical touch, even platonically, is in some cultures compared to others who view it as a more intimate exchange. This can be particularly challenging in cross-cultural relationships where different partners may have culturally based assumptions the extent of which they are unaware.

Meaning-making also influences personal identity, such as the extent to which a person identifies with one or more cultures. Consider how complex cultural identity would be for those who grow up in mixed cultural contexts. It is common for immigrants and refugees from collectivistic cultures to transition to individualistic locations. This can introduce complexities around cultural loyalties and impact their experience of co-occurring systems.

Culture and Co-occurring Systems

Let's break down how culture is an influencing factor at all levels of ecological systems. As mentioned repeatedly, one's culture(s) are part of one's macrosystems. These macrosystems will have different norms and ideas of what optimal health and functionality looks like, both individually and systemically. There can be different rules in the system such as acceptable behavior and communication. For example, some cultures or families may be more comfortable bringing in a third person to try and solve problems than others. That third person could be a friend, relative, or even a therapist. Therefore, we must be mindful of this possible discomfort letting someone into their private lives and be as respectful and appreciative as possible. Rushing the person to share and change could be a version of enforcing your values on them, which would not be appropriate, particularly as a therapist.

Exo- and mesosystems can be experienced similarly, depending on the culture. For many, there is prominent and intentional division in one's microsystems. This would mean there is very little overlap between microsystems (mesosystemic overlap), and intentional minimization of influence by indirect environments (exosystemic overlap). This is like having a rigidly closed system. Some cultures may view this as ideal – such as individuals who feel unsafe to express their transgender identities in a professional setting or around certain family members. Unfortunately, general observations indicate that this lack of consistent identity and internal incongruence can cause more anxiety and increase disconnect between those mesosystems. This can, unfortunately, result in dissolution of one or more of those systems. (Remember structural determinism? This would be an example of that concept.)

An additional multisystem consideration across cultures is the definition of family. Generally, it is the blood- and/or emotionally bound system that circulates influence individually, dyadically, intergenerationally, and through all levels of systems in the ecological model. Families also hold the expectation that the system will be governed by similar rules and do so with the distinctly human quality of seeking balance between individuality and meaningful connection with others. By these broad descriptions, we are potentially able to have families in several contexts. But these are often restricted to a phase of life, setting, or generation. For the most part, clinically and practically, we want to allow each microsystem and immediate self to define "family" for themselves. Family can include spiritual family, work family, and family that includes "adoptive" parenting and child figures such as family friends and extended family members others might consider essential and nuclear. This is where the tool of structural therapy, the family map, may be more practical than the Bowenian genogram. It is formatted to allow for more familial and cultural flexibility.

Boundaries across Cultures

Perhaps more than any other family systems theory concept, boundary norms and acceptable behaviors vary drastically across cultures. This is due to the dramatically varied preferred balance of cohesion and adaptability. Cohesion was explored a bit in the earlier section about cultural experiences of holism,

210 Additional Considerations

where differentiation of self was the indicating balance of individuality and togetherness, structure and flexibility. Theoretically, differentiation of self is the ability to cope with distress; therefore, it also impacts adaptability. It is the lifelong process and pursuit of balance between boundaries, both your own and that of others.

In different cultures, different types and means of reinforcement may be considered acceptable or not. Remember, in collectivistic cultures, sacrifices are frequently made not out of selfless martyrdom but out of respect to shared interest, such as keeping a house clean because it is the best interest of everyone who lives there. It is each person's responsibility to keep the house clean out of respect to one another in the home and one's relationship with them. Asking others to keep a clean space is not a cost incurred or a favor to be cashed in on a later date. The giving mentality is very practical when shared among the system; however, it can become problematic when others in the system view a giving relationship as give-and-take.

Unfortunately, a collectivistic perception can view the setting of boundaries as harsh and harmful to the relationship. They may personalize the process and view themselves as burdensome. They may now perceive the boundary-setter as unsupportive or a conditional friend. A lack of boundaries can be viewed as proof of dedication, not proof of dependence in need of correction. Exploring the meaning and intention of boundaries – to improve the relationship, not damage it – will be an essential step, especially when multiple cultural perspectives are in consideration.

An unfortunate reality is that people frequently do not respect boundaries set by others. Or some may expect others to hold their cultural values (including boundaries) without openness to exploring otherwise. Inside a family, boundaries may vary including gender roles – even what defines gender versus sex, for example. Gender oppression, often maintained through strict adherence to gender roles and assumed hierarchy between sexes, is part of established hierarchies that are maintained by rigid boundaries. This persistence can be very present and influential in some cultures and will potentially influence therapeutic goals, even who sets them in the system. Adhering to traditional gender norms could be a type of cultural boundary some hold to with greater intentionality while others allow more fluidity. The same could be said of gender expression.

In the United States, there is a growing observation of gender as socially constructed perception in some parts of the world, but for many, gender remains synonymous to biological sex. These perceptions allow gender to be a spectrum or keep it binary (man or woman with nothing in between or instead). Here's some objective definitions:

- *Sex:* Biologically defined, typically distinguished by the presence of a penis (male) or vagina (female). Even in this narrative, there are individuals who do not fit into either category due to biological divergences at birth.
- *Gender:* Socially constructed experience and expression of one's sex often rooted in interests, desires, mannerisms, behaviors, and perceived roles.

Cultural Considerations 211

- Each of these is different from one's *sexual orientation*, which determines what gender(s) a person finds sexually attractive, if any.

It can be difficult to describe gender since it is so socially constructed and therefore flexible: "But how do you know?" is an incredibly common question cisgender (those whose biological sex and mental perception of their gender match) individuals may have for transgender individuals. Sometimes normative language can be used to describe the dysmorphia when someone is not cisgender. I've heard it described "being in the wrong body [based on sex] is like wearing shoes that don't quite fit. It leaves blisters, squeezes uncomfortably, and makes it so you can't really do everything you want to. Coming out as transgender" – changing one's gender appearance to match between one's gender identity and expression, often through physical change to one's body – "was like finally learning I could take those shoes off and put on ones that fit better and let me live life more fully."

Respecting someone's gender expression can be a way of respecting their boundaries. There are several ways this can appear, including those related to gender roles. Some perceptions of feminism assume feminists seek to empower women at the cost of men's rights. Others know feminism aims to encourage all people, including women, to pursue the fullest version themselves rather than be satisfied with a "smaller slice of the pie." This means encouraging people to pursue their interests and desired career paths, even when that career path is to a stereotypically feminine industry. It does not have to be a professional position of power; a feminist can just as well be a stay-at-home parent as a business owner or contributing employee. Despite its name, feminism does not only aim to help women; instead, it seeks to strengthen the influence of all minorities across genders, disabilities, and anyone who faces discriminatory "isms." However, how this is expressed can still be controversial in some cultures.

Even in cultures such as the United States, where individual freedoms are considered a cornerstone of the country's identity, many struggle to respect others' identity expression and personal rights. They struggle to respect that boundary set by another person, even when it does not impact them. There can be disagreements as to what "freedom" really means. For another example, to some, sex work empowers women, to others, it is degrading and objectifying. This is a perfect example of meaning-making as an essential step in exploring as part of boundary-setting and personalization of when and how others set boundaries, too.

Culture Impact on Change and Circular Causality

Culture deeply influences how individuals and systems perceive capacity to change. It also impacts their receptivity to the concept of circular causality. This perception can be grounded in attachment.

Attachment theory highlights circularity between family-of-origin and nuclear family. The cultural backgrounds of each family-of-origin coming

212 *Additional Considerations*

together into a nuclear family can introduce some additional challenges. Attachment theory is based on observing and intentionally addressing what draws people together, what drives them apart, and intergenerational influence. According to the theory, attachments and connections between people are learned early in life and replicated in future relationships. This can be done securely or through avoidant or ambivalent connection. However, these can appear differently across cultures based on the needs of the individuals and systems within it. What some call secure others view as coddling. What some see as ambivalent others view as appropriately independent. This all depends on systemic dynamics, structures, roles, boundaries, and power differentials – ideas that are present both in families and culture-wide.

Consider the refugee population. Some cultures steeped in economic and political turmoil do not have the luxury of pursuing self-actualization in the chaos of life-or-death daily stressors. Those trapped in low social class – restricted by lack of income, education, occupation opportunity, wealth, or access to resources – are particularly susceptible. Especially with these high-risk populations, language of circularity can be misheard as victim-blaming and actually discourage meaningful attachment. Therefore, depending on the culture, attachment-based change may seem insignificant compared to the constant risk of losing the person with whom one is supposed to be building attachment. This perception can contribute to maintaining homeostasis as a survival mechanism that discourages change because of the unknown dangers that change may bring.

Homeostasis exists at a cultural level, too; individual change can be nearly impossible when faced against a wider context. Lasting change must persevere through a phase of uncertainty and distress. This is when some members of the system resent and/or resist the change, often with harmful results. At a cultural level, this can be seen in those who resist public policy changes that embrace previously unacceptable practices, such as the early twenty-first center shift in the United States to call bans on same-sex marriages unconstitutional. This effectively legalized same-sex marriage, allowing those couples the legal benefits of the spousal title. Many who held to the religiously rooted assumption that marriage should only be between one man and one woman struggled with this transition.

This struggle presented itself through economic distress; challenging the legality of the judicial decision; and reintroducing other legislation that holds to those same religious beliefs, such as restrictive access to abortion and limiting rights for transgender individuals. These disagreements centralized around clashing cultures even within the same country. Those who consider the United States to be a Christian nation questioned this decision as it challenged their perception: What does it mean to be a citizen of their country/culture that they do not feel represent their values? This all happened in the United States since 2015. In the midst of social progression toward equal rights, several efforts were made to thwart the very same. These opposing positions demonstrate why systemic change is so difficult – it is frequently supported by a portion of the culture and undermined by another.

Always keep in mind that healthy is not the same as normal; we must aim to respectfully explore a person's normal and how it serves and deters their health. As homeostasis – the status quo – attests, normal is not always the healthy goal. In fact, some cultural practices are downright unethical, such as mistreatment of women or children through abuse, neglect, or disrespect. Even in cultures where these behaviors are normalized, it is our responsibility as therapists and humans to stand against oppression and discrimination – neutrality is not an option and silence reinforces the oppressive voice (McGoldrick & Ashton, 2012). Discrimination impedes on personal senses of safety, which interrupts optimal functionality of individuals and systems.

The Culturally Competent Therapist

According to work from the American Psychological Association, there are four mechanisms a therapist will move through to demonstrate the cultural competence to bridge across differences from clients. These are comparable to the shift from awareness to sensitivity to competence. However, in this approach, sensitivity is split into two areas, one focused on empathy toward others and the other on increasing mindfulness of the therapist's own power and influence in the room based on their own cultural identities. These mechanisms appear to have been written with the assumption that the therapist is of the dominant culture – for example, a white, cisgender, heteronormative individual. While this is true of many therapists, it is important to reflect how our cultural identities may influence our clients and the work we do with them. This is true regardless of what those are and whether they fall into the dominant cultural narrative.

Mechanism 1: Worldview and Value Differences

The first challenge of the therapist is to demonstrate basic awareness of cultural differences. These include how those identifiers may influence the client's beliefs and values. It also includes views on mental health such as symptoms, causes, expression, treatment expectations. Therapists are challenged to ask about client preferences and values, accepting and normalizing these without cultural shaming. Of course, this can be challenging when the therapist perceives the client's cultural values to not be normal or healthy. We must be careful how this is conveyed, if so. The final task of this mechanism is mindfulness of one's own biases, including *ethnocentrism* – the restrictive lens through which you view and understand the world – such as assumed superiority of eurocentrism.

Mechanism 2: Experiences and Contexts

At this stage of competence development, the therapist increases their awareness of other cultures' history, including how it has been treated by other cultures (discrimination, oppression), any "isms" found in the culture (sexism,

214   *Additional Considerations*

racism, ageism, ableism, etc.), and additional stressors the culture has placed on the client system such as a restrictive caste system or perceptions of their own capacities for change.

In this mechanism, the therapist is responsible to identify and speak to the layers of influence these cultural identities may play on a person. They must also make efforts to individualize treatment for the client, not making assumptions about the client based on their culture, and considering the client systems' challenges navigating within the dominant cultural setting. This could be considered a form of *cultural brokering*, or overseeing the mental and emotional shift from one culture to another. Any formal test measures should be reliable and valid for the client's culture (not just the dominant culture) to the best of the therapist's ability. Overall, it is the therapist's responsibility to begin introducing not just awareness of the client system's unique cultural identity but offer sensitivity to it. A final piece of this mechanism is the therapist's increase self-awareness. This can be any racial privilege they carry, such as white privilege, and any other privileged identities. Along with this personal awareness, the therapist must be intentional to consider the structural paradigms the dominant culture puts in place that enable these advantages and disadvantages.

Mechanism 3: Power Differences between Therapist and Client

At this second half of sensitivity mindfulness on the way to competence, this mechanism highlights the issues of power, respect, and inclusivity at a macrosystemic level that may influence clients at a microsystemic level. Here, the therapist is called to consider the client's cultural identities and the stigma, shame, unfair media portrayals, and instance of exclusion they may have experienced as a result. Additionally, consider the dominant cultures' role in creating and perpetuating these, such as white supremacy. We consider how the culture contributes to perceptions of the client system's problems and potential solutions.

This is also the mechanism that begins to turn cultural limitations on their head. We increasingly emphasize the client system's strengths and positive intentions both including and despite the cultural factors. We also begin to bring in the postmodern and family systemic perception that clients are the experts of their own lives. This includes the extent to which they allow cultural "isms" and stressors to impact them, how their cultural identities can be sources of resilience and advocacy, and opportunities to create institutional change that might have previously been overlooked by the client. At this time, we focus more and more on strengthening the client, often through the relationship with their culture and next, with the therapist.

Mechanism 4: Felt Distance between Therapist and Client System

At this mechanism of cultural competence, the therapist demonstrates the height of awareness, sensitivity, and client empowerment. The therapist will be consistently mindful of nonverbals and how those are culturally interpreted. They demonstrate second-order cybernetics of "I'm in this with you," through intentional joining/alliance-building. They use the assessment and interventive tool of a cultural genogram, which connects the client to their cultural identities and reflects on how these may impact treatment process and goals (Hardy & Laszloffy, 1995). Lastly, the therapist is able to reflect on past instances – both theirs and the clients' – of stereotypes. All parties ideally feel safe to acknowledge past therapeutic reactions and disservices to different cultures structurally, interpersonally, and intrapersonally. This affirms that you, the clinician, view these as wrong and asserts you are open to learning and striving to do better. Overall, this mechanism emphasizes that there may be cultural differences between client systems and their therapist; this difference does not have to be a weakness when the therapist is considerate and respectful of those differences.

Summary

This chapter reflects on how family systems theory, though based on individualistic and western philosophies, still can be helpful in other cultures, including collectivistic perspectives. It can be flexible to consider how other cultures view holism, communication, context, co-occurring systems, boundaries, and circular causality. These include culture facets beyond ethnicity and race. It can include sex and gender, sexual orientation, religiosity, nationality, age, socioeconomic status, formal and informal education, peer class, employment, neurodivergence, disability, and many other aspects that contribute to a person's identity.

My hope is this chapter communicates more than the importance of cultural awareness and sensitivity. I hope it highlights the many facets of cultural competence. This includes mindfulness around client system identities that are founded in their cultural experiences and values. It also includes personal reflection on your own cultural identities and how these influence you as a person and clinician. More than anything, I hope this chapter highlights how we all are humanly responsible to constantly grow and learn, including in our understanding of how culture impacts a person and how people impact their cultures systemically, too.

Conclusion

The purpose of this book was to introduce readers to the core concepts of family systems theory and expose them to how a few models of therapy use those concepts. Unfortunately, it would be impossible to cover every therapeutic model – you would be reading this book for the duration of your professional career! Not that this would be entirely terrible; I hope you will return to read these ideas periodically, refresh your memory and application of its concepts.

As you read through each chapter, you may have noticed a trend. While so many models of therapy may appear different, they have origins in family systems theory that can benefit any client. And some of those interventions start sounding pretty similar. At the end of the day, these models demonstrate the idea of equifinality – there are many paths to the same end. There are many means to help others achieve their preferred future. There is not one right model for all problems, all clients, and all therapists.

Part of your professional development as a therapist will potentially include identifying specific models of therapy you will predominantly practice. The model(s) you select will likely match your worldview about holism, communication, context, co-occurring systems, boundaries, and circular causality and change happen. Finding that model (or integration of models) that achieves this will be an ongoing process. I would argue that is why so many models of therapy exist – so many therapists design models that fit what works for them and hope to offer that insight to others!

That being said, a therapist's comfort in a model of therapy significantly impacts a client and their relationship with the therapist. Your comfort and confidence radiate and help the client feel more comfortable and confident, too. They grow in comfort and confidence in you and your practice and within themselves. This can be some of the first flavors of hope for them, and hope is an essential step toward resilience and meaningful change.

Overall, I hope this book encourages therapists to remain curious and open-minded, continuing to be mindful of the foundational role of family systems theory in the many models of therapy a professional may be exposed to throughout their career. I revel in the idea of being a constant student of my field and industry; I hope you feel the same. I hope to ceaselessly challenge myself to learn more, self-assess more, and take proactive steps toward being a

DOI: 10.4324/9781003088196-16

Conclusion   217

better therapist and better person. For those who do not go on to be therapists, I hope this text still teaches you the influence we have on one another – past, present, and future.

As a final note, let us stay deliberate in our application of these concepts. Let us be mindful of self and others without harsh judgment toward self or others. Let us consider how important it is to both be whole and part of a whole. Let us reflect on the constant presence of communication, even in the smallest and seemingly insignificant ways. Let us be discerning of how context influences us and considerate of how it influences others. Let us acknowledge all the circles of influence, all the systems of which we are members, and how they influence one another and our sense of personal congruence and authenticity. Let us examine assumptions we make about the act of setting and bending boundaries. Let us recognize how life is circular in all ways, not linear; even as we grow and age, we influence others who are growing alongside us, even at different stages of life. Let us be open-minded about how different change can look and feel to different people. Let us be compassionate to others, even in the face of adversity and vast differences. Through all this, let us be intentional. Let us be intentional in our interactions personally and systemically. Let us be wise and always remember the words of philosopher Søren Kierkegaard: "Life is not a problem to be solved but a reality to be experienced."

References

Ackerman, C. E. (2019). *What is psychodynamic therapy? 5 tools & techniques*. Positive Psychology. https://positivepsychology.com/psychodynamic-therapy/

Adler, A. (1973). *The practice and theory of individual psychology*. Adams.

American Psychological Association (2016). *Understanding psychotherapy and how it works*. APA Help Center. www.apa.org/helpcenter/understanding-psychotherapy

American Psychological Association (2020). *What is cognitive behavioral therapy?* Clinical Practice Guideline for the Treatment of Posttraumatic Stress Disorder. www.apa.org/ptsd-guideline/patients-and-families/cognitive-behavioral

American Psychological Association Dictionary (n.d.). *Culture*. https://dictionary.apa.org/culture

Anderson, H. H. (1946). Directive and nondirective psychotherapy: The role of the therapist. *American Journal of Orthopsychiatry, 16*(4), 608–614. doi:10.1111/j.1939-0025.1946.tb05424.x

Anderson, J. R. (2019). Inviting autonomy back to the table: The importance of autonomy for healthy relationship functioning. *Journal of Marital and Family Therapy, 46*(1), 3–14. doi:10.1111/jmft.12413

Bandura, A. (1991). Social cognitive theory of self-regulation. *Organizational Behavior and Human Decision Processes, 50*, 248–287. www.uky.edu/~eushe2/Bandura/Bandura1991OBHDP.pdf

Bateson, G. (1963). The role of somatic change in evolution. *Evolution, 17*(4) 529–539. doi:10.2307/2407104

Bateson, G. (1972). *Steps to an ecology of mind: Collected essays in anthropology, psychiatry, evolution, and epistemology*. University of Chicago Press.

Bateson, G., Jackson, D. D., Haley, J., & Weakland, K. (1956). Toward a theory of schizophrenia. *Behavioral Science, 1*(4), 251–254. https://solutions-centre.org/pdf/TOWARD-A-THEORY-OF-SCHIZOPHRENIA-2.pdf

Baumeister, R. F., Vohs, K. D., & Tice, D. M. (2007). The strength model of self-control. *Current Directions in Psychological Science, 16*(6), 351–355. doi:10.1111/j.1467-8721.2007.00534.x

Becvar, D. S., & Becvar, R. J. (2018). *Systems theory and family therapy: A primer (3rd ed.)*. University Press.

Benito-Gomez, M., Williams, K. N., McCurdy, A., & Fletcher, A. C. (2020). Autonomy-supportive parenting in adolescence: Cultural variability in the contemporary United States. *Journal of Family Theory & Review, 12*, 7–26. doi:10.1111/jftr.12362

Bennett, S. S. (2014). Negotiating your way to better boundaries and relationships. In S. S. Bennett (Ed.), *Children of the depressed* (pp. 115–143). New Harbinger.

References 219

Berger, C. R., & Chaffee, S. (1987). Communication as a science. In C. R. Berger & S. Chaffee (Eds.), *Handbook of communication science* (pp. 15–19). Sage.

Blumenthal, E., & Notman, M. (2006). Psychoanalysis: Theory and treatment. *Harvard Women's Health Watch.* www.health.harvard.edu/newsletter_article/Psychoanalysis_Theory_and_treatment

Boszormenyi-Nagy, I. (1966). From family relationships to a psychology of relationships: Fictions of the individual and fictions of the family. *Comprehensive Psychiatry, 7*(5), 408–423. doi:10.1016/S0010-440X(66)80070-6

Bott, D. (2002). Client-centred therapy and family therapy: A review and commentary. *Journal of Family Therapy, 23*(4), 361–377. https://doi.org/10.1111/1467-6427.00190

Bowen, M. (1978). *Family therapy in clinical practice.* Rowman & Littlefield.

Bowen, M., & Kerr, M. W. (2009). *Family evaluation.* Norton.

Bozarth, J. B., & Shanks, A. (1989) Person-centred family therapy with couples. *Person-centred Review, 4:* 183–209.

Bratter, T. E. (1976). The psychotherapist as advocate: Extending the therapeutic alliance with adolescents. *Journal of Contemporary Psychotherapy, 8*(2), 119–126. doi:10.1007/BF01812965

Bretherton, I. (1993). Theoretical contributions from developmental psychology. In P. G. Boss, W. J. Doherty, R. LaRossa, W. R. Schumm, & S. K. Steinmetz (Eds.), *Sourcebook of family theories and methods: A contextual approach* (pp. 275–297). Springer.

Broderick, C. B. (1993). *Understanding family process: Basics of family systems theory.* Sage.

Bronfenbrenner, U. (1979). *The ecology of human development.* Harvard University Press.

Burgess, E. W. (1926). The family as a unit of interacting personalities. *Family, 7*(1), 3–9. https://journals.sagepub.com/doi/10.1177/104438942600700101

Canadian Mental Health Association, BC Division. (2015). *What's the difference between CBT and DBT?* Heretohelp. www.heretohelp.bc.ca/q-and-a/whats-the-difference-between-cbt-and-dbt

Carey, M., & Russell, S. (2003). Re-authoring: Some answers to commonly asked questions. *International Journal of Narrative Therapy and Community Work, 3.* https://narrativepractices.com.au/attach/pdf/Re-Authoring_Commmonly_asked_questions.pdf

Center for Substance Abuse Treatment (1999). Enhancing motivation for change in substance abuse treatment. Substance Abuse and Mental Health Services Administration (US). *Treatment Improvement Protocol, 35.* www.ncbi.nlm.nih.gov/books/NBK64964/

Chen, S., Boucher, H. C., & Parker Tapias, M. (2006). The relational self revealed: Integrative conceptualization and implications for interpersonal life. *Psychological Bulletin, 132*(2), 151–179. doi:10.1037/0033-2909.132.2.151

Cheung, G., & Chan, C. (2002). The Satir model and cultural sensitivity: A Hong Kong reflection. *Contemporary Family Therapy, 24*(1), 205–221. doi:10.1023/A:1014338025464

Christman, J. (2004). Relational autonomy, liberal individualism, and the social constitution of selves. *Philosophical Studies, 117*, 143–164.

Chun, Y. J., & MacDermid, S. M. (1997). Perceptions of family differentiation, individuation, and self-esteem among Korean adolescents. *Journal of Marriage and the Family, 59*, 451–462.

220 References

Cioffi-Revilla, C. (2017). *Introduction to computational social science: Principles and applications (2nd ed.)*. Springer.

Cohler, B. J. (1983). Autonomy and interdependence in the family of adulthood: A psychological perspective. *The Gerontologist, 23*(1), 33–39.

Combrinck-Graham, L. (2014). Being a family systems thinker: A psychiatrist's personal odyssey. *Family Process, 53*(3), 476–488. doi:10.1111/famp.12090

Cooley, C. H. (1902). *Human nature and social order*. Scribner.

Davies, M. (2019, March 20). The four stress communication styles and how to 'level' for harmony in relationships. *Medium.com*. https://medium.com/@amattdavies/four-stress-communication-styles-b804de9f5c6

Davies, N. (2018, October 22). Designing the therapeutic space: Using layout, color, and other elements to get patients in the right frame of mind. *PsychiatryAdvisor*. www.psychiatryadvisor.com/home/practice-management/designing-the-therapeutic-space-using-layout-color-and-other-elements-to-get-patients-in-the-right-frame-of-mind/

Deissler, K. G. (2013). Beyond paradox and counterparadox. In G. R. Weeks (Ed.), *Promoting change through paradoxical therapy (revised ed.)* (pp. 60–98). International Psychotherapy Institute. https://library.um.edu.mo/ebooks/b31685377.pdf

Dreikurs, R. (1967). *Psychodynamic, psychotherapy and counseling*. Alfred Adler Institute.

Dreikurs, R. (1972). Dreikurs sayings. *The Individual Psychologist, 9*, 38–45.

Erdem, G., & Safi, O. A. (2018). The cultural lens approach to Bowen family systems theory: Contributions of family change theory. *Journal of Family Theory & Review, 10*, 469–483. doi:10.1111/jftr.12258

Eron, J., & Lund, T. (1996). *Narrative solutions in brief therapy*. Guilford Press.

Fenton-O'Creevy, M., Nicholson, N., Soane, E., & Willman, P. (2010). Trading on illusions: Unrealistic perceptions of control and trading performance. *Journal of Occupational and Organizational Psychology, 76*(1), 53–68. doi:10.1348/096317903321208880

Fishbain, D. A. (1994). Secondary gain concept. *APS Journal, 3*(4), 264–273. https://doi.org/10.1016/S1058-9139(05)80274-8

Fischer, S. L. (2017). Relational attitudes in gestalt theory and practice. *Gestalt Review, 21*(1), 2–6.

Fisher, J. (2017). *Healing the fragmented selves of trauma survivors: Overcoming internal self-alienation*. Routledge.

Fitzpatrick, M. A., & Ritchie, L. D. (1993). Communication theory and the family. In P. G. Boss, W. J. Doherty, R. LaRossa, W. R. Schumm, & S. K. Steinmetz (Eds.), *Sourcebook of family theories and methods: A contextual approach* (pp. 565–585). Springer.

Foley, V. D., & Everett, C. A. (Eds.) (n.d.) *Family therapy glossary*. American Association for Marriage and Family Therapy.

Fosshage, J. L. (2003). How does change occur within the psychoanalytic encounter? *Journal of Religion and Health, 42*(4), 281–299.

Franklin, C., Bolton, K. W., & Guz, S. (2019). Solution-focused brief family therapy. In B. H. Fiese, M. Celano, K. Deater-Deckard, E. N. Jouriles, & M. A. Whisman (Eds.), *APA handbook of contemporary family psychology: Family therapy and training* (pp. 139–153). American Psychological Association.

Freud, S., & Hall, G. S. (2019). *Introductory lectures on psychoanalysis*. digiReads.

Frew, J. (2017). Key concepts from gestalt therapy for non-gestalt therapists. *Counseling Today (Online)*. https://ct.counseling.org/2017/06/key-concepts-gestalt-therapy-non-gestalt-therapists/

References 221

Frosh, S. (1995). Postmodernism versus psychotherapy. *Journal of Family Therapy, 17*, 175–190. https://doi.org/10.1111/j.1467-6427.1995.tb00012.x

Gilbert, R. M. (1992). *Extraordinary relationships: A new way of thinking about human interactions.* Wiley.

Gilmore, H. (2016 Dec). Reflections on applied behavioral analysis: ACT (acceptance and commitment therapy) ... a summary. *Psych Central Professional.* https://pro.psychcentral.com/child-therapist/2016/12/act-acceptance-and-commitment-therapy-a-summary/

Goodell, K. A., Sudderth, B. G., & Allan, C. D. (2011). The self of the therapist. In L. Metcalf (Ed.) *Marriage and family therapy: A practice-oriented approach (1st ed.)* (pp. 21–38). Springer.

Guttman, H. A. (1991). Systems theory, cybernetics, and epistemology. In A. S. Gurman & D. P. Kniskern (Eds.), *Handbook of family therapy, vol. 2 (1st ed.).* (pp. 41–64). Routledge. https://doi.org/10.4324/9781315803944

Guzzardo, P., & Pina-Narvaez, L. (2019). Structural family therapy. In L. Metcalf (Ed.), *Marriage and family therapy: A practice-oriented approach (2nd ed.)* (pp. 203–227). Springer.

Hall, A., & Fagen, B. (1956). Definition of system. In L. von Bertalanffy & A. Rapoport (Eds.), *General systems, vol 1* (p. 18). University of Michigan Press.

Hardy, K. V., & Laszloffy, T. A. (1995). The cultural genogram: Key to training culturally competent family therapists. *Journal of Marital and Family Therapy, 21*, 227–237. doi:10.1111/j.1752-0606.1995.tb00158.x

Hargrave, T. D., & Pfitzer, F. (2003). *The new contextual therapy: Guiding the power of give and take.* Routledge.

Harris, R. (2017). Making self-as-context relevant, clear and practical. *I'm Learning ACT.* www.actmindfully.com.au/upimages/Making_Self-As-Context_Relevant,_Clear_and_Practical.pdf

Hastings, C. (2002). So, how do you become culturally competent? *Family Therapy Magazine, 1*(2), 18–25.

Havighurst, R. J. (1972). *Developmental tasks and education.* McKay.

Heath, L. (2001). Triangulation: Methodology. In N. J. Smelser & P. B. Baltes (Ed.), *International Encyclopedia of the Social & Behavioral Sciences* (pp. 15901–15906). Elsevier.

Hill, R. (2020, Jan 2). Implementing a curiosity-oriented approach. *The Science of Psychotherapy.* www.thescienceofpsychotherapy.com/implementing-a-curiosity-oriented-approach/

Hofmann, S. G., Asnaani, A., Vonk, I. J. J., Sawyer, A. T., & Fang, A. (2012). The efficacy of cognitive behavioral therapy: A review of meta-analyses. *Cognitive Therapy and Research, 36*, 427–440. doi:10.1007/s10608-012-9476-1

Hubble, M. A., Duncan, B. L., Miller, S. D., & Wampold, B. E. (1999). *The heart and soul of change (2nd ed.).* American Psychological Association.

Jaccard, J., & Jacoby, J. (2010). *Theory construction and model-building skills.* Guilford Press.

Jesser, C. J. (1975). *Social theory revisited.* Dryden.

Johnson, S. (2004). *The practice of emotionally focused couple therapy: Creating connection.* Routledge.

Kağıtçıbaşı, Ç. (1996). The autonomous-relational self. *European Psychologist, 1*, 180–186. https://doi.org/10.1027/1016-9040.1.3.180

Keeney, B. P. (1983). *Aesthetics of change.* Guilford Press.

222 References

Kelly, S., Bhagwat, R., Maynigo, P., & Moses, E. (2014). Couple and marital therapy: The complement and expansion provided by multicultural approaches. In F. T. L. Leong (Ed.), *Handbook of multicultural psychology* (pp. 479–497). American Psychological Association. https://doi.org/10.1037/14187-027

Kiecolt-Glaser, J. K., & Newton, T. L. (2001). Marriage and health: His and hers. *Psychological Bulletin, 127*(4), 462–503. https://pubmed.ncbi.nlm.nih.gov/11439708/

Kim, H., Prouty, A. M., Smith, D. B., Ko, M. J., Wetchler, J. L., & Oh, J. E. (2014). Differentiation of self and its relationship with family functioning in South Koreans. *American Journal of Family Therapy, 42*, 257–265. doi:10.1080/01926187.2013.838928

Koestler, A. (1967). *The ghost in the machine*. Hutchinson.

Lambert, M. J. (1992). Implications of psychotherapy outcome research for psychotherapy integration. In J. C. Norcross & M. R. Goldfried (Eds.), *Handbook of psychotherapy integration* (pp. 94–129). Basic Books.

Larner, G. (2008). Towards a common ground in psychoanalysis and family therapy: On knowing not to know. *Journal of Family Therapy, 22*(1), 61–82. doi:10.1111/1467-6427.00138

LaRossa, R., & Reitzes, D. C. (1993). Symbolic interactionism and family studies. In P. G. Boss, W. J. Doherty, R. LaRossa, W. R. Schumm, & S. K. Steinmetz (Eds.), *Sourcebook of family theories and methods: A contextual approach* (pp. 135–163). Springer.

Laveman, L. (1997). The macrosystemic model of psychotherapy: Autonomy and attachment in family systems. *Journal of Psychotherapy Integration, 7*(1), 55–74.

Lipchik, E. (2002). *Beyond technique in solution-focused therapy: Working with emotions and the therapeutic relationship*. Guilford Press.

Lynch, J. E., & Lynch, B. (2005). Family and couples therapy from a gestalt perspective. In A. L. Woltd & S. M. Toman (Eds.), *Gestalt therapy: History, theory, and practice.* (pp. 201–218). Sage.

Manzi, C., Vignoles, V. L., Regalia, C., & Scabini, E. (2006). Cohesion and enmeshment revisited: Differentiation, identity, and well-being in two European cultures. *Journal of Marriage and Family, 68*, 673–689. doi:10.1111/j.1741-3737.2006.00282.x

Marchal, J. H. (1975). On the concept of a system. *University of Chicago Press, Philosophy of Science, 42*(4), 448–468. www.jstor.org/stable/187223

Markus, H., & Cross, S. (1990). The interpersonal self. In L. A. Pervin (Ed.), *Handbook of personality* (pp. 576–608). Guilford Press.

Maslow, A. H. (1943). A theory of human motivation. *Psychological Review, 50*(4), 370–396.

Maslow, A. H. (1966). *Religions, values, and peak experiences*. Penguin.

Massey, R. F. (2017). Paradox, double binding, and counterparadox: A transactional analysis perspective. *Transactional Analysis Journal, 16*(1), 24–26. doi:10.1177/036215378601600105

McGoldrick M., & Ashton, D. (2012). Culture: A challenge to concepts of normality. In F. Walsh (Ed.), *Normal family processes: Growing diversity and complexity (4th ed.)* (pp. 249–272). Guilford Press.

Merkel, W. T. & Searight, H. R. (1992). Why families are not like swamps, solar systems, or thermostats: Some limits of systems theory as applied to family therapy. *Contemporary Family Therapy, 14*(1), 33–50.

Milton Erickson Foundation. (n.d.) *Milton Erickson biography*. www.erickson-foundation.org/biography/

References **223**

Minuchin, S., & Fishman, H. C. (2004). *Family therapy techniques.* Harvard University Press.

Montero-Marin, J., Pardo-Abril, J., Demarzo, M. M. P., Garcia-Toro, M., & Garcia-Campayo, J. (2016). Burnout subtypes and their clinical implications: A theoretical proposal for specific therapeutic approaches. *Revista de Psicopatología y Psicología Clínica, 21*(3), 231–242. doi:10.5944/rppc.vol.21.num.3.2016.15686

Musick, K., & Bumpass, L. (2012). Re-examining the case for marriage: Union formation and changes in well-being. *Journal of Marriage and Family, 74*(1), 1–18. doi:10.1111/j.1741-3737.2011.00873.x

National Council of Family Relations. (2014). *F. Ivan Nye: In memoriam.* www.ncfr. org/news/memoriam/f-ivan-nye-95

Neff, K. (2011). *Self-compassion: The proven power of being kind to yourself.* William Morrow & Co.

Newman, B. M., & Newman, P. R. (2018). *Development through life: A psychosocial approach (13th ed.).* Cengage.

Nichols, M. (1984). *Family therapy: Concepts and methods.* Gardner Press.

Nye, F. I. (1958). *Family relationships and delinquent behavior.* John Wiley.

Nye, F. I. (1978). Is choice and exchange theory the key? *Journal of Marriage and Family, 40*(2), 219–232. doi:10.2307/350754

O'Leary, C. J. (1999). *Counselling couples and families: A person-centred approach.* Sage.

Olson, D. H. (2000). Circumplex model of marital and family systems. *Journal of Family Therapy, 22*(2), 144–167. doi:10.1111/1467-6427.00144

Olson, D. H. (2010). *FACES-IV manual.* Life Innovations. www.facesiv.com

Owen, J., & Hilsenroth, M. J. (2014). Treatment adherence: The importance of therapist flexibility in relation to therapy outcomes. *Journal of Counseling Psychology, 61*(2), 280–288. doi:10.1037/a0035753

Pacer Center (2015). *Tantrums, tears, and tempers: Behavior is communication.* www. pacer.org/parent/php/php-c154.pdf

Papero, D. V. (2011). Responsibility for self. In O. Cohn Bregman & C. M. White (Eds.), *Bringing systems thinking to life: Expanding the horizons for Bowen family systems theory.* (pp. 67–74). Routledge.

Parsons, T. (1975). *Social systems and the evolution of action theory.* The Free Press.

Perls, F. (1969). *Ego, hunger and aggression: The gestalt therapy of sensory awakening through spontaneous personal encounter, fantasy, and contemplation.* Vision Books.

Pieters, H. C., Ayala, L., Schnieder, A., Wicks, N., Levine-Dickman, A., & Clinton, S. (2018). Gardening on a psychiatric inpatient unit: Cultivating recovery. *Archives of Psychiatric Nursing, 33*(1), 57–64. doi:10.1016/j.apnu.2018.10.001

Pitts, E. (2019). Narrative therapy with families. In L. Metcalf (Ed.), *Marriage and family therapy: A practice-oriented approach (2nd ed.)* (pp. 289–310). Springer.

Popovic, M. (2019). Bowen family systems theory. In L. Metcalf (Ed.), *Marriage and family therapy: A practice-oriented approach (2nd ed.)* (pp. 43–69). Springer.

Popper, K. (1963). *Conjectures and refutations.* Routledge.

Rapoport, A. (1968). Foreword. In W. Buckley (Ed.), *Modern systems research for the behavioral scientist.* Aldine.

Rapoport, A., & Horvath, W. J. (1960). The theoretical channel capacity of a single neuron as determined by various coding systems. *Information and Control, 3*(4), 335–350.

Raskin, N. J., & Rogers, C. R. (2005). Person-centered therapy. In R. J. Corsini & D. Wedding (Eds.), *Current psychotherapies* (pp. 130–165). Thomson Brooks/Cole Publishing Co.

224 *References*

Ray, W. A., & Schlanger, K. (2008, Sept.-Oct.). Family therapy pioneers: A directory. *Family Therapy Magazine*, 23–60. www.aamft.org/members/familytherapyresour ces/articles/08_FTM_05_23_60.pdf

Rhodes, S. L. (1981). Psychoanalytic theory and family systems theory: A complementary view. *International Journal of Group Psychotherapy, 31*(1), 25–42.

Rivera Walter, I. (2017, January 31). Family of origin exploration for the therapist: Family rules and structure. *Family Therapy Basics*. https://familytherapybasics. com/blog/2017/1/31/family-of-origin-exploration-for-the-therapist-family-rules-and-structure#:~:text=When%20Minuchin%20(1974)%20defined%20bou ndaries,within%20the%20family)%20within%20it.

Robbins, J. (2020). Ecopsychology: How immersion in nature benefits your health. *Yale Environment 360*. https://e360.yale.edu/features/ecopsychology-how-immersion-in-nature-benefits-your-health

Robinson, K. J. (2019). Satir human validation process model. In L. Metcalf (Ed.), *Marriage and family therapy: A practice-oriented approach* (pp. 165-182). Springer.

Robles, T. F., & Kiecolt-Glaser, J. K. (2003). The physiology of marriage: Pathways to health. *Physiology & Behavior, 79*(3), 409–416. doi: 10.1016/s0031-9384(03) 00160-4

Rogers, C. R. (1942). *Counseling and psychotherapy*. Houghton Mifflin.

Rogers, C. R. (1957). The necessary and sufficient conditions of therapeutic personality change. *Journal of Consulting Psychology, 21*, 95–103.

Satir, V., Bandler, R., & Grinder, J. (1976). *Changing with families*. Science and Behavior Books.

Satir, V., Banmen, J., Gerber, J., & Gomori, M. (1991). *The Satir model: Family therapy and beyond*. Science and Behavior Books.

Schwartz, R. & Sweezy, M. (2020). *Internal family systems therapy (2nd ed.)*. Guilford Press.

Schwarz, S. (2018). Resilience in psychology: A critical analysis of the concept. *Theory & Psychology, 28*(4), 528–542. doi:10.1177/0959354318783584

Segal, L., & Beavin Bavelas, J. (1983). Human systems and communication theory. In B. B. Wolman & G. Stricker (Eds.), *Handbook of family and marital therapy* (pp. 61–76). Plenum Press.

Selvini Palazzoli, M., Boscolo, L., Cecchin, G., & Prata, G. (1971). *Paradox and counter-paradox*. Jason Aronson, Inc.

Shannon, C. (1949). The mathematical theory of communication. In C. Shannon & W. Weaver (Eds.), *The mathematical theory of communication* (pp. 1–25). University of Illinois Press.

Shearer, C. (2020, August 20). *The cultural implications of silence around the world*. CultureWizard, RW3, LLC. www.rw-3.com/blog/cultural-implications-of-silence

Shen, M. (2020, November 1). A collectivist's discomfort in an individualistic culture. *Mojia Shen*. https://mojia.medium.com/a-collectivists-discomfort-in-an-individu alistic-culture-6b458270890e

Smuts, J. C. (1926). *Holism and evolution*. Macmillan Publishing.

Stevenson, H. (2018a). Holism, field theory, systems thinking, and gestalt consulting: How each informs the other—part 1, theoretical integration. *Gestalt Review, 22*(2), 161–188. doi:10.5325/gestaltreview.22.2.0161

Stevenson, H. (2018b). Holism, field theory, systems thinking, and gestalt consulting: How each informs the other—part 2, practical application. *Gestalt Review, 22*(2), 189–207. doi:10.5325/gestaltreview.22.2.0189

Suppes, B. (2019). Self-care of the therapist. In L. Metcalf (Ed.), *Marriage and family therapy: A practice-oriented approach (2nd ed.)* (pp. 25–39). Springer.

Tuason, M. T., & Friedlander, M. L. (2000). Do parents' differentiation levels predict those of their adult children? And other tests of Bowen theory in a Philippine sample. *Journal of Counseling Psychology, 47*, 27–35. doi:10.1037/0022-0167.47.1.27

Von Bertalanffy, L. (1968). *General systems theory: Foundations, development, applications.* George Braziller, Inc.

Ward, M. (1995). Butterflies and bifurcations: Can chaos theory contribute to our understanding of family systems. *Journal of Marriage and the Family, 57*, 629–638.

Warner, M. S. (1989). Empathy and strategy in the family system. *Person-Centered Review, 4*, 324–343.

Watzlawick, P., Beavin, J. H., & Jackson, D. D. (2011). *Pragmatics of human communication (2nd ed.).* Norton.

Watzlawick, P., Weakland, J. H., & Fisch, R. (1974). *Change: Principles of problem formation and problem resolution.* Norton.

Whitchurch, G. G., & Constantine, L. L. (1993). Systems theory. In P. G. Boss, W. J. Doherty, R. LaRossa, W. R. Schumm, & S. K. Steinmetz (Eds.), *Sourcebook of family theories and methods: A contextual approach* (pp. 325–352). Springer.

White, H. C. (2008). *Identity and control: How social formations emerge (2nd ed.).* Princeton University Press.

White, M. (1992). Deconstruction and therapy. In D. Epston & M. White (Eds.), *Experience, contradiction, narrative, & imagination: Selected papers of David Epston and Michael White, 1989-1991.* Dulwich Centre.

White, M. P., Alcock, I., Grellier, J., Wheeler, B. W., Hartig, T., Warber, S. L., Bone, A., Depledge, M. H., & Fleming, L. E. (2019). Spending at least 120 minutes a week in nature is associated with good health and wellbeing. *Scientific Reports, 9*(7730). doi:10.1038/s41598-019-44097-3

Index

acceptance and commitment therapy 103, 109–11, 171–2, 177–9
action theory 12
active listening *see* attending skills
adaptability 17, 21, 142–3, 144, 167, 192, 194, 209–10
adult-centered family 4
affect theory 14; *see also* social-exchange theory
AGIL paradigm 13
alignments 115
alternative narratives 58, 102, 107
alternative stories *see* alternative narratives
attachment theory 194, 211–12; attachment injuries 179
attending skills 42
autonomy 38, 139, 145, 193–4, 205
autopoiesis 117–18

Bandura, Albert 16
Bateson, Gregory 18–19, 21, 35, 70–1
Bateson Project 18, 21, 29, 70–1
Beck, Aaron 30
Bertalanffy, Ludwig von 9, 21, 122–3; *see also* general systems theory
bias 15, 100–1; bias in language 79, 100; biased networks 54; dominant stories 102; family contributions 102, 121; therapist biases 98, 100–1, 121, 213
body language 42, 69, 73, 206
Boszormenyi-Nagy, Ivan 18, 20, 21
boundaries: clear 140, 145; communication 143–4, 148; definition 137; diffused 140; disengaged 140–1, 144; enmeshed 140–1, 144, 149; flexible 143, 144; goals 145; purpose 137–8; rigid 140–2, 144, 209–10; self-care 47, 149–50; setting/asserting

139–40, 145–7; structured 143, 144; subsystems 138–9
Bowen multigenerational therapy 34, 56–7, 60–1, 123–5, 130, 170, 176–7, 188, 201, 205
Bronfenbrenner, Urie 118–19
Burgess, Ernest Watson 18, 21
burnout 48

case studies (by name): Billy's Night Job 127; Candice's School Anxiety 59–60; Cassie and Dan's Disconnect 80–1; Erik's Dilemma 174–5; Jimiyu's Big Move 104–5; Lola's Limits 152–3
change 10, 20, 30, 101, 195, 197, 209; circular causality 167–8, 211–12; definition 192; first-order 24–5; second-order 24–5; *see also* adaptability
chaos theory 168
child-centered family 4, 154
chronosystem 121, 189
circular questioning 80, 89
circularity 162, 192, 194–5, 211–12; causality 162–5, 167–8; definition 162; faults and responsibility 166–7; versus linearity 163–4
circumplex model 141–5
client-centered therapy *see* person-centered therapy
coalitions 115
co-constructing reality *see* consensual domain
cognitive-behavioral therapy (CBT) 30–1
cohesion 141–2, 144, 148, 154, 192, 209
communication: analog 69–70, 90; complementary 74; digital 69–72; dysfunctional styles 78; failure to communicate 74–5; interpretations 72–3; message 70–1, 75; meta

message 70; pragmatic 73; principles 70–2; semantic 72, 75; symmetrical 73–4; syntactic 72; theory 68; verbal/nonverbal 42, 68–9
consensual domain/second-order consensual domain 100
constructivism 99
content 28, 38, 196
context 32, 90, 100; contextualizing 101; emotional environment 92–5; inevitability 98–9; over time 95–8; physical 90–2; significance 101
contextual family therapy 79–80, 88–9, 102–3, 107–9, 149–50, 156–7, 170
co-occurring: definition 114
coping skills 195
core self *see* internal family systems therapy
cost-benefit analysis 13–14
counter-paradox *see* paradox/counter-paradox
creating safe space 41
creative self 191
creative synthesis 51
culture 44, 122, 157, 194, 198; awareness 44, 199, 213; competence 199, 213–14; context 105; cultural brokering 214; definition 198; sensitivity 199, 206, 213
cybernetics 10–12, 16, 21, 24, 35–6, 117, 215; first-order 10; second-order 11; thermometer/thermostat metaphor 11–12

developmental task theory 17
dialectical behavioral therapy (DBT) 30
dominant stories *see* dominant narratives
dominant narratives 58, 102, 106–7; culture 213–14
double-bind: criteria 76–7; theory 21, 76–7, 80, 206

ecological systems theory 118–22, 188, 190, 208–9
Ellis, Albert 30
emotional logic 98, 101
entitlement 79–80, 149, 156, 170; constructive 80; destructive 149
entropy 168
epistemology of participation 102
equifinality 168, 216
equipotentiality 168–9
Erickson, Milton 19–20, 21
Erikson, Erik 17, 29

ethnocentrism 213
exosystem 120–1, 209
experiential family therapy 26; *see also* symbolic experiential therapy
externalization 58, 64, 107

family map: Olson's couple and family map 143–4; structural 57–8, 62, 148, 155, 209
family of origin 3, 51, 60, 103, 108
family theory 23
feedback loops 10, 165, 190, 195; *see also* circularity
fluid reality *see* constructivism
free association 29
Freud, Sigmund 3, 29

gender 210–11
general systems theory (GST) 9–10, 21
genogram: Bowenian 56–7, 61, 124, 130–1; cultural 215
gestalt: definition 27; empty chair technique 28, 129; exaggeration technique 28; insight 27; phi phenomenon 27; theory 52, 191; therapy 27–8
goal-seeking *see* goal-setting
goal-setting 52–4
Goodman, Paul 27

Haley, Jay 20, 21, 35
Havighurst, Robert 17
hexaflex 103, 110, 171, 178
hierarchy 53, 122, 129, 138, 154, 210
holism 51–3, 114, 167; criticism 56; culture 204
holon 52–3, 114, 190, 204–5
homeostasis 20, 24, 167–8, 199, 212–13
horizontal relationships 4, 57
Horvath, William 54
humanistic theories 28

immediate self 119, 124, 206, 209
individuality 188, 194–5; and togetherness 137, 189, 192, 205; versus collectivism 193, 201, 205, 209
information: definition 68–9
intergenerational transmission 201
internal family systems therapy 59–60, 64–7, 125–6, 134–5, 151–2, 159–60, 188–9

Jackson, Don D. 18–19, 21, 35
Jesser, Clinton 16, 56
Jung, Carl 1, 194

Koestler, Arthur 52

ledgers 80, 88, 102
limitations: family systems theory 31–2; theory 31; therapeutic modality 32–3

macrosystem 120–1, 124, 194, 198–9, 208–9, 214
manifest and latency, 12; *see also* structural functionalism
Maslow's hierarchy of needs 53, 59
mental health 185–7, 191, 213
mental illness 185–7, 193; diagnoses 34–5, 54, 185–6
Mental Research Institute 18, 21, 77
mental wellness 185
mesosystem 120, 209
microsystem 119–20, 124, 189, 193–4, 198, 208–9
Minuchin, Salvador 20, 21, 137, 140, 148, 154
morphogenesis 168, 192
morphostasis 168
multidirectional partiality 42–3, 108, 150
multigenerational transmission process 170, 201

narrative family therapy 36, 58–9, 63–4, 102, 106–7
negative entropy/negentropy 168
negative feedback loops 165, 171; *see also* feedback loops
nominalism 56
non-diagnosing stance 34–5
non-purposeful drift 168
not-knowing stance 43
nuclear family 4, 111, 124, 205, 211–12
Nye, Ivan 14, 21; *see also* social-exchange theory

Palo Alto Team 18–20, 21, 76–9, 185, 193
Parsons, Talcott 12, 21; *see also* structural functionalism
paradox/counter-paradox 77, 82–3, 169
Perls, Fritz and Laura 27–8, 52
person of the therapist 44
person-centered therapy 26–7, 37
perturbances 168
polyvocality 36
Popper, Karl 32
positive feedback loops 165, 172–4; *see also* feedback loops
preferential attachment mechanism 54

process/processing 28, 38, 196
psychoanalysis 28–9
psychodynamic *see* psychoanalysis

Rapoport, Anatol 54
recursion 165–6, 192
reflecting 62
reframing 77–8, 85, 102, 149
relationship satisfaction 51, 144
resilience 19, 192, 194, 203, 214
resistance 43
rituals 4, 12, 208
Roger, Carl 26–7, 37–8
roles: boundaries 140–3; family roles 4, 17, 54–6, 85, 122, 148; social roles 93–4, 122–3, 191; triangles 116–17
rules: boundaries 137–8, 140, 142, 145; family rules 4, 28, 85, 103, 121–3, 143, 209; social rules 94–5, 165

Satir, Virginia 18, 20, 21, 27, 78–9, 84–5, 150–1, 202–4
self-care 45–8
self-compassion 45–6
self-differentiation 60, 188, 201–2
self-disclosure 47
self-focus 177
self-leadership 1, 66, 152, 159, 188–9
self-reference 44–5
self-regulation theory 15–17; components 15; steps 15; means 16; impulse control (*see* self-control); self-control 16–17; sex 210–11
sexual orientation 211
Shannon, Claude 74–5
Smuts, Jan Christian 51
social-exchange theory 13–15, 21, 96; core tenets 14; resources 14; social theory 23
solid self *see* immediate self
solution-focused therapy 79, 86–8, 125–6, 132–3
strategic family therapy 27, 77–8, 81–3, 169–70, 175–6, 208
structural family therapy 57–8, 61–2, 123, 128, 148–9, 153–5, 209
structural functionalism 12–13, 21, 23
structured/structural determinism 99, 209
subsystems 114–18, 121–3, 138–9, 152
supra systems 114–15, 121–2
symbolic experiential therapy 78–9, 83–6, 150–1, 157–9, 202–4

Index 229

systemic therapist 34; modern 35–6; postmodern 36–7; directive 37; nondirective 37–8; client advocate 39–40; flexibility and patience 43; curiosity 43–4

therapeutic modality 24; difference from theory 25

therapy theory: definition 23; difference from modality 25

transference 29; counter transference 47

triangles 116–17; interlocking triangles 117; triangulation 62, 116–17; detriangulation 116

unconditional positive regard 26

verbal tracking *see* attending skills
vertical relationships 3, 57
vicious cycles 166
vocal qualities 42

Watzlawick, Paul 12, 18–19, 21, 72
Weakland, John 18–19, 21, 35
Wertheimer, Max 27
Wiener, Norbert 10, 21; *see also* cybernetics
worldview 2–3, 31, 33, 43, 45, 57, 186, 191, 213

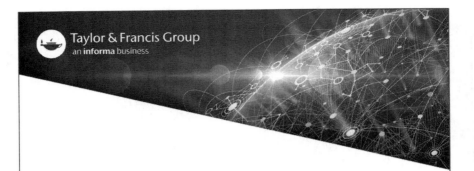